i can only IMAGINE

i can only IMAGINE

Becoming the worshipper you long to Be

mercyme
with Jeff Kinley

Nelson Bibles
Nashville
A Division of Thomas Nelson, Inc.
www.ThomasNelson.com
www.Xt4J.com

i can only imagine

Scripture quotations are taken from the following sources:

THE NEW KING JAMES VERSION. Copyright ©
1979, 1980, 1982, Thomas Nelson, Inc. Publishers.

The Holy Bible, New Century Version,
copyright © 1987, 1988, 1991 by Word Publishing,
Nashville, Tennessee 37214. Used by permission.

ISBN 0-7180-0170-2

Printed in the United States of America
02 03 04 05 RRD 5 4 3 2 1

contents

CHAPTER I

Turn Down the Radio

Beyond the music

He who despises music, as do all the fanatics, does not please me. Music is a gift of God, not a gift of man. After Theology, I accord to music the highest place and greatest honor.

—Martin Luther

The aim and final end of all music should be none other than the glory of God and the refreshment of the soul.

—Johann Sebastian Bach

Why should the devil have all the good music?

—Larry Norman

July 13, 2001, is a day Cody Clawson will never forget. The Utah Boy Scout and the rest of his buddies from Troop 241 headed out for a few days of hiking and camping in Targhee National Forest located about a mile south of the Yellowstone National Park boundary and about forty miles north of Jackson, Wyoming. Each of the boys was looking forward to the trip with great anticipation. But as the scouts were setting up camp, young Cody lost his sense of direction while carrying supplies from a vehicle to the campsite at Loll Boy Scout Camp. In a matter of minutes he was completely turned around in the thick forest. Shortly afterwards, around 2 P.M. on that day, Cody was discovered missing by his troop leaders and fellow scouts.

They looked for four hours before finally contacting search and rescue personnel from Idaho and Teton County in Wyoming.

Soon night fell, and the search was postponed until the morning. Despite the summer season, it was nevertheless sufficently cold in the darkness of the secluded Yellowstone forest that night. Making matters worse, that evening the rain came down, washing away any tracks of evidence where Cody had been. With his alternatives limited, and wearing only a T-shirt, shorts, and sandals, the young Boy Scout took cover under a rock outcropping and waited for morning.

As dawn approached that Tuesday, the search resumed at 6 A.M. By this time a Wyoming Air Patrol plane, along with several private aircrafts, had been employed in the operation. Though family and friends feared the worst, all anxiously waited for any news regarding the boy's whereabouts, hoping for the best. At about 8:30 A.M., after over two hours of flying, a diligent and skilled helicopter pilot finally spotted Cody. Swooping down, he carefully maneuvered the aircraft, landing nearby.

Tired, cold, hungry, and drenched, thirteen-year-old Cody Clawson climbed to safety inside, surprised to learn he had wandered about ten miles away from the Scout Camp. He had been separated from his troop for over fourteen long hours. But that wasn't Cody's biggest surprise that summer morning. Imagine his astonishment upon discovering the man flying that helicopter was none other than Harrison Ford! The famous actor, a part-time Jackson resident, regularly volunteers his helicopter flying skills for rescue missions. A proficient pilot, Ford and another rescuer had spent two hours that morning scanning the landscape for any sign of the lost boy.

Flying back to safety, Harrison turned and looked at Cody through his aviator sunglasses.

"Boy, you sure must have earned a merit badge for this one."

Can't you see one side of Ford's mouth slightly turn up in his trademark halfsmile?

"I already earned that badge last summer," Clawson replied. The famous actor chuckled as he flew the boy back to his family.

"Did you get an autograph?" his fellow Boy Scouts later asked.

"No," replied the grateful thirteen-year-old. "I got something better than an autograph out of the deal. I got a hug and a handshake."

And you can bet Cody also got a few lessons from his mom and his scoutmaster about knowing where you are at all times. Maybe he should get a compass on his next birthday.

Now, there is a good chance you have never been lost overnight in the Wyoming wilderness. But in the unlikely event you have, there is even less of a chance you were rescued the next morning by Indiana Jones. But where we all do tend to lose our sense of direction at times is in the Christian life. It seems we have an inherent inclination to wander off the path—to stray off course personally and spiritually. In a culture given to radical extremes, we often trivialize the essential things in life while making icons out of the insignificant ones. In the process, we not only lose our sense of direction, but our perspective as well. We develop spiritual vertigo, forgetting which end is up. Our vision gets fuzzy, and we end up emphasizing all the wrong issues. We take good things and elevate them to a place of unhealthy importance. Because of this, every now and then we should pause and perform a diagnostic self-examination, checking ourselves to see if our perspective and vision on life is still 20/20.

Take music for example, an integral and needed part of our lives. Have you ever stopped to wonder what it is about music that appeals to us so much? Why do we spend multiple billions of dollars on CDs and digital recordings? Why are there so many wannabe musicians, thrashing away after school in neighborhood garage bands? Ever thought what your car would be like without a radio, CD, or cassette player?

Music is unique because it stirs up something in the soul, awakening the emotions. Imagine a great movie without a soundtrack or background music. Boring! But insert a beautiful composition at just the right moment in the movie and we can be moved to tears and sadness or inspired to do something more heroic—like conquer a nation! It's the reason you wanted to stand up and cheer when Roy Hobbs crushed that game-winning homer in *The Natural*, and it's why you were scared spitless at that suspenseful thriller you saw last month. The background music working in concert with the action on the big screen, either massaging or messing with your emotions, elicited your response.

There's just something about a good song, isn't there? Music can motivate us to do great things. It pricks and prompts our hearts to joy and celebration. It has the ability to touch us way beyond just our auditory senses. Like a beacon, it hones in on our inner person, influencing and impacting our mind, emotions, and will. And yes, at times it can even move our bodies to dance.

In fact, melody's ability to energize the human soul is perhaps more powerful and universal than any other art form in history. It's obvious that our Creator programmed us to enjoy music and be touched by it. It then comes as no surprise that throughout Scripture, music finds a comfortable home in our worship of God. Is it any coincidence that this present age will officially end with the sound of a musical instrument?[1] Make no mistake about it, music has always been an integral component of our worship.

Is it any wonder that God chose a musician to write the official hymnal of Scripture—the *Book of Psalms*? King David tuned up his stringed instrument to enhance his worship experience of God. And he urges all of creation to make music to our God.[2] In fact, had David been born in our day instead of his, the Psalms might have been *recorded* instead of *written*. He would have been forced to produce a 100-plus track CD anthology.

Have you also noticed how David encourages his readers to make use of virtually every musical instrument available, including tambourines, harps, trumpets, guitars, strings, flutes, and cymbals?[3] Can you imagine this sound? The Psalmist's purpose is to confidently declare, "If you can praise God with it, use it!"

But it's not just instrumentals. We're also encouraged to sing praises to our God.[4] God wants us to use our voices to praise Him too. This is an exercise that is both enjoyable and fitting for worship. We lift up our voices in adoration and celebration to our great Savior. Combined with those instruments, we now have a kicking band plus great vocals. We're talking some awesome music.

What exactly pops into the minds of many when they are asked to define the word *worship*? Most definitions include a musical element. Maybe a concert where we close our eyes, singing out loud in praise? Or perhaps it's a scene composed of a large group of believers lifting their voices to heaven? Could worship occur with 1,200 adrenaline-filled seventeen-year-olds, whipped into a frenzy, crowd surfing and jumping up and down like kangaroos? Or is it confined to the stillness of 150 baby boomers, standing in silent awe of God? The truth is, the landscape of worship in our country and culture is as varied as the topography itself. We have the Christian musical equivalent of hills, valleys, mountains, rivers, beaches, deserts, and forests. Bottom line: There is truly something for everybody in music today.

We don't want to create a division in the body of Christ, but we do want to be discerning. In our argument and divisions over the subject of worship, sometimes nobody wins and everybody loses. Instead, perhaps God has something for you to learn through your struggle with the worship in your church. Or maybe He is calling you to be a firm, but loving agent of change. If so, then go for it. Fortunately, a large number of churches today have awakened this need, and are including contemporary choruses and modern hymns into their Sunday worship. Some traditionalists cry out in terror that we have left the faith to do such a thing. And to be fair to them, not every contemporary hymn written today contains a whole lot of depth. But, on the other hand, some are not intended to. They simply express an honest emotion or state of being, kind of like some of David's great psalms. Just because a song was written in the past five years doesn't automatically condemn it to the category of unorthodoxy or bad theology. All of our classic hymns were at one time contemporary songs, right? Some of them borrowed melodies from local pubs and most all were relevant to the time in which they were written. Martin Luther's chosen melody for "A Mighty Fortress is Our God" was an old German beer chugging chorus. It's the modern-day equivalent to singing "Shout to the Lord" to the tune of Jimmy Buffet's "Margaritaville!"

Some of those old hymn writers were pretty wild. And clearly, what has kept some of those other old songs in our hymnals is text alone, because the melody can be awkward, difficult to sing, and outdated. Other old hymns have incredible melodies, but fail to say very much to this generation.

Then there are classic old hymns that are sure to be sung in heaven—songs like "When I Survey the Wondrous Cross" or "All Hail the Power of Jesus' Name." These and scores of many other great hymns speak to every generation. It is simply wrong to ignore the great hymns and choruses that have become anthems for the Christian church throughout many centuries. But it is also equally wrong to believe God only moved musicians and song-writers to compose good worship music in the hundred years that made up the eighteenth century. In each new generation of believers, God raises up writers, composers, and musicians who are gifted to lead us in worship.

Ultimately, however, worship is really not about music. It's not about what you wear to church, how old you are, or even the style of your wor-ship that is the real issue here. It's not about whether we use organs or orchestras, electric guitars or violins, keyboards, choirs, or congas. It's not really about hymns vs. choruses. Music is merely a medium, a method, *a way*—not *the* way we worship God. It's a tool used to prompt us to worship. Praising God goes way beyond the music. It's really all about the heart of the worshipper, right? Or at least it's supposed to be. In reality, life is really about knowing God in a personal way. After all, as we'll discuss in Chapter Three, you can't worship God very well if you don't know Him. And how you view that God in your mind has a whole lot to do with how you will relate to Him. A.W. Tozer wrote, "The most important thing about you is what comes into your mind when you think of God." Counterfeit, bogus perspectives of God need to be exterminated from our thinking. We need to attack these false images of God as we would a life-threatening disease. And why is it so important to have a proper view of God? Well, one reason it's important to have a true image of God in our minds is because every-thing else is simply idolatry.

So with that in mind, let's take aim and blow away a few of these false views of God. Each of the following unbiblical ideas represents an incomplete, inaccurate, or distorted picture of God's character and what He is really like.

false image #1—God the Distant Deity

This one says He's out there . . . somewhere, but He really doesn't bother with humanity. You can talk about Him; you just can't talk *to* Him.

But Scripture says God isn't distant at all, but rather He is very near to us.[5] He created you and He's much closer and more accessible than you think.

false image #2—God the Gentle Grandparent

This view is that He allows us to sow our wild oats and will forget about it in the end. Do what you want. He'll just wink and say, "Boys will be boys, you know."

But Scripture says God is holy and must punish every sin.[6] He doesn't look away when we disobey, but lovingly corrects and disciplines us.[7]

false image #3—God the Strict Schoolteacher

Whenever we start enjoying life, God yells, "Hey, cut it out down there! Stop having fun . . . or else!" God has a furrowed brow and is always frowning whenever He looks down on us.

But Scripture says God isn't against having fun at all. He wants us to enjoy life to the fullest.[8] He is a God of great joy!

false image #4—God the Punishing Policeman

This one subtly states that every problem you experience is somehow a direct punishment for a sin you have committed. You can trace every bad circumstance back to some mistake in your life. You are to blame.

But Scripture says though God does discipline His children, He certainly isn't looking for ways to punish us. Instead, He wants to provide a better way for us.[9] In other words, every time you stub your toe or lose your car keys doesn't mean God is getting you back for a sin you committed.

false image #5—God the Generous Genie

You see, God owes us at least three wishes. We just have to know how to rub the magic prayer lamp . . . in Jesus' name, of course. He's the celestial Santa Claus, there to answer our every whim.

But Scripture says God doesn't exist to serve us, but instead we exist to serve Him. Though He is giving and generous, He doesn't cater to our every wish.[10]

false image #6—God the Faceless Force

God is a strong universal influence of good—a power, an entity, but not a personal Being. And He is also an energy that can take many forms. Who God is to you may differ from who He is to someone else. He's whoever you want Him to be, really.

But Scripture says God is not an it or a thing or whatever you want Him to be . . . He is not different things to different people. He is our Creator who can be known in a personal way.[11] And He is who *He* says He is, not who we *think* He is.

false image #7—God the Callous Creator

He really doesn't care about us. It's up to us to solve our problems, struggle through this life, and ultimately correct our mistakes and atone for our sins.

But Scripture says God isn't uncaring, but cared so much about us that He even became one of us,[12] atoning for our sins at the cross.

Can you see what's wrong with each of these views? Do you see how they fall far short in accurately describing who the God of the Bible really is? And how does all of this relate to worship? Here's how: The image of God you have in your mind right now greatly affects your perception of Him. And your perception of Him radically influences your relationship with Him. For example, if He is a *Punishing Policeman*, you will want to hide when you make a mistake or break His law. If He is the *Callous Creator*, you surely aren't going to bring your hurts and problems to Him. That is why it is so important to have a true image of God in your mind. It purifies your worship. And isn't that what you really want?

So what is worship to you? Perhaps a better question would be what is worship? What constitutes a worship experience? What does it really mean to praise God? What does that look like? What does it feel like? And how do you know when you have done it? Though our contemporary Christian culture has, perhaps unintentionally, misled us to believe that worship is, or at least must include, some sort of music or singing, the truth is that worship goes way beyond our music. Just as there is more to evangelism than merely sharing a gospel tract or going door-to-door, so worship involves far more than our music. And that is exactly what the rest of this book is all about.

Think of it this way: The stadium of worship is much bigger than just one music section. The journey of praise involves far more than focusing on the great sound coming from your stereo speakers. So, just for a few pages, turn down the volume on the radio and join us as we take some time to look at the road and the surrounding scenery. Together, let's pull over and stop a few minutes, long enough to check the map, long enough to make sure we're on the right path. Let's get a fresh perspective on worshipping our God.

CHAPTER 2

Human Hard Drive

wired for worship

We are here to be worshippers first, and workers second.

—A.W. Tozer

No-Brainers

There are some things in life that take great effort to learn and perfect. These are the activities, skills, and disciplines that just don't come that easy for most of us. They require effort, exercise, and sometimes even excruciating practice. They test our patience and sometimes even our sanity. Try as we might, these activities seem to exist in a realm just beyond the reach of our fingertips. We just can't quite succeed at them.

But what is more sick are those individuals who appear to effortlessly master difficult things with great ease. These people can be positively annoying, because for some reason, what is complex and difficult for us is simple and second nature for them. We struggle for years to be proficient at the things that are a breeze for them. You know, things like algebra, ice-skating, playing the piano, speaking a foreign language, or conquering a half pipe on a skateboard.

What is it for you? What things, while attempting to conquer them, have instead sent you into emotional orbit? Well, don't freak out about it or be discouraged. There are surely some things you can do that others can't. Like the guy in your senior class who scored a 1590 on his SAT, but never learned how to swim or ride a bicycle. Or the girl who kept winning all those beauty pageants growing up but was completely inept on the soccer field. Everyone has his or her own strengths and skills. And yours are as unique as theirs are. But for the sake of everyone, there are also countless activities that come pretty natural to most all of us. In fact, they're so habitual and routine that they require virtually no effort whatsoever. These are the nobrainers in life that appear to run by some autopilot system hidden deep within our collective psyche. They just happen . . . all by themselves. No worries about forgetting these things. They occur with frightening regularity. We don't have to work at them or practice them. They are human habits. Some of these activities even border on instinctual behavior.

Like oversleeping. Could there possibly be a more natural behavior than that? Millions do it every day, especially those in their late teens and early twenties. Don't you think by now this activity ought to be considered a Division I college sport? Sure, though we dabbled in it during our high school years, we *perfected* it during the four . . . er . . . five years we spent away at college. It's an actual art form to some. What student hasn't abruptly awakened, glanced at the alarm clock exclaiming within, *Oh no! I overslept . . . again!?* Now, the two most common responses to this reccurring morning mistake are to jump out of bed like a frantic fireman, throw on the clothes nearest to your bed, slap a hat on your bed-head hairdo, slide into a pair of shoes, and race to class, or to smash the snooze button, roll over, and go back to sleep. It's unlearned. Unplanned. Unexpected. And very natural.

Among our other natural habits is cheering when our team scores a touchdown. Last time you were at the video store, did you notice the instructional video on this subject? Probably not. It just happens, right? It's second nature to us. Or how about that confusing look we give the pavement immediately after tripping over our own two feet (usually in plain sight of your crush)? We glance back at the ground with a confused, quizzical, and disturbed facial expression that says, *There must have been something in my path that caused me to trip because everyone knows I would never trip on my own. I'm not even close to being that uncoordinated or clumsy. I'm just too cool for that.*

You know you've done that. C'mon, admit it.

Truth is, our lives are filled with movements, motions and mannerisms that occur without any conscious prompting, things like breathing, blinking, swallowing, dreaming, watching, resting, playing, loving . . . and worshipping.

Hey, wait a minute, some might say. *Did you say* worshipping? *I mean, let's be real here. How can you say that worshipping is a natural, unlearned activity that all people do? I thought only the religious crowd was into that.* Well, that depends on how you personally understand the concept of worship. Actually, worshipping is something we all do as regularly and as unconsciously as breathing. Like inhaling and exhaling, worship is what we effortlessly and naturally do everyday as human beings. In fact, it may be the most common and consistent habit we ever practice. But how can this be? And why?

A&E Biography

To discover the answer to this, we have to take a few minutes and go back to the beginning, to the original pair God created. Scroll to the *menu* section in your memory file and press *scene index*. Now choose *Adam and Eve*. Remember them? This first ever couple was made as the prototype of the race of human beings that would follow them. Of course we all know Adam and his beautiful bride Eve were made in the image of God.[13] And as a part of that image they (and we) were given the awesome ability to think and reason on a level far above all the animal kingdom. As such, we remain the ultimate crown of God's great creation.

But there is a privilege that is even better than that. Something more unique and honorable. Inherent within this image of God in us is the awesome capacity for *relationship*—specifically, a relationship with God. Put simply, their relationship with God was just like their relationship with their environment and with each other—perfect and complete, lacking in nothing. They were made to worship God and walk with Him. They had everything imaginable at their disposal in this new world. For them, finding paradise didn't involve a flight to Maui. They looked no further than their own backyard. They didn't dream of a better life. They already had one! And they lived that dream 24/7. It was their own little version of heaven on earth and they possessed it all, right there in the Garden.[14] They were *complete*.

But it wasn't always that way. There was a time when things were not good for Adam. It was during his B.E. period, or Before Eve. God knew Adam needed a counterpart, and he did something about it. "Then the Lord God said, 'It is not good for the man to be alone; I will make him a helper suitable for him.'"[15] So He made Eve. Guys, this gal was the ultimate woman. Not only did she possess all the physical characteristics of history's first supermodel, but she was also the total package *inside* as well. Her personality was ideal and emotionally, she was perfect. In fact, so perfect was Eve, that when Adam asked her, *What's the matter, honey?* she never, ever answered, *Oh, nothing. That's* how perfect! She had body, brains, and balanced emotions. She was every godly guy's fantasy. Well, at the time she was actually the *only* guy's fantasy. But, fortunately for this particular guy, his fantasy came to life right before his very eyes. Eve was tailor-made for her man. Scripture recounts what happened:

And the Lord God fashioned into a woman the rib which He had taken from the man, and brought her to the man. And the man said, This is now bone of my bones, and flesh of my flesh; She shall be called Woman, because she was taken out of Man.[16]

Upon God's official presentation of his newly fashioned female gift, Adam must have been very excited to see her. However, Eve wasn't the only ultimate person in the Garden. Adam was also the pinnacle of perfection as well—a hunk of a man who perhaps sported a chiseled physique to match his rugged but gentlemanly charm. Girls, he was the original hottie. A real stud-muffin. Adam didn't need a cool car to attract women. He was the prototype chick magnet. So what if there was only one chick? Nonetheless, she was very attracted to him. Adam was also the total package, inside and out.

Here was a pair literally made for each other. It was the first match made in heaven and seen on earth. And as such, they were complete, lacking in absolutely nothing. But wait, it gets even better.

They were also unashamed.

> For this cause a man shall leave his father and his mother, and shall cleave to his wife; and they shall become one flesh. And the man and his wife were both naked and were not ashamed.[17]

In other words, Adam and Eve were originally created au natural—in the buff—and that was cool. But even after being made by God, they remained naked. That's because there was no need for clothing in a perfect environment where the temperature was just right at all times. There were no such things as clothes yet. Beyond this, they would have had no reason to cover their nakedness. The absence of physical clothing was something designed by God as an outward picture of the inward spiritual and emotional intimacy they shared with one another. There was no guilt regarding their nakedness because there was no sin associated with it. They had total freedom, perfect love, and intimacy with God and each other. As co-regents with God, they exercised dominion over creation and did it in the context of a perfect environment.[18] And though God did set one simple boundary for them concerning a certain tree, there weren't a whole lot of rules in the Garden. Noticeably absent are commands such as the one the Lord later gave His people, namely, "You shall worship the Lord your God only." After all, why would God need to issue this command? Plainly, there was no need for Him to tell them to do what came so naturally for them. Imagine this: Their capacity to love God was virtually unlimited. They worshipped Him without any prompting whatsoever. They needed no reminders. No wake up calls. No encouragement and no accountability. They simply worshipped

Him because they were engaged in a love relationship with Him. Things were very good in the Garden, and the forecast looked great for the human race. What more could a man, woman, or couple possibly want? They were totally fulfilled. Nothing could possibly go wrong, right?

Wrong.

food poisoning

Something did go wrong. Very wrong. Adam and Eve lost it all. Everything. They went bust. The bottom fell out and they declared bankruptcy. Their personal stock crashed and burned. But how? How could anyone possibly screw up a great situation such as this? What were they thinking? Well, you can be sure Adam and Eve didn't plan it that way. (Who would?) They didn't set out to ruin their lives and, in doing so, indelibly mark ours. Quite the contrary, it happened like most of our failures do—subtly, and in a seemingly harmless manner. Their first mistake was that they listened to the wrong voice.

Now the serpent was more crafty than any of the wild animals the Lord God had made. He said to the woman, Did God really say, 'You must not eat from any tree in the garden'?[19]

Up to this point, there was only one voice Adam and Eve recognized, only one voice they had respected—God's. They knew Him. They followed Him. They worshipped Him. But now, for the first time, they listened to the voice of another. Even though it was the wrong voice, it didn't necessarily *sound* eerie or evil to them. Otherwise, they wouldn't have been so persuaded by it. On the contrary, this voice was soothing and very conversational. It also didn't seem to surprise them that a serpent spoke out loud to them.

But this conversation did mark the first time Adam and Eve opened themselves to other ideas about God, life, and truth. This historic moment began what progressively became a downward spiral. It was one mistake that opened the door to a whole series of unfortunate events. In reality, Adam and Eve were persuaded to believe a lie about God.

The woman said to the serpent, "We may eat fruit from the trees in the garden, but God did say, 'You must not eat fruit from the tree that is in the middle of the garden, and you must not touch it, or you will die.'"

"You will not surely die," the serpent said to the woman. "For God knows that when you eat of it your eyes will be opened, and you will be like God, knowing good and evil."

When the woman saw that the fruit of the tree was good for food and pleasing to the eye, and also desirable for gaining wisdom, she took some and ate it. She also gave some to her husband, who was with her, and he ate it.[20]

As the former worship leader in heaven, Satan had been expelled from there after leading an unsuccessful rebellion against God. Because of this, he was opposed to God and His children. Created in God's image, Adam and Eve were a bitter reminder to Satan of his former prestige, position, and subsequent punishment. This couple was a walking audiovisual, reminding Satan of what he had forfeited by his attempted coup against the Creator. Their presence in Paradise personified his pain. And he hated them for it.

And so, noticing the innocence of Adam and Eve, he seized upon the opportunity to get his revenge. Inhabiting the body of one of God's creatures, the devil manifested himself via the vocal chords of the snake. As a superior intellectual being, this Satan-filled serpent communicated as much with his inflection of voice as he did by the words themselves. Translated from under his breath and through the tone of his voice, Lucifer calmly whispered his sinful sales pitch to the unsuspecting newlyweds. It went something like this:

You know, the three of us have a lot in common. This God you worship, I too have worshipped. In fact, I have known Him a long, long time. Longer than you. And I am well acquainted with all His ways. Indeed, I was a part of a very select few who got to see Him up close and personal. And because of my easy access to Him, I was privileged to know things about Him that none of the other created ones knew. But I must tell you how disappointed I soon became. What I learned both shocked and disturbed me. In fact, I became disillusioned. Imagine my surprise at discovering that, instead of being the good God He professes to be, He is in fact a deceptive deity. You see, He teases you by allowing you to look, but not touch. Then He says you can touch, but not taste. Taste but not swallow. Swallow, but not enjoy! I discovered He really isn't so good after all. He doesn't want you to know what He knows, because by knowing, you will then become His equal. He's insecure and selfish. And He's holding out on you, too. There is so much more to life than what He offers. There is real living outside this Garden. Trust me, I know. I've been outside this place, and it's great. As a result, I now have worshippers like He does. Wouldn't you also like to be a god? Then you can experience something far greater than merely serving Him. You can be worshipped, too. I mean, I'm only telling you these things because I just don't want to see someone else hurt by Him like I was. Somebody has to blow the whistle here and tell the truth. But don't take my word for it. Go ahead. See for yourself. Take and eat. This God of yours, trust me . . . He isn't worth worshipping.

Of course, all this sounded pretty convincing to Eve and her hubby, so much so that they bought into the lie and signed on the bottom line. But in doing so, they made a much bigger mistake than buying non-existent land in the Everglades. Their faux pas was that they chose to believe that fulfillment awaited them outside of God's provision. They embraced this new and novel idea that there actually was something better than being a worshipper of the true God. And so, with their destiny hanging in the balance, and human history hinging on this one single moment, all of creation paused and held its breath.

And they ate.

But amazingly, nothing happened to the honeymoon couple. No lightning bolts from the sky. No sharp pain in their stomachs. No Montezuma's Revenge. In fact, just the opposite happened. Their first sensation was the sweet and satisfying taste of this fruit. Like the first bite of a juicy hamburger or the inaugural taste of that first piece of pizza, it felt great. Mmmmm. It was moist. Succulent. Rich. Ripe. Pleasing to the eyes *and* to the taste buds. In short, Adam and his bride initially discovered what Scripture later affirmed—that sin can often be very fun.[21] Let's not deny it. There really is pleasure associated with sin. None of us would ever be tempted if there weren't! Temptation involves things that are appealing, not things that are repugnant. Think for a moment: we wouldn't commit the same sin over and over unless it brought us some sort of pleasure. From the feeling of superiority we enjoy when we put another person down to the drug-like sensation of immoral sex, sin always tastes good. Well, at least initially.

And for Adam and Eve, sin's first fruit did indeed "taste great" but, as they would soon discover, was also "less filling." Since their creation, they had worshipped and pursued God alone. Now the story line took a wicked twist. They had come upon a hairpin turn, and instead of slowing down, they pressed the pedal and floored it, running straight through the guardrail and over the cliff. Against all logic and sound judgment, they had trusted a creature instead of their Creator. They had bowed down to an altar of self in a momentary act of spiritual insanity. And just for a brief moment, it felt so good. So right.

The wonderful world of sin

But the buzz of sin's narcotic high left them in a flash almost as soon as it had come. Unlike a bad feeling the morning after an all-night binge, their hangover set in before the party was even over. And when it did, they began crashing—hard and fast. They had taken the bait, the hook was set deeply, and Satan began reeling them in. Simultaneously, their eyes opened as the door of their souls closed. In an instant, they passed through an unseen portal. It was a one-way path leading into another world altogether. It was a world where they would experience things their virgin minds had not even the capacity to imagine in their previous life. The consequences of their act of disobedience soon came on them like an unforeseen tidal wave of nausea. "Then the eyes of both of them were opened, and they realized they were naked."[22]

Up to this point, the man and woman had not known the always-present consequences to disobedience. Though it's an old maxim, it still rings true: Sin will take you father than you want to go, force you to stay longer than you want to stay, and make you pay more than you want to pay. For Adam and Eve, they had maxed out their credit card and the bill arrived at their doorstep just seconds after swiping the card. They had pushed a button that set in motion a long-lasting avalanche of negative and damaging consequences. What they now began experiencing were things they had never known before—things like shame, guilt, grief, pain, sadness, loneliness, loss . . . and confusion.

A hollow emptiness now echoed in their souls. It was now barren. Dark. Cold. Unoccupied. Silent. Lifeless. They had voluntarily opened the front door, allowing thieves to plunder their new heart-home. This horrible sin of self-worship changed every conceivable part of their person, influencing every function of their humanity. Spiritually, they instantly died, afterward only producing offspring of like nature. It took only one generation to show how this deceiving drug of self-worship they induced would cause fatal flashbacks for the rest of human history.

Like a deadly virus infecting their bodies, sin also took over their minds. Their thoughts would no longer naturally turn to God. Instead, it now required a concerted effort to think on those things that are godly and right. Sin caused a sort of brain damage. Adam and Eve lost a certain mental ability that day in the Garden. Parasitic untruths and self-generated lies now had the potential to find a welcome home in their minds. But sin also affected their emotions. Formerly strong and balanced, they would now be weak, volatile, and unstable. From that point on, humankind would battle a roller-coaster emotional experience from day to day, and relationships since then have suffered because of it. This emotional collapse would eventually give rise to anger, hatred, hostility, murder, depression, despair, and a seemingly endless chain of bad feelings. Like a smoldering train wreck, their emotions would be a mess that no medication could possibly cure. But that's not all. Their ability to choose was also now handcuffed by sin's power. It became more work for them to choose to follow God. Their free will was conquered and enslaved to sin's power. An unholy trinity of masters now dominated their lives. Working in sinister cooperation with one another, the manipulating control of sin, Satan, and self took up residence in the heart home once owned and occupied by God alone. The first couples' lives were now officially under new management. And as if all this isn't enough, their bodies now began the slow process of dying. Disease and death, formerly foreign concepts to their world, made their presence known as time went on.

Hey, isn't sin wonderful?

cover girl

But there's one more thing. The combined effect of this single, sinful act caused Adam and Eve to lose something else. They lost their sense of identity. Like unwanted guests, chaos and confusion invaded their world of security and order. It was as if they now suffered from a kind of prehistoric amnesia. Once so sure of who they were and their purpose in life, sin had deleted their sense of honor and distinctiveness so prominent in their pre-serpent encounter. They now had no identity. They found themselves strangers in a strange land. All at once, they felt very out of place. Their garden of paradise had become a patch of thorns. But perhaps what was even worse was that they didn't even have enough presence of mind to exclaim, *Oh no! What have we done?* Instead, they aggressively tried to cover up the effects of their sin with a false sense of security. "So they sewed fig leaves together and made coverings for themselves."[23]

And mankind has been in the fig leaf business ever since, franchising the industry in every continent and country, town and tribe, hillside and hamlet. By pursuing the trivial and worshipping things that offer a temporary feeling of self-importance and security, we have all sentenced ourselves to a futile and fruitless struggle for that original Garden fulfillment. But as Adam would tell you, it's a pointless, dead-end journey until we rediscover our identity as worshippers of the only true God.

Though our fig leaves are somewhat less obvious than their original designs, we wear them nonetheless. We have more sophisticated fig leaves now, and they mostly have very little to do with clothing. We conceal our insecurities and emotional nakedness with more acceptable coverings. Things like self-righteousness, religiosity, success, and financial independence. We create our own stunt double identities through our preoccupation with academics, appearance, athletics, possessions, partying, fashion, having the right friends who boost our image, achieving popularity, attaining position, or obsessing over our careers. Of course, none of these is inherently sinful, but they become so when we consciously or unconsciously trust them to bring us the satisfaction that only comes from being a worshipper of God. They became substitutes because what they provide for us is a close enough facsimile to the real thing, or so we think.

By the way, have you noticed that some are better than others at this game? Some of our self-minted soul currency looks pretty close to the real thing, while others' looks more like Monopoly™ money. And that is what's fundamentally wrong with us. We humans have a fatal flaw, a virus implanted long ago in our spiritual hard drive. Our original design was faultless. Unblemished. Immaculate and untarnished. But as a result of diverted worship, we now fail to boot up properly. Sure, we function okay, but just not in the best way. Without God, we have the ability to manufacture character, but it's counterfeit and cheap. We can produce love, but it's conditional; happiness, but it's temporary; peace, but it's circumstantial. We have developed a thin, but see-through layer of security. And though Scripture teaches that none of us are born seeking God as we were designed to, we are still nevertheless born seekers. It's an undeniable compulsion within us—an irresistible inclination, so powerful that we might conclude it is somehow undetectably encoded in our DNA. The truth is, we are simply predisposed to worship, because when we worship, we fire on all the pistons, enjoying the ultimate level of the human experience. We are born bent in that way, always leaning towards the person, thing, or experience that seems to give us what we need. Like the gravitational pull of a planet, that inner compulsion to worship always draws us to something greater than ourselves. It's such an influential magnetism that even a temporary, false substitute still gives us a bit of that Garden thrill we all desperately seek.

It's like we're born color-blind, while at the same time possessing an insatiable desire to see color. We were made for color, but we live in a gray, dull world. However, because of our condition, we say brown is blue and red is green. *So then, doesn't anyone still genuinely seek God?* Unfortunately, no. Due to the fact that we are spiritually dead,[24] our inherent nature prevents us from seeking the true Person of God.[25] Until we trust Christ for salvation, the restraining power of sin forbids us to pursue God. So, we spend the better part of our lives striving and scraping for whatever we can get. Ironically, those pursuits end up being the things God alone can sufficiently and satisfactorily provide: happiness, significance, fulfillment, purpose, love . . . basically all the things that make life worth living. In other words, we seek for things only God can give, but not God Himself. We want to worship, but we just don't want it to be God. Worship then is our inner compass. It's our true north. The problem is that we are attracted and drawn to all the wrong things.

Natural-Born Worshippers

In the end, we all end up worshipping something. We have to, for we cannot not worship. It's just not possible. We are compelled from within to focus on *something*. We submit ourselves to this pursuit in an attempt to achieve that which we passionately long for. Resisting worship is like holding your breath. Good luck. Hold it for a while and you can pass out. Do without air long enough and you check out. Those who make the choice to stop worshipping soon die for they lose their purpose for being. To live is to worship, to seek something greater, bigger, and better than you, something that gives you what you need. This is one reason why there are so many world religions. Every continent and community, every race and religion, every nation and neighborhood are all populated by seekers and searchers. We're all thirsty. We're natural-born worshippers hopelessly lost in a sea of substitutes.

Fortunately for Adam and Eve, God wasn't content to let them live off those cheap Brand X substitutes the world and Satan had to offer. Though they chose to pursue something other than Him, God still chose to pursue them.

Wait. Stop. Time out. Go back and read that last sentence again. Slowly this time.

This one reality may be the most significant truth you ever contemplate this side of eternity—maybe even the deepest thought you ever entertain in your head while you have breath in your lungs. In spite of your sin and turning away from Him, God still chooses to passionately pursue a relationship with you. Take a minute before reading further and let that one thought settle into your brain like feet into a sandy beach. Let it go past the front gate of your mind, past that guard standing there who continually says, *Yeah, yeah. I already knew that.* Allow this truth to gain access to a deeper, more real and authentic part of you. Hear it knocking on the door of that room where intimacy dwells. Now open the door and invite it in. Just stare at that truth with the eyes of your mind just like you would a favorite photograph. It's one of those things that, considered properly, causes you to shake your head in near disbelief. *God loves me in spite of my sin. He pursues me. He wants me.* That's the kind of God He is. Do you believe this? Really believe it? Do you? If so, then why do you pursue other people and things to make you happy?

> Then the man and his wife heard the sound of the Lord God as
> he was walking in the garden in the cool of the day, and they hid

from the Lord God among the trees of the garden. But the Lord God called to the man, "Where are you?" He answered, "I heard you in the garden, and I was afraid because I was naked; so I hid." And He said, "Who told you that you were naked? Have you eaten from the tree that I commanded you not to eat from?"[26]

Now c'mon. Did God really need to know where they were? After all, He's God and He knows everything, right? He wasn't playing cosmic hide-and-go-seek in the Garden with His children. He knew precisely where they were. He didn't need to discover their location. He did, however, want them to know where *He* was. He also didn't use one of these you're-in-deep-trouble-now tones of voice either. You know, like the one your parents used after discovering that huge dent in the side of the car. It's that tone of voice that is usually accompanied with your mother using your full name. Yikes! But this wasn't that kind of tone.

God's was not a condemning call, but rather a compassionate one. It was not the call of a cold Creator, but instead one of a caring Father. That's because Adam and Eve were more than just a part of His creation. They were more than just subjects of the King. They were His children. And He loved them. In calling out for them, God was giving them an opportunity to come back to Him. He wanted them to be *found* . . . by Him. Needless to say, God could have merely written them off, cast them aside and started the human race all over again with a brand new couple. Pressing the reset button, He could have scratched the original plan and simply given humanity another try. Or He could have just as easily exercised His righteousness and sent them both straight to hell. And in doing so, He would have been perfectly just. After all, they clearly violated His holy command, knowingly and willingly breaking His standard. They deliberately disobeyed. They deserved judgment and they expected a Judge to be waiting on the other side of that bush.

What they got instead was a Father.

God was calling our first parents to a place of confession, repentance, and restoration. Confession is important because they needed to agree with Him concerning their sin. He wanted them to repent, or to change their minds, doing an about-face in their attitude towards Him. But they also needed to change their minds about His plan as well, agreeing that His way really was best for them. They needed to believe again He really was a good God and that in Him they would find all they needed for life and fulfillment. They needed to agree that life was not found in the deceptive bargains offered by the devil. They needed to realize that unlike the devil, there was no hidden fine print in God's promises to them. In short, they needed to trust their Father again.

And why would God want them back? So that He might love and redeem them. They were valuable to Him and He was plainly demonstrating it here. He wanted to repair the tear in their relationship, using His own love to sew up the rip in the fabric. Like a rock band trashing a hotel room, their sin had effectively and thoroughly ruined the relationship. But God had plans to remodel, renovate, and restore that.

God wanted Adam and Eve to be themselves again, to once more become true worshippers. And the whole rest of the Bible is the story of how God did just that for them . . . and for us.

So have you ever thought of yourself as a natural worshipper? Specifically, that you were born incomplete, with a critical component of you missing? That missing piece of your soul's puzzle is demonstrated by your unexplainable desire to be a part of something bigger than yourself. From the most primitive island dweller to his counterpart in the big city, and every one of us in between, we are all irresistibly drawn to submit to something or someone. That's why, when as Christians we finally worship God, we feel so *complete*.

And we are.

Our very purpose is to worship. It's why the blood runs in our veins. It's the reason our heart beats seventy-plus times every minute. Every beat begs to worship God. It's why our eyes open each morning and why our feet move from the bed to the floor. Though the object of worship for some may be a religion, a person, or a passion, it really makes no difference. Every person out there is worshipping. Every student dashing to the next class. Every workmate in the office. Every player on the field. Every one. No one escapes the soul's gravitational pull of worship. The human race was designed with this need, capacity, and desire. It's in our motherboard, forever cemented in our circuitry.

We're wired for worship.

So have you felt this familiar ache in the heart? Have you come to believe that missing part is satisfied only when you fulfill your destiny in becoming a worshipper of the God who made you? It is only then that you will understand just how natural it can be. It's as native, innate, unlearned, and instinctive as breathing.

And if that's what you really want, turn the page and breathe deeply.

CHAPTER 3

An Audience of one

focusing your worship

When we see Him, we will wonder that we ever could have disobeyed Him.

—j. oswald chambers

Many faiths, one god?

In the wake of our national tragedy of 9–11–2001, a huge amount of attention was focused on spirituality and religion. On the one hand, Bible sales skyrocketed all across the country. Prominent radio and TV talk show hosts, not known for their religiosity, made on-air promises to pray for victims and their families who had suffered in the attack. In general, prayer itself even enjoyed a surprising comeback to the American way of life. But sandwiched between the bookends of prayer and our freshly found national God-consciousness was also a renewed emphasis on tolerance. Sprinkled like salt, the word was spread over virtually every broadcast conversation following the aftermath of our national nightmare. As a country, we slowly began the long process of dealing with our grief and loss. And in the midst of it all, we decided that though we desired revenge and justice, misplaced anger was to be avoided at all costs. And rightly so. The concern was that traditional Judeo-Christian America might rise up, declaring our own national brand of jihad, or holy war. It was made clear in a consensus that the United States' citizens should not seek retaliation for what radical Islamic extremists had done, acting on orders from madman Osama Bin Laden.

And though there were a few minor isolated acts of violence, Americans responded as expected, with proper restraint and trust. We agreed to allow our government and military to take care of justice overseas, while we would remain relatively tolerant here at home. Not long after the terrorist attack, President Bush hosted a national memorial service. Dignitaries and politicians packed out the National Cathedral in Washington, D.C. It was a national time to mourn, remember, and to make our resolve strong. We pledged to remain united as a country while at the same time seeking to bring to justice the ones behind this master plot of terror and destruction. As part of that service, representatives from the world's major religions were invited to attend in a visible effort to demonstrate the diverse spiritual life present in America. Jewish, Muslim, Hindu, Sikh, and Christian ministers were seated in chairs lining the front of the church. At the appointed time, the Reverend Billy Graham, aged and weak, ascended the steps to the pulpit. Once there, he was in his comfort zone. His almost regal snow-white hair shining with Moses-like glory, Reverend Graham stood and delivered a timely sermon. But his wasn't the only message delivered that day. Clearly through the vast diversity of the religious leaders present, we were also being visibly reminded that ours is a country of many faiths. Late night talk shows and news programs followed suit by featuring Jewish, Muslim, and Christian clergy, all unanimously agreeing that though we take different paths to Him, we all nevertheless still worship the same God.

But do we? This belief of merging all religions into one is what theologians call syncretism. But this practice is nothing new, really. As far back as the book of Exodus, we see Israel blending their faith with other religions of the day. This became a huge problem for God's people when they began conquering the Promised Land. But it even began way before that time.

Remember when Moses went up to the top of Mount Sinai to receive the Ten Commandments?

sin At sinai

Moses was up on the Mountain forty days and nights, and his brother Aaron, along with a very large congregation of people, grew weary of waiting for their fearless leader to come back down. Perhaps they figured he had lost his way in the darkness or perished in the fire. But in reality, Moses was just fine up there. It's just that he was more than a little preoccupied with listening to the voice of Almighty God speak to him. Moses really didn't have the luxury of leaving whenever he wanted to. God had a lot to tell the former son of Pharaoh, and He wasn't quite finished speaking yet. Among the many things He told him up on that mountain was that Moses should instruct the people to bring Him an offering of gold, among other valuable items. But meanwhile, down at base camp, things were getting out of hand. Here's what happened.

> When the people saw that Moses was so long in coming down from the mountain, they gathered around Aaron and said, Come, make us gods who will go before us. As for this fellow Moses who brought us up out of Egypt, we don't know what has happened to him. Aaron answered them, "Take off the gold earrings that your wives, your sons and your daughters are wearing, and bring them to me." So all the people took off their earrings and brought them to Aaron. He took what they handed him and made it into an idol cast in the shape of a calf, fashioning it with a tool. Then he said, "These are your gods, O Israel, who brought you up out of Egypt." Then he built an altar in front of the calf and announced, "Tomorrow there will be a festival to the Lord." So the next day the people rose early and sacrificed burnt offerings and presented fellowship offerings. Afterward, they sat down to eat and drink and indulge in revelry. (Exodus 32:1–6)

Now it should be brought to your attention that among Bible scholars, there is some debate as to what Aaron's actual intentions were in this idolatrous exercise. Many believe the molded golden calf was a mistaken attempt to physically represent the invisible God who had brought them out of slavery. After all, Aaron was there with his brother Moses when God did those miracles before Pharaoh. It wasn't like he didn't know God was real. At the same time, he wasn't the one on top of the mountain hearing the voice of God say, "You shall have no other gods before me." Besides, the people needed reassurance that their God was real and that He was still with them. They wanted a God they could see and touch. They needed some symbol to look at. And keep in mind also that the people of Israel, about two million strong by this point, had been living in a pagan land (Egypt) for four hundred years. They all grew up there, as did their fathers and grand-fathers for centuries before them. As far as they knew, Egypt was home. For generations, their families had been a part of Egyptian culture. During that four-hundred-year time span, there was no Bible, no prophets, no worship services, no temple of God, and no one to spiritually lead them. Naturally, many, if not most Jews would have adopted many of the customs and prac-tices of the pagan religions native to Egypt. After all, they did this in every other land in which they later lived.

But there is yet another clue suggesting the making of this golden calf was an effort to blend the true God with their Egyptian religion. The Hebrew word translated *gods* (*elohim*, pronounced "el-o-heem") is simply the name of God in its plural form. Keep in mind also that after being redeemed from Egypt, the nation had enjoyed seeing the *shekinah*, the glory of God, lead them, but now it was veiled. So they were looking for something visible and tangible to symbolize the divine presence of God. Perhaps they reasoned that this golden god could go ahead of them just like the pillar of fire had done.

At first glance, we might be tempted to initially cut Israel some slack because of their harsh slavery experience. After all, they were somewhat ignorant of this new Redeemer God. And besides, at least they were *trying* to worship God. It's just that they didn't know any better, right? Wrong.

Prior to their little arts and crafts calf-making experience, consider what God had told them.

> Then the Lord said to Moses, "Tell the Israelites this: 'You have seen for yourselves that I have spoken to you from heaven: Do not make any gods to be alongside me; do not make for your-selves gods of silver or gods of gold'" (Exodus 20:22–23). When Moses went and told the people all the Lord's words and laws, they responded with one voice, **"Everything the Lord has said we will do."** (Exodus 24:3)

Busted.

Due to an irresistible desire to worship and celebrate their redemption from Egypt, (or maybe they were just impatient and bored), the people of God held a very weird and wild worship service including, among other things, gluttony and sexual orgies. Now the gluttony part we can partially understand, seeing as how we love to pig out on Sunday after church. But this was one serious potluck dinner on the grounds, with gross and exces-sive eating. Combined with sexual perversion and immorality, it was a scene resembling modern-day Mardi Gras. And God was not pleased.

But here's what happened next: Moses finally comes down from the mountain, hearing what sounded like a celebration of war victory. As he approached the camp and saw the calf and the dancing, his anger burned and he threw the tablets out of his hands, breaking them to pieces at the foot of the mountain. He took the calf they had made and burned it in the fire; then he ground it to powder, scattered it on the water and made the Israelites drink it.

He said to Aaron, "What did these people do to you, that you led them into such great sin?"

"Do not be angry, my lord," Aaron answered. "You know how prone these people are to evil. They said to me, 'Make us gods who will go before us. As for this fellow Moses who brought us up out of Egypt, we don't know what has happened to him.' So I told them, 'Whoever has any gold jewelry, take it off.' Then they gave me the gold, and I threw it into the fire, and out came this calf!"

Moses saw that the people were running wild and that Aaron had let them get out of control and so become a laughingstock to their enemies.

So he stood at the entrance to the camp and said, "Whoever is for the Lord, come to me." And all the Levites rallied to him. Then he said to them, "This is what the Lord, the God of Israel, says: 'Each man strap a sword to his side. Go back and forth through the camp from one end to the other, each killing his brother and friend and neighbor.'" The Levites did as Moses commanded, and that day about three thousand of the people died.

Admittedly, this was not a pleasant scene. Aaron and the people learned the hard way that God refuses to share His glory with another. It was a very high price to pay for a night of sin. The prophet Isaiah would record centuries later, "I am the Lord; that is my name! I will not give my glory to another or my praise to idols" (Isaiah 42:8). Translated, this means that the God of the Bible demands to be worshipped exclusively. He is the only God, and only His religion is authentic.

So what about that syncretism thing, then? Blended religions? Do all faiths really worship the same God? Can we legitimately combine Yahweh worship with that of any other so-called god, faith, or religion? The Lord says, *No way. Never.* If that sounds a bit narrow, it's because it is. But when you're the only true God, you can make statements like that.

Fast forward now to Jesus' day, when the most celebrated city in the world was Rome. Supposedly founded in 753 B.C., by the time the New Testament was written, Rome was enriched and adorned with the spoils of the world, containing a population estimated at 1,200,000—half of which were slaves, including representatives of nearly every nation. It was distinguished by its wealth and luxury. An elaborate series of paved highways were constructed all over the Roman Empire, enabling travelers to make their way to the greatness of that monumental city. But while all roads may have led to Rome, not all roads lead to God. Never have. Never will. Jesus reaffirms this truth, claiming in John 14:6 to be "the way, the truth and the life," adding, "no man comes to the Father except by Me." And those are His original words, not merely the claims of narrow-minded Christians.

So since that's true, let's take a time out to respond by asking ourselves a few follow-up questions. Why worship this one and only God? What's the goal of our worship? What inspires worship in us? What factors determine how we worship Him? How are we supposed to know how to worship? How important is our knowledge of God? What is the role of our life experiences? How much of God do you need to know in order to truly worship Him? How can we deepen our personal worship experience? Okay, let's see if we can tackle a few of these together.

it's who you know

First, we need to understand that it is God's revelation of Himself that first prompts us to worship Him. In other words, when God reveals who He is and what He has done for us, the most natural response is to worship. Or put another way, we worship God because of His character and His great deeds. As we said earlier, your view of God will ultimately determine your worship of Him. And the more you know about God's greatness, the greater your capacity to declare His praise. Unfortunately, the image of God many people have in their minds is, in reality, more of a caricature than an accurate portrait. Like a cartoonist's sketch, many have a distorted picture of who He is and what He is like. As we saw in Chapter One, many see God as a harsh, weak, distant Deity or even some kind of faceless force. And while it's true that God created man in His own image, due to man's fallen nature, he returned the favor, creating God in *his* own image. He has imagined Him to be what he would *like* Him to be.

We want a God that is fair and loving . . . but only as *we* define those terms. The God of man's mental creation must be a God who answers prayer . . . but does so in *our* timing, and in the way *we* want them answered. We certainly don't want a God who is too harsh, but on the other hand, we do want Him to execute swift justice on all those who are not as righteous as we are. We prefer a God who gives out crowns, not crosses—a God who provides eternal salvation, but who doesn't demand too much of us this side of eternity. We desire a God who let's us get to Him any way we choose. Poll most people concerning what God is like, and they are prone to respond this way: I *think* God is like this . . . or I *feel* God wouldn't ever do *that* . . .

Here's the problem: If our ideas about God stem from our own thoughts and feelings, we end up using the brush stroke of our brains to paint a Picasso-like portrait of the true God. It becomes a hit and miss thing, and we can never really know for sure whether those thoughts and feelings are accurate. Does that make sense? Suppose you were led into a room containing an eight-foot tall partition down the middle. You are seated at a table on which is a pen and paper. You are told that on the other side of the partition is a woman. You are then told to draw a portrait of the woman, the only rule being that you can't see or hear her. Obviously, you will never be able to accurately draw the woman. And why not? To begin with, you have never seen her. You would miss accurately portraying her because you have no idea what she looks like. Oh, you might take a stab at it and draw her with long hair or wearing a dress or something. But still, your best effort would fall short of duplicating what she really looks like. Now if you could peek around that partition, you might have a chance of representing her image with pen and paper. Let's apply this to our view of God. Left to ourselves, we really have little information about Him. So when we try to conjure up images of what He is like from our own imaginations, our best efforts will fall short. Our only hope is that God would step around the partition to reveal Himself to us. That's the only way we can ever know what He is really like.

So if we are ever going to confidently know who God is and what He is like, then *He* must reveal Himself to us. We are totally dependent on His revelation. Without it, we are doomed to stumble about in the darkness of our fallen vain imaginations. It's like putting together a jigsaw puzzle without the picture on the box and with most of the pieces missing. To truly understand who God is, we desperately need Him to speak to us. When we worship what we do not know, we are no different than an uncivilized jungle native bowing down to the sun. But fortunately for us, God has not been silent. On the contrary, He has spoken loudly to us through a variety of ways and on many different levels. Generally speaking, creation reveals God to us, telling us of His power and greatness. Our inner conscience also helps us know right from wrong, thereby revealing His moral nature. But if we are to know more and get specific about God, we have to consult Scripture. He has spoken to us in His word, and He has not stuttered (2 Timothy 3:16–17; Hebrews 4:12). Our understanding of God must primarily come from His written Word. He reveals His true nature and character to us in the only book He ever wrote. Isaiah penned these words: "The grass withers, the flower fades, but the word of our God stands forever."[27]

Contained within the pages of your Bible is the real truth about God. And because He wants you to know Him, He has utilized virtually every literary device available in Scripture to help you get it, including autobiography, biography, poetry, history, narrative, and prophecy. In Scripture, you find drama, action, suspense, and satire. There is a variety of ways in those sixty-six books that God has communicated to you. It's His book written for you. Of course, God's ultimate and final revelation of Himself was through His Son, Jesus Christ (John 1:14,18).

> . . . but in these last days he has spoken to us by his Son, whom
> he appointed heir of all things, and through whom he made the
> universe. (Hebrews 1:2)

We could summarize it this way. So great was God's desire for us to know Him that He revealed Himself outwardly (through Creation), inwardly (through conscience), and completely (through Christ). Then He permanently put it all in print for us to read and understand. But rather than simply deliver a huge laundry list of God's characteristics to increase our knowledge so we can feel better about ourselves, let's focus instead on a small portion of that written record. Let's discover a bit of who God really is, putting those truths in the context of real life.

There is no debating that we live in dark times. Our world is as uncertain as it ever has been. Governments change hands overnight. Injustices increase. Evil flourishes. Wars never cease. The innocent and righteous suffer while the guilty and criminals prosper. But lest we think these things are unique to our time and culture, things were no different in Isaiah's day. The nation Israel was suffering in captivity to a godless Assyrian nation. Judah (her southern sister) would follow in just one hundred years, becoming a captive of Babylon. Into this dark era stepped the prophet Isaiah, and he had a word *from* God *about* God. If they ever needed a word from heaven, it was then. And what was Isaiah's message of hope to a hurting people? Was it social reform? A motivational speech? A government grant? A comedy routine? Hardly. Isaiah, under the inspiration of the Holy Spirit, was much smarter than that. What he does in Chapter 40 of the book that bears his name is simply declare to Israel who God really is. He tells them God alone is worthy of their worship. But why? What specifically moves us to worship Him? Quoting God directly, Isaiah records three essential truths about who He is.

I AM THE GREATEST
(Isaiah 40:12–20)

Mohammed Ali was the best boxer of all time. Regardless of how you feel about his political views or religious affiliation, when the former Cassius Clay strapped on the gloves and stepped into the ring, he made history with almost every blow. And yet, with all due respect to the Champ, who's most famous catchphrase was *I am the greatest*, there is Someone much greater than he. Granted, it sure *sounds* wonderful for God to say He is the greatest, but what in the world does that really mean? Of course, He knew you were going to say that so He specifically mentions four reasons why He alone is worthy of your heart's worship and allegiance. He gets a little more specific for us with the following claims:

I am Great in creation

> Who has measured the waters in the hollow of his hand, or with
> the breadth of his hand marked off the heavens? Who has held
> the dust of the earth in a basket, or weighed the mountains on
> the scales and the hills in a balance? (Isaiah 40:12)

Next time you take a walk outside at night, or even when you're standing alone on the back porch, take a long look up into the sky. For sixty seconds, try and count the stars staring down at you from above. On a clear night
out in the country, with no man-made lights dimming the night sky's bright-
ness, the human eye can spot approximately four thousand luminaries. Of
course it's doubtful you'll take the time to count all four thousand, but assuming you did, think on this: What do you suppose lies beyond those stars you
can see with your eyes?

Astronomers now estimate there are some ten billion stars in our
galaxy . . . ten billion! But that's not all. They also believe there is sufficient
evidence for the existence of some ten *million* galaxies like ours contained
within our universe. Feeling small yet? In addition, remember from science
class that the distance from one end of our Milky Way to the other is millions of light years in time and distance. Considering light travels approximately six trillion miles in a year's time, that's quite a road trip! Okay, now
ponder this: God made it all. He's bigger than all of it *combined.* Unlike some
of our modern, misguided, self-appointed galactic gurus, it is both illogical
(not to mention just plain stupid) to worship the cosmos. Imagine admiring
a masterpiece painting without recognizing the one who painted it. If the
painting draws our praise, how much more so should the painter. Duh!

Or suppose you attended the concert of your favorite band. How disappointed would you feel if, after the lights dimmed and the music began
playing, onto the stage walked a lone roadie carrying their "Greatest Hits"
CD. Perched on a stool all by itself, giant background screens projected an
image of the band. Then the contents of the CD blasted away for two hours

over a killer sound system until at last the final track was played and faded to silence. Then the same roadie returns to the stage, retrieves the CD and disappears offstage. Do you have the suspicion that some angry fans might want their money back? Or maybe even storm the stage? No chance the fans will stomp their feet or hold lighters in the air for an encore. But why? Easy answer: Because when you go to a concert, you do so to see the *band*, not to hear the band's CD. You can listen to the CD in your car anytime. It's far more valuable to see the band in person than it is to simply hear a recording of them. Though you can hear the greatness of the band through the recording, the recording is not the band. It never will be. It's just a creation of that band. At a live concert, it's never a substitute for the real thing. Besides, without the band there would be no CD.

So next time you're standing on a snow-packed Colorado mountaintop, pause and take in the spectacular view. The great God you worship formed those same mountains. Walk to the edge of the Grand Canyon and feel your heartbeat raging like a wild drum solo. It's His handiwork you're witnessing. Body surf the North Shore waters off Oahu and marvel at His ability to create such a paradise. Pluck a leaf from a tree. Gaze at a freshly fallen snowflake. Follow the flight of a hawk. Hear the rhythm of the raindrops. Trace the path of a stream through the woods. Find your favorite cartoon character in the clouds. Feel the summer sun heat up your face. All of this comes from Him. Creation is His invention, and it plainly tells every one of us that God is powerful, creative, and eternal (Psalm 19; Romans 1:19–20). The sheer enormity of creation screams the power of God. Contemplating His work in the universe puts both us and our world into fresh perspective. It tells us there is a God after all, and He has not left Himself without a witness. Look at what Paul affirmed:

> Since what may be known about God is plain to them, because God has made it plain to them. For since the creation of the world God's invisible qualities— his eternal power and divine nature— have been clearly seen, being understood from what has been made, so that men are without excuse. (Romans 1:19–20)

Attempting to refute the reality of a Creator is to simply suppress the truth (Romans 1:18, 21–22). It's an exercise in futility. It is also denial in its worst form. But God goes even farther than just surrounding us with an outward witness of Himself. He also placed an inward witness in us as well. Implanted within each of us is an inner compass, a built-in database that bears witness to His existence and to a basic right and wrong (Romans 2:14–16). And as we will discuss more in Chapter eight, it wasn't just the earth God created, but you as well (Psalm 139). He not only gave you life while in your mother's womb, but He was also intricately involved in personally creating you. You are not a result of random chance or even a case of simple parental genetics taking its natural course. God Himself made you. And He loves what He makes. Do you stand in awe of God's supremacy as Creator?

But God tells us a second reason He is the greatest.

I Am Great in Wisdom
(Isaiah 40:13–14)

Consider the following mind-melting realities about God's intelligence: No one gives God directions or tells Him what He can and cannot do (Psalm 115:3). As we will soon see, He does whatever pleases Him. God has never needed counsel or advice. No one instructs Him in wisdom. No one can or could. It is reasonable to say that God possesses more knowledge than all of man's combined knowledge and wisdom. No amount of data could possibly match God's. Silicon Valley will never find the word to describe the massive post-gigabyte memory capacity unique to God. However, theologians have found a way to describe it. They call it omniscience, or God's infinite knowledge. You may remember this word infinite from math class. It's a term meaning without end. God's omniscience just means He is all-knowing. Try to grasp the following thought: It is impossible for God to learn anything new. He cannot be taught any new information. From eternity past, God has owned all knowledge. He has always possessed knowledge of all facts, figures, reasons, and dates. He has always known every minute detail of history. At no point in time or eternity has He had ever had a Eureka! experience. He has never discovered something He didn't previously know. God's vast knowledge extends to the past, present, and future. He even possesses all knowledge in the realm of possibility and theory. In other words, He knows every what if and contingency possible to mankind, history, world events, and even your life. Ever wondered what you would be like had you been born in another country, of another race, or in another time? God knows it completely. What if you had been awarded that athletic scholarship and gone on to play pro ball? What about that life-changing event that happened to you when you were ten years old? How would your life be different today had it not occurred? What if you had been born to different parents? God sees that scenario right now. He knows it all. He has known it from eternity past. His knowledge is both perfect and perpetual. It never ends. And God is also the origin and source of all wisdom and understanding (Proverbs 1:7). Even these profound thoughts about God did not originate with the prophet Isaiah, but were given as divine revelation from heaven.

As you think about your life, with so many different potential paths still ahead of you, which one will you choose? God knows the best and most excellent way. And combined with His love for you, He has even promised to guide you there (Psalm 32:8; James 1:4). Is that a deal or what?! He has a perfect and wise plan for your life that cannot be improved upon (Jeremiah 29:11; Romans 12:2). Like an infinitely wise online search engine, God has already instantly surveyed a few billion possibilities for your life, immediately drafting for you the best blueprint imaginable. His wise plan is perfect because it is based on the greatest wisdom available. And it is wise because it is birthed out of a wisdom that is both eternal and infinite (Romans 11:33–36). You cannot add one single thing that would in any way enhance His plan for you. Your suggestions would only damage and detract from it. But wait, there's more. God wants us to know. Now catch your breath for a minute, because we're about to take an adventure into the deepest nature of your God.

ı Am Great in sovereignty

Look at this portion of Scripture:

> Surely the nations are like a drop in a bucket; they are regarded
> as dust on the scales; he weighs the islands as though they were
> fine dust. . . . Do you not know? Have you not heard? Has it not
> been declared to you from the beginning? Have you not under-
> stood from the foundations of the earth? It is He who sits above
> the vault of the earth, and its inhabitants are like grasshoppers,
> Who stretches out the heavens like a curtain And spreads them
> out like a tent to dwell in. It is He who reduces rulers to nothing,
> Who makes the judges of the earth meaningless. Scarcely have
> they been planted, Scarcely have they been sown, Scarcely has
> their stock taken root in the earth, But He merely blows on
> them, and they wither, And the storm carries them away like
> stubble. "To whom then will you liken Me that I should be his
> equal?" says the Holy One. (Isaiah 40:15,21–25)

This paragraph from Isaiah illustrates part of what we refer to as God's
sovereignty. God's sovereignty simply means He is God and God alone. He
is self-sufficient. Independent. Free. Self-governing. A law unto Himself.
And He does whatever pleases Him. You may be thinking, *Wow! That sounds
a whole lot like my boss at work!* Well, while it may be true that some people
try to function this way, there is still only One who actually does. So what
would God have us know about His sovereignty? What does it mean?

First, it means God is on His throne, controlling all things. He's in charge.
He is the ultimate Commander-in-Chief. Heaven is the real Supreme Court
and God is the Chief Justice. He manages the affairs of the world in such a
way that accomplishes His purposes. Look at how Job, David, and Isaiah put
it: "I know that Thou canst do all things, and that no purpose of Thine can be
thwarted" (Job 42:2). "But our God is in the heavens; He does whatever He

pleases" (Psalm 115:3). "Whatever the Lord pleases, He does, in heaven and in earth, in the seas and in all deeps" (Psalm 135:6). "Even from eternity I am He; and there is none who can deliver out of My hand; I act and who can reverse it?" (Isaiah 43:13).

Now let's take this truth off the top shelf so we can see it up close. One way we can understand God's sovereignty is to realize He doesn't have to consult anyone before He acts. No one tells Him what to do or controls Him. He is self-existent and self-fulfilling. In other words, He has need of nothing. He doesn't need heaven, angels, or people. But in His sovereignty, He chose to create them all. And because God is independent and free, it means He has no inherent obligations to His creation. In other words, He owes no man anything (Romans 11:33–36). No man can point a finger at God and say, *Hey, You owe me!* God is totally free to give and do as it pleases Him. The only obligations God has to us are those He has decided to place upon Himself as recorded in His Word.

In America, we have a cherished document called The Bill of Rights where our freedoms under the Constitution are outlined and protected— things like freedom of speech and freedom of religion. You can even go to Washington and view this wonderful document. It's your right to do so as an American. We are used to hearing a lot about individual rights these days—things like civil rights, the right to free speech, the right to a fair trial, etc. Our rights involve everything from praying to protesting. And it seems like someone's rights are constantly being violated. People march in the streets, demanding their rights. But have you ever stopped to consider that God has rights too? Simply because of Who He is, as the King of the Universe, as a Citizen of Himself, He possesses certain inalienable rights. In reality, He has the right to say or do anything. It's His prerogative as God. And yet, even among Christians, there isn't much talk about God's rights. True, we could never trust any mere man with this kind of limitless sovereignty, but we can trust God to do whatever He wants because He always does what is good, fair and right (Psalm 111:7–8).

So first of all, God's sovereignty means He does whatever He pleases and that He is accountable only to Himself. He is the King and answers to no one. But secondly, His sovereignty also means He rules over all.

In light of this great power, wisdom, and sovereignty, can you see how the great nations of the earth, with their influence and power, are insignificantly small compared to God? This comforting truth would have been especially meaningful to the people of Israel to whom Isaiah spoke. They were suffering under the hand of Assyria, the most powerful empire on the earth at the time. Such a kingdom must have seemed bigger than life itself to the tiny Jewish nation, for it affected their daily lives. But compared to God, even the world's mightiest country or coalition of nations is no more significant than the *drop* of water which condenses on the outside of the bucket (Isaiah 40:15). God says whatever nation threatens the welfare of His children is as irrelevant as the *fine dust* that is leftover on a pair of market scales (verse 15). Like a speck of dust easily blown away with a whisper, so are His enemies. When compared to Him, it's almost like they don't even exist (Isaiah 40:17). Such nations are *meaningless* (verse 17). By the way, has anybody seen Assyria the great lately? On the other hand, the tiny nation Israel thrives to this very day. Ever wonder why?

God is very jealous about His authority. He will share it with no one. Even so, there have been some earthly rulers who thought *they* had a better idea on how to run the world than God did. As we read earlier in Isaiah 40, God gets specific concerning how He disposes of powerful and arrogant rulers. There have been some who challenged God's authority—and regretted it. Maybe you've heard of these cocky criminals. He reduced them to nothing.

It is true of the Napoleons, Hitlers, Lenins, Stalins, Husseins, and Bin Ladens. Those who refuse to bow before God will not stand before Him. These men thought they could outrank the God of heaven. Big mistake! They opposed His authority to rule and to control the affairs of men. But ultimately God proves He is the greatest. He even changes the hearts of world rulers to do what He wants them to do (Proverbs 21:1). Man proposes; God disposes. God shares His glory with no one, and because He rules, no nation is a threat to Him.

Thirdly, God's sovereignty means that He is in control (Daniel 4:35; Isaiah 43:13; Job 42:2). This is what theologians call the Decree of God (now don't freak out). This truth simply means that God is in absolute control of everything that occurs and everything that exists. It means His sovereignty has everything under control. It means all things happen only under the purpose, plan or permission of His divine will. Think of it this way:

- God *causes* some things,
- God *allows* other things, but
- He is in *control* of all things.

The Bible teaches us that God is working behind the scenes, bringing history along to conform to His perfect and beautiful plan (Ephesians 1:11). He has mapped out a blueprint for history that is always right on schedule and accomplishing exactly what He desires (Isaiah 55:8–11).

But wait a second, you may be thinking. *How can God be in control of all things? How can He be in control over sin and evil?*

That is a very perceptive and spiritual question. And here's the answer. Above all, you can be confident that, because of His holy and righteous nature, God is never the author of sin or evil. He cannot touch sin in any way or be affected by it. But we would all admit He does allow its existence. And He does permit people to choose to sin. But why? Ultimately, God allows sin to occur for reasons known only to Him. We know that one day, perhaps soon, He will bring all sinners to judgment. In the meantime, God does not permit sinners to go beyond the boundaries He has fixed before-hand for them (Job 1:12). Though many things work against the sovereignty of God (such as sin), His purposes are nonetheless always established. And (are you ready for this?) because He is so sovereign, God even *uses* sin and sinners to accomplish His purposes.

And we know that God causes all things to work together for good to those who love God, to those who are called according to His purpose (Romans 8:28). Sin and sinners are a part of all those things He *causes* to work together for His purposes. For example, He even used the greatest and most horrific *sinful* act of all mankind (the brutal and bloody murder of His Son) to bring about the greatest *good* for all mankind (the salvation of all who would believe). Look at one of the first-ever prayers offered up by New Testament believers in Jerusalem.

> For truly in this city there were gathered together against Thy holy servant Jesus, whom Thou didst anoint, both Herod and Pontius Pilate, along with the Gentiles and the peoples of Israel, **to do whatever Thy hand and Thy purpose predestined to occur**. (Acts 4:27–28)

That is how much God is in control. Can you say, Wow?

100% chance of Reign

So are there any benefits of God's reign? What practical difference does knowing about God's ability to rule over all make in our everyday lives? There are several areas of blessing we can experience from knowing that God is in control. Here are a few of the biggies:

He reigns in our personal life (Romans 10:9; Philippians 2:10–11). One of the implications of God being a sovereign Lord is that He has an inherent, inalienable right to rule, not just the world, but the people in it as well. Of course, some have a real problem with God demanding His right to rule in their lives. We often hear the Savior characteristics of God expressed—His love, mercy, goodness, etc.—but His Lordship and Sovereignty are another matter. In our sin, we still want autonomy. Is that any surprise? The thought of climbing down off the throne of our hearts and submitting to someone else is offensive to our sin nature. Simply put, we want to be in control. We fear not being in control and we are often unwilling to give up the reins to anyone other than ourselves. This is sad because God's rule in our lives is such an awesome thing. As we submit to God, we become truly free, receiving the ability to be who we were created to be. Besides, who better to run our lives than the One who created us, pursued us, died, rose again for us, and has promised to lead us into the abundant life?

But second, *He reigns in our salvation* (Ephesians 1:4–5, 11; 2:1–2; Romans 9:18; I Peter 1:1–2). Before becoming Christians, we were spiritually dead, unable to seek after God, clearly having no chance of salvation on our own. Considering this, God had to first initiate a relationship with us if we were to have any hope of heaven. And that is exactly what He did. We now love Him because He first loved us (I John 4:19). Consider these truths about God's sovereignty in your salvation:

- He set His heart on you before the foundation of the earth (Ephesians 1:4).
- He chose you before you chose Him (John 15:16, Colossians 3:12, I Peter 2:9).
- He loved you before you loved Him (I John 4:19).
- He made you spiritually alive in Christ (Ephesians 2:1–5).
- He attracted you to His Son for salvation (John 6:44).
- He saved you, because of His own will, not because of your effort (John 1:12–13).

And all this He did sovereignly because He desired to do it. It simply pleased Him to save you. Now we can see why the psalmist wrote, "Salvation belongs to the Lord" (Psalm 3:8).

Third, *He reigns in our suffering* (Romans 5:3–5; 8:28). Only a sovereign God could take tragedy and turn it into triumph, right? But does God's sovereignty really help us in our suffering? Yes! First, when we suffer, we can rest assured that God is still in control. Nothing takes Him by surprise. He is still on the throne and in control. Heaven never pushes the panic button. Though your world may crumble, *you* don't have to because God's still in charge.

But also, when you suffer, you can know He will somehow turn your suffering into good for you (Romans 8:28), and that when you suffer, you can know God is conforming you into Christ-likeness (Romans 8:29; Job

23:10). Remember Joseph? God ultimately turned his horrible circumstances into triumph and redemption for the entire Jewish nation (Gen. 37:20–28; 50:20). Who would've thought it? Only a sovereign God could take a Calvary and turn it into an Easter.

And fourth, *He reigns even over our sin* (Romans 6:1–2, 6; Philippians 1:6). Perhaps the most amazing thing of all is the wondrous way God exercises His sovereignty over our sin. Only God can transform our moral defeats into victories. He turns our stumbling blocks into stepping-stones. And He has been doing this for His children since time began.

Are you beginning to get the idea that God is on your side? That He is *for* you? That's good news! No, make that *great* news! And it calls to mind those words found in the New Testament.

> What, then, shall we say in response to this? If God is for us, who can be against us? He who did not spare his own Son, but gave him up for us all— how will he not also, along with him, graciously give us all things? (Romans 8:31–32)

It's an argument from the greater to the lesser, really. If God's rule is not threatened by our suffering or even our sin, then what should we fear? If He has bound Himself to be for us, why should we worry? If God has declared you righteous in Himself, who can possibly say you are otherwise? Who or what could possibly remove the salvation God has given to you? Is any power greater than God's? Don't think so! No hardship humanly imaginable will ever disconnect you from Him. No sin too bad. No power too strong. Right now, could you just shout, or at least pause, close your eyes and thank Him for this? Even if an entire pagan nation comes against you, take heart, friend. God isn't cowering. He isn't running for cover. Your Deliverer and Defender will come! And in the unlikely event the mountains crumble down around you, don't sweat it (Psalm 46). Instead, be still and worship this God who is greater than your circumstances.

Ruling in our hearts. Ruling in salvation. Ruling in suffering. Ruling over our sin. The implications of these truths are staggering. All praise to our sovereign God!

And God's conclusion? *Who is like Me?*, God says. And *to whom will you compare Me?* God shouts to the earth, *Do you know anyone like Me?* and silence blankets the entire universe! Not even a cricket chirping.

But God isn't quite finished yet. Isaiah now dips his pen in ink and positions his hand to write one more for us. God says,

I Am Great in Righteousness
(Isaiah 40:16)

"Lebanon is not sufficient for altar fires, nor its animals enough for burnt offerings."

The forests of Lebanon were not only the largest in the known world, but it's wood was the finest quality—used in temples, government buildings and the interiors of wealthy home-owners.

God is saying, *I am so righteous and worthy that if you cut down every tree in that great forest, and kill every animal and lay all of this on an altar, setting it on fire in an attempt to satisfy My righteousness, it would still not be enough.* The righteous demands of God's holy nature cannot be satisfied or appeased with religious sacrifice no matter how great or sincere. That's because an infinite God requires an infinite sacrifice (Isaiah 64:6; I Peter 1:18–19). Nothing can appease God's wrath (I John 2:2)—nothing except the perfect, permanent sacrifice of the Messiah will do. And again, God asks us, "Who is like Me?" (Isaiah 40:18–20) Are you beginning to see how even our highest thoughts of God fall far short of Him?

In summary, God is unique. He is not like us. He is above us all, and very great. God is awesome and supreme. So think high, deep and lofty thoughts of Him! Worship Him because He is so great! Worship Him because He proves Himself to the greatest in creation, wisdom, sovereignty, and righteousness. Worship Him because He is God. He is our only audience, and the only One who really matters. Let's be a generation with a zero tolerance worship policy. May we not allow ourselves to worship anyone but God and to worship Him because of His great character and attributes. Worship is really not about us, is it? It's not even about worship. It's about God and God alone, the One who rightfully deserves our deepest devotion and highest praise. Don't settle for anything less than that in your worship experience!

CHAPTER 4

The Grace Factor
Motivation for worship

His grace has brought me safe thus far, and grace will lead me home.
—Amazing Grace by John Newton

To live by grace is to live solely by the merit of Jesus Christ.
—Jerry Bridges

Any fool can make a rule.
—Henry David Thoreau

cheap grace

The world is full of oxymorons. You know, those two-word phrases which appear to negate themselves, canceling out their combined meaning. Of the thousands of contradictory terms out there, here are some of the better ones.

act naturally · advanced basic · alone together · casual sex · computer jock · clearly ambiguous · seriously funny · conservative liberal · deafening silence · definite maybe · designer jeans · diet ice cream · exact estimate · extensive briefing · minor miracle · found missing · freezer burn · friendly fire · genuine imitation · government organization · healthy chocolate · hells angels · half naked · ill health · instant classic · black light · jumbo shrimp · least favorite · legally drunk · minor crisis · modern history

Now here's the most outrageous of them all:

Boring worship.

These are two words that have no business hanging out with each other. They are polar opposites. Contradictory terms. An unequally yoked couple, boring worship is an oxymoron if there ever was one. When we see who God is, with His great character and essence, how can we not worship? How can we worship this kind of God and be bored? How can we see him for who He truly is and not be moved? How can we walk away unchanged? When we begin to understand His greatness, there is an almost involuntary reaction leading us to this One who is so wonderful. We can actually know the Creator of the Universe! Hello? How could that possibly be boring? And yet, it often seems that way for some. Aren't you tired of people who mis-represent our great God in this way? Doesn't it just give you a pain to see people who advertise a blasé Savior?

You know this kind of person. They are filled with knowledge about God. They have been in church since they were in their mother's womb. They have seen every Bible picture book ever written. They have made every imaginable craft known to man out of popsicle sticks while in Sunday School and Vacation Bible School (has anyone noticed there seems to be a lot of school in church?). They have memorized more Bible verses than there are Bible verses, even receiving awards for doing so. They have taken special training classes. They can share their faith with an avowed atheist. They can even disarm a cult leader's philosophy with one Testament tied behind their back. They are defenders of the faith. Their Bibles are filled with study notes and their calendars are filled with religious activities. They are morally upright people, theologically orthodox, believing all the right things about God. But there's just one small problem—they don't have a vibrant, alive relationship with Him.

In the last chapter, we discussed the greatness of God, and rightly so. Knowing who He is essentially enhances our worship. Once again, we can't worship a God about whom we know nothing. But sometimes we fall into the deceptive and subtle trap of pursuing knowledge about God for knowledge's sake. We mistakenly assume that the more facts we gather about Him, the more spiritual we become. Surely there is more to it than that! If that's all there is, then we become nothing more than contestants for the Bible Jeopardy game. If simply knowing facts about God, as mind-blowing as those truths are, is what constitutes the Christian life, then our worship is incomplete. And after a while, it would indeed be very boring. However, that is exactly where some people's relationship with God ends—right there with the facts. Oh, they think they have a real relationship with Him. But in reality, it's only a relationship with a set of rules or a system of beliefs. Their idea of the Christian life is bound up in trying to be right in everything. To be real honest, if that's all you're looking for, you can get it from any one of many world philosophies, political parties, and religions.

Granted, it's true that God could have made us as mere subjects in His royal kingdom and nothing more. He could have said, *Here is my Book. Just live by these rules and I won't destroy you.* But thank God His plan extends beyond that . . . way beyond that. God desires us to know Him not only as Creator and King, but also as Savior and Father. And that's where our second motivation for worship enters the picture.

We saw earlier that after mankind first fell into a state of sin, God came after them with a compassionate call. His plan was to redeem them, restoring them to the place where they could once again enjoy a relationship with Him. However, to accomplish this, He would have to devise a master plan, something that would effectively remedy their sin problem and conquer their corrupt human nature. And that's exactly what He did. But to fully appreciate God's grace, we need to first understand and appreciate the context in which that grace is applied to us.

Perhaps you know one of those talented people who enjoy locating old cars in junkyards, towing them home, and completely refurbishing and rebuilding them. From rusted metal, corroded bumpers, deteriorating fabric, cracked dashboards, peeling paint, and missing parts, these craftsmen can, with great skill, intense labor, and sometimes a wad of cash, give the old car new life again, making it virtually brand new. In fact, many times these cars end up as classics, becoming even better than new. Wading through those junkyards, these automobile artisans possess the ability to see beyond the wrecks and ruins stacked high and deep. They see more than what those old heaps *are*, but instead what they can *become* through the miracle touch of a master craftsman.

Similarly, when God finds us, we are in a state of sin. All of us. We have failed to live up to God's standard of perfection. This means we are spiritually dead, a condition we unfortunately inherited from our first parents, Adam and Eve (Psalm 51:5). Because of this, our inborn sinful identity is as much a part of who we are as our physical DNA. In fact, it's even more a part of who were are. Unlike our physical bodies, it is possible to take our sinful condition with us into eternity. But this spiritual death also means we are separated from the life of God, unresponsive to spiritual things, and unable to change our condition, just like a dead person. That's what Paul was communicating to the Ephesian Christians when he wrote:

> As for you, you were dead in your transgressions and sins, in
> which you used to live when you followed the ways of this world
> and of the ruler of the kingdom of the air, the spirit who is now
> at work in those who are disobedient. (Ephesians 2:1–2)

So because we are all in this sinful boat together (Romans 3:23), no one of us is any better than another. In the sight of God, the hate-filled terrorist, the Wall Street executive, the do-gooder, and the Scripture memory champ all stand on equal ground before Him. No outward accomplishment, good or bad, can change the fact that we are all spiritually dead, guilty of sin—sentenced to be separated from God forever. What does that mean? (Okay, tighten your seat belt. We're encountering some turbulent air now.)

It means that for eternity, the unbeliever will never experience even one solitary good thing associated with God—things like light, freedom, relationships, rest, security, love, peace, comfort, hope, goodness, etc. But that's not all. In place of those things, God ignites the holy fire of His righteous wrath and hatred for sin upon that person. Because God is righteous, He must punish sin. It is an offense to His holy nature for one single sin to go unpunished. His nature demands it. Therefore every sinner is condemned to suffer under this terrible wrath. And we all remain under this death sentence until the time when we trust in Christ's payment for our sin (John 3:36). Pretty heavy stuff, huh?

Taking Your Case to Court

Okay, so with that as background, consider the following scenario: Imagine over the course of a few years you managed to max out all your credit cards. About this time, suppose you also lose your job because of missed work due to a recurring illness. On top of this, you begin to suffer from depression stemming from your financial problems. Are we having fun yet? And as if that's not enough, you are also being harassed by your landlord because of delinquent payments. Suddenly, your debt balloons like an atomic mushroom cloud, amassing into well over $100,000 dollars. Because you have no job, you are left with no possible way to repay that debt. Your only hope is to file for personal bankruptcy, conceding that your future credit will be ruined, not to mention what will happen to your reputation. Already people are beginning to talk about you behind your back. But since the alternatives are lawsuits and a potential all-expenses-paid vacation in a luxurious state corrections facility, you go ahead and meet with a bankruptcy attorney. Finally, after several weeks, your day in court arrives, and it's not a pretty sight. Deep in debt and even deeper in depression, you mentally and emotionally resign yourself to what is sure to be a miserable future.

But wait! Pause the tape. What if, with just minutes left before the judge slams down his gavel, a well-dressed man walks through the courtroom door carrying an aluminum briefcase? Strolling up to your attorney, he identifies himself as a distant relative, on your mother's side. You don't recognize him, so you wonder what he could be doing there. Privately whispering to your lawyer, the two men then ask for permission to approach the judge's bench. After convening a few more minutes, the judge finally slams down his gavel with an echoing thud. *Case Dismissed!*, he proclaims. *This court is adjourned.*

Confused, you turn to your attorney with a quizzical look blanketing your entire face. He simply smiles and motions for you to follow him and the unknown relative into an adjoining room. Once there, he shuts the door behind you, places the briefcase on a table and flips open the latches. Upon opening it, your eyes gaze on neatly stacked $100 dollar bills lining the inside from left to right, top to bottom. It's packed with cold, hard cash. And the total? $133,331.48. It exceeds by $10,000 the amount you owe Visa, MasterCard, American Express, the bank, your attorney, and the three friends you swore you would pay back. For just a millisecond, you secretly wonder how long $133,000 would last in Rio de Janeiro. Then you snap back to reality. You blink repeatedly, pinching yourself, convinced this has got to be some sort of a dream. But it's no dream. It's very real. Also included in the briefcase is a letter of reinstatement from your employer and an envelope addressed to you. Opening the envelope, you unfold the note, which contains just five words:

All this for you. Enjoy.

The attorney begins making arrangements to pay off all your creditors. *This is not happening to me,* you say out loud. *Its unbelievable . . . just to good to be true.* You turn to thank the unknown relative who brought the money, but he has left. You fall back into a chair, breathless. Suddenly, you sense a heaviness lift from your shoulders like a black cloud of despair leaving you. In its place is now hope and a smile. In just a matter of seconds, you have moved from cynicism to celebration. You jump up, pumping your fists in the air, shouting *Yessss! Yessss! Yessss!*. Hardly able to contain yourself, you find yourself dancing for the first time in months.

But suppose for a moment you hadn't owed $130,000 dollars, but rather just $13 to Visa for lunch for two at El Café Gordo? How would you feel if someone paid off *that* debt for you? Grateful? Well, sure, but compared to the feeling you would experience after having the $130,000 paid off in your near bankruptcy fiasco, that's nothing. Are the two feelings the same? Of course not, but why not? What makes the difference?

It's the size of the debt, isn't it?

The truth is that our sin-debt towards God is infinitely greater than a few hundred thousand dollars in cash. And though you probably don't have that kind of money lying out on the bedside table, there are people who actually do possess that kind of wealth. But no one—not a single person on the planet—has what it takes to pay off his or her sin—debt to God. Through an attitude of indifference towards God and choosing to go our own way, each of us has amassed a huge sin-debt with interest and penalties. And we are completely unable to repay the massive balance due. Well, there is one way: to suffer in utter darkness and separation from God forever. That's what we deserve and we know it. But that's where the good news kicks in! The Bible says Jesus Christ became both our attorney and our rich relative when He hung on the cross. Suspended between heaven and earth, God the Judge slammed down the gavel of His righteous wrath, landing squarely and forcefully on His Son. The hatred, penalty and punishment for our sin (your sin) fell on Him as the Great Substitute. He went to Hell for us, in our place. And we get to walk out of that courtroom debt-free from sin's penalty and power. Free to pursue a new life. Plus, the bonus cash we get comes in the form of a new lease on life. The good news doesn't end with just paying off our sin debt!

But all this begs a question: Why on earth would Jesus do something like that? Why, when we rightfully deserved the punishment for sin, would He take it on Himself instead? And why would He forgive all our sin, wiping our slate clean and clearing our record of any wrongdoing? There is only one answer. Are you ready for this?

It's grace.

Admittedly, it's a simple word. Just five letters. But bound within that word like the power of the atom are untold megatons of meaning. Christ's payment for your sin was an act of grace, pure and simple. God did this for you because He loves you. So now that you know how deeply you were in debt and now are totally debt-free, how do you feel about this grace? Are you a little breathless? Blinking your eyes, wondering how this could be true? Feel like pumping your fists in the air knowing you will never, ever experience one drop of God's anger (Romans 8:1)? Feel like worshipping a little? We thought so.

I Kissed Legalism Goodbye

It really is overwhelming to ponder the magnitude of God's grace for us in salvation. But what about now? How does this grace translate into our relationship to God *today*? It's not unusual, after clearly understanding God's rich outpouring of undeserved grace and mercy, to be overcome with a desire to live a life that somehow pays God back for all He has done for us. We feel obligated, don't we? But though it is a fairly natural response, it is nevertheless misguided and unbiblical. And here's why. As we attempt this impossible task of paying God back for His great gift of grace, we discover all the more how we fall short of His perfect standard. In other words, we fail. We end up not living the kind of life we desire. This leaves us very frustrated, not to mention feeling very guilty. It becomes so hard to live the life that we wonder if it's even worth it. So we do what comes naturally. We try harder. We recommit ourselves. We rededicate our lives to Him over and over again. We vow to live by the rules, promising to do better this time. But this time comes and we find ourselves pulled right back into the guilt trap. The futility grows as we spin our wheels, getting nowhere real fast. Unfortunately, our churches become populated with moral, well-meaning, sincere people who are trying their best to do right. They are passionate about earning God's favor and approval through their obedience. But this is nothing new really. The apostle Paul confronted a group of believers who were doing exactly the same thing. In revealing the truth about law and grace, he teaches us how to properly respond to God's gift of goodness and mercy. Surveying Paul's letter to the Galatians, we uncover four myths about keeping the rules. Like Jack and the Beanstalk, these bedtime stories sound good, but they are nevertheless still just fairy tales.

Myth #1—Obeying God's rules can save me
(Galatians 1:6–9; 3:24; 5:1–4)

If Satan would lie to us about anything, it would be concerning how we gain salvation and maintain a holy standing before God. That was precisely the lie he pitched to the Galatians, and they bought it. They took the works-salvation bait—hook, line, and sinker. Paul referred to those who promoted this teaching as *false brethren* (Galatians 2:4). These men were deceivers who had crept into the church, convincing believers a person was declared righteous (justified) by faith in Christ plus some external deed or act. Paul was shocked that the Galatian Christians had allowed these teachers into their fellowship, so he wrote them to combat this heresy. Specifically, the false teachers were claiming that salvation must include the works of the Law (Galatians 3:1–3). They taught that the works of the Law were necessary for salvation and for staying righteous before God. This was very upsetting to Paul! In other words, he was ticked off. He was so frustrated that he called the Galatians *foolish* (meaning spiritually dull or having a low spiritual IQ). *Hey,* Paul says, *don't you guys know better than this? What's the matter with you?!* He also said they had become *bewitched* (charmed, and deceptively fascinated) by this slick teaching concerning works-righteousness. But having said that, it's still fair to ask, *Exactly why can't faith in Christ plus good works (or obedience to God's rules) save a person?* Paul says, *I was hoping you would ask that,* and replies with five convincing reasons:

1. God's rules were never intended to save (Galatians 3:23–25). Look at Paul's reasoning here.

"Before this faith came, we were held prisoners by the law, locked up until faith should be revealed. So the law was put in charge to lead us to Christ that we might be justified by faith. Now that faith has come, we are no longer under the supervision of the law."

In other words, Paul is saying that the Law (or God's rules) merely served as our tutor, leading us to Christ (Galatians 3:24). God gave us the law to demonstrate our inability to keep it. And why would He do that? So that in our futility and hopelessness, we would realize our need for a Savior.

He wanted us to see our need for someone else to accomplish salvation for us (Romans 8:3–4). Obeying God's Law cannot save us! Neither can obeying His rules keep us saved. It never could. It never will.

2. If keeping the Law saves you, then who needs Christ (Galatians 5:1)? If you could get to Heaven on your own, by keeping the rules, then you wouldn't need a Savior. Christ set us free from having to keep the Law, so that we do not have to be enslaved to it again now that we're Christians. Besides, your chances of earning your way to Heaven are the same a corpse has of running a marathon!

3. If you trust in your own good deeds, Christ will be of no benefit to you (Galatians 5:2). These were stern words reminding us that salvation is found in Christ alone plus *nothing. Pick one*, Paul says. *Choose to depend on works or Christ. But keep in mind that when you do, the other will be worthless to you as far as salvation is concerned.*

4. If you keep any of God's rules, you have to keep them all (Galatians 5:3). Paul says, *Don't stop there. You must obey all the Law if you obey any of it.* Put another way, you would have to keep every one of the Ten Commandments perfectly in letter and in spirit for a lifetime to achieve perfection before God. To break one of God's commandments is to break them all (James 2:10). Only one link has to be broken for the whole chain to be broken. This means you are not allowed one unclean thought, unkind word, or unloving deed. Anybody think they're up for this? *I didn't think so . . . alrighty then*, Paul's reasoning concludes. So why even try to keep the rules? That's Paul's point exactly. Stop *trying* to keep the law and start *trusting* God with your life.

5. If you try to combine law and grace, you will forfeit (lose) grace (Galatians 5:4). Place one drop of deadly cyanide into a glass of tea and the tea becomes undrinkable. Paul's argument here is that the only way to fall from grace is by refusing to trust in it. The way of grace is the only road to salvation. Keeping the law is a dead end.

Now you may be thinking, *Isn't this a bit elementary? I mean, doesn't everybody know this stuff already?* Well, not exactly. Though it's a basic teaching of our faith, there are churchgoers all over the world who think through their good deeds they are storing up points for heaven. The bottom line blowing away this myth is by answering the following two questions:

- What are you really trusting to get you to heaven?
- What is your hope of attaining righteousness before God?

God's answer is that it must be solely, completely, and exclusively in Jesus Christ, plus nothing.

Grace is free, and grace that is earned isn't really grace at all. If you earn it, it's wages, or what you deserve, but it's not grace. Grace is a gift for the guilty, not a reward for the righteous. You can't earn grace. That's impossible. It's a gift. And it's free. The truth about grace is out there, but so are the deceptive lies. And here is another popular fib, a prevalent fabrication many people believe.

Myth #2—As a Christian, obeying God's rules improves my standing before God
(Galatians 3:24–26)

This second unspiritual law, which Paul refers to as things taught by demons (I Timothy 4:1), applies more to believers than non-believers. This subtle belief states, *If I don't do all the bad things, and if I keep myself clean from all the evil out there in the world, then God will accept me and be pleased with me.* For example, consider the following checklist.

If I don't:
- do drugs
- drink
- dance
- smoke
- listen to rock music
- curse or swear
- have my body pierced or tattooed
- associate with bad people

- go to R-rated movies
- cheat on my spouse
- rebel against authority
- cheat on my taxes
- abuse my family
- go to Mardi Gras
... *then* I will be spiritual.

But is that really what makes a person godly? The problem with this list is that a person can avoid all these things and still miss salvation altogether. You can keep this list of don'ts and still remain unchanged by Christ's power. As a Christian, you can steer clear of all these activities and still be self-centered and self-righteous in your heart, and thus not please God at all. It is self-deception to equate self-denial with spirituality. Look at what Paul wrote to the Colossians on this subject:

> Since you died with Christ to the basic principles of this world, why, as though you still belonged to it, do you submit to its rules: Do not handle! Do not taste! Do not touch!? These are all destined to perish with use, because they are based on human commands and teachings. Such regulations indeed have an **appearance of wisdom**, with their self-imposed worship, their false humility and their harsh treatment of the body, but they lack any value in restraining sensual indulgence.
>
> Since, then, you have been raised with Christ, set your hearts on things above, where Christ is seated at the right hand of God. Set your minds on things above, not on earthly things. (Colossians 2:20–3:2)

We have to be very careful of equating our position and standing before God with certain external measurements. If spirituality is nothing more than simply obeying a list of thou shalt nots, then any self-disciplined person can be spiritual. But godliness is much deeper than just having outward right-eousness. Just ask the Pharisees. Of course, some of the aforementioned practices in our don't list are, in fact, wrong and sinful. But simply avoiding them will in no way improve your standing before God. Who you are in Christ was once for all determined by what Jesus did for you at the cross—nothing more, nothing less, and nothing else. It was His righteousness, not yours, which purchased your salvation and won your freedom. He did for you what you couldn't have done for yourself in a million lifetimes. Now that's grace!

As a result of Christ's accomplishment at the cross, God's view of you as being holy will never change (2 Corinthians 5:21). He now sees you clothed with the very righteousness of Jesus Himself. Your standing before God is forever fixed, and based on His work, not yours. Self-denial cannot improve your righteous position in Christ. How could we ever think we could improve on the salvation God Himself has already provided for us?

But here is where things get a little sticky. What you couldn't accomplish through the thou shalt nots can also never be accomplished through the thou shalts. In other words, if you do all the good things a Christian is supposed to do, you will still not improve your position before God. For example:

- Giving
- Tithing
- Prayer
- Scripture memory
- Evangelism
- Church attendance
- Teaching a class
- Studying the Bible

All these are great things, right? But remember that there is no Christian deed you can do which will motivate God to see you as more holy or accept-able in His sight. None of these awesome things can in any way improve your standing before Him because He already sees you covered with the righteousness of Christ. In fact, none of these godly activities means anything to God unless they are motivated by grace and born out of a personal relationship with Jesus Christ. Blind obedience and Christian busyness is a poor substitute for a relationship with God. This is one of the primary reasons why many young people today who grow up in Christian homes bear little or no resemblance to the God their parents claim to worship. Why not? After all, they have received all the right facts about God from nursery school to grad school. However, for various reasons, they somehow missed out on the part about God being personal to them. Or perhaps they had the rules shoved down their throats so hard and so often that they blatantly rejected their parents' faith. They just played the game long enough to keep their mom and dad off their back. But after pacifying their parents and upon arriving at college, they were finally able to live the way they wanted to, making their own decisions about life. Is it any wonder why there is such an enormous generation gap between so many Christian parents and their children today? These well-meaning and sincere people diligently passed on the rules, but failed to pass on the relationship! They had their kids in God's house every Sunday, but failed to bring Him home after the service was over. Maybe that scenario in some way describes your experience.

The point is, as a Christian, no matter what you do, you will never be any more loved or accepted by God than you were at the moment you received Christ. Are there commandments in Scripture? Of course. Lots of them. Does God have standards of thought and conduct that He desires us to obey? Absolutely. Yes! But God's commandments must be communicated in a context of love, not law. We should follow Christ willingly, not out of obligation or duty. We are to obey God out of a loving relationship and heart for Him, not out of a cold compulsion to keep the rules. Unfortunately, this is not the case for the legalist. For him, the rules are just another opportunity to feel good about himself, earn God's approval, boost his self-righteous image and exalt his pride. Have you ever fallen into this trap? Have you ever embraced this myth as truth? Let's move on now to the third fairy tale.

Myth #3—Living by the rules is the best way for me to mature in Christ

Would you ever stick your hand in a rattlesnake's den? Probably not. But we still play around with another animal equally as deadly. That ferocious animal is legalism. Seemingly harmless while hiding its fangs, it waits until we bring it home to our lifestyle before slowly injecting its venom into our bloodstream. And as the poison takes effect, we begin losing our ability to think clearly, believing things that just aren't true. We start pursuing standards we believe will make us more acceptable to God instead of resting and relying on His accomplished work on our behalf. As it travels to our central nervous system, we soon lose feeling and grow numb to the sensitive touch of God's grace. But the good news is that there is an antivenom. And as with a snake, this antidote is also extracted and developed from the original poison. Through looking at what legalism eventually does to us, we can see more clearly how to purify ourselves from it. Freedom from the poison of legalism comes through changing our belief system concerning the rules. But again, to effectively do this, we need to see exactly just what it does to us as Christians. Here is what keeping the rules eventually does to us.

10 Deadly Effects of Being a Legalistic Rule-Keeper

1. **It breeds pride and contempt for other people** (check out Luke 18:10–14). It deceives you into thinking you're something that you're not, creating a false sense of spirituality. It's like a spiritual narcotic, giving you a phony feeling of moral superiority and self-righteousness.

2. **It distorts the true Gospel of Christ** (Ephesians 2:8–9). Salvation is by grace alone. Period. Not by works or keeping the commands and demands of the Law.

3. **It causes people to major on the minors.** It takes peripheral issues, or gray areas (like dancing or style of music) and makes them more significant than they actually are. It says things the Bible never says, making issues of all the wrong things.

4. **It creates a judgmental spirit.** This is the worst form of Phariseeism (Matthew 23:13–15).

5. **It short-circuits spiritual growth.** It creates an improper and unbalanced fear of God, which prevents you from experiencing a biblical and loving relationship with Him.

6. **It catapults you back into bondage to sin again.** You discover you are still living under the Law, just like before. Nothing has changed (Galatians 5:1–2).

7. **It creates frustration because rules can never restrain or tame your sin nature** (Colossians 2:23; Romans 7:18). Being crucified with Christ and resting in God's grace is the only remedy for dealing with the sin nature (Galatians 2:20; 2 Corinthians 12:9).

8. **It robs you from experiencing genuine Christian liberty.** Legalism is the archenemy of grace and wisdom. Legalists turn general principles into specific commands. But if all you need to do is keep the rules, there is no need for wisdom or the Holy Spirit (or a relationship with God, for that matter). Legalists fear biblical liberty. They are terrified that people will abuse their freedom, and so out of this fear they use man-made rules (or God's rules misapplied) to keep them chained to the law.

9. **It removes peace from your life.** You can never be sure if you're ever totally pleasing God. You can never be good enough. There will always be some minor rule or command you have missed.

10. **It prevents you from enjoying the abundant life Jesus promised** (John 10:10). In legalism, you're way too busy stressing over whether you have been good enough today to really enjoy the life God intended you to have.

Keep in mind:

- Legalism cannot produce holiness (Mark 7:15, 21–22).
- Legalism cannot restrain fleshly desires (Colossians 2:19–23).
- Legalism cannot set you free from sin (Galatians 5:1; Acts 15:10).

Legalism is anything we do or don't do in order to earn favor from God. It is primarily concerned with rewards to be gained or penalties to be avoided.

Legalism insists on conformity to man-made religious standards or God's rules improperly applied. It's checklist Christianity. It's the spoken and unspoken dos and don'ts of a particular Christian circle. But the problem is complicated when this legalistic belief is forced on others. (Jesus addressed this in Mark 7:6–8). God calls us to be free and actually exhorts us to stand firm in our Christian freedom (Galatians 5:1). We are to fight against legalism like an enemy that threatens to destroy us. And why? Because God knew there would be legalists who would try and rob us of our joy and freedom in Christ. Unfortunately, they are much more concerned about someone abusing his freedom in Christ than they are that he gets caught up in sinful legalism. Grace frightens these people. Legalists are afraid someone might give into the flesh through freedom but ironically, that is exactly what legalism produces. Through pursuing a legalistic, self-righteous lifestyle, the sinful and proud flesh is fed and pampered. Legalism is as much a deed of the flesh as immorality or anger. Through legalism, the sinful nature's power only grows.

Legalistic thinking in your life will produce either self-righteous Phariseeism or cause you to consistently fall into the performance and failure trap. Living under the rules means your conscience and behavior is controlled by your active righteousness (whatever you can manage to do that day for God). However, living under God's grace means your conscience and behavior is controlled by your passive righteousness (what Christ has already done for you). Legalism is motivated from outward pressure to conform, from external rules and expectations. Grace is motivated from within, from a relationship of love. Legalism requires that which the Scriptures do not require and forbids that which the Scriptures do not forbid. Rules without reasons lead to ritual and legalism. And rules without relationship lead to ruin.

We are called to a Person, not to a persuasion, right? Christianity is not a subject to be learned, but a life to be lived. It's not about *our* righteousness. It's about *His*. It's not about trying to get God to love and accept us. It's about responding to the love and acceptance we already have in Him! So you have to be careful of the snake-handlers out there who traffic this poison. You must decide whether you are going to please people or God. You have to learn to be free and to let others be free as well. Controllers are those people who are not willing to let you live your life before God as you believe He is leading you. Love them, but don't listen to them. The truth of the Word of God is your lamp. Let it light your way.

Myth #4—Under Grace, I Can Now Sin All I Want
Galatians 5:13

Lest we commit another equally harmful mistake, let's not swing the pendulum the other way and conclude that Scripture endorses unbridled freedom. This highlights our need to be alerted to yet another dangerous and deadly doctrine. This lie says, *It doesn't really matter what I do now because I am saved. I can live any way I want to now that I'm a Christian! Since my standing before God is secure and unchanging, I can just go and sin all I want!*

Buzz!! Wrong answer. Hey, but thanks for playing our game. We have a lovely parting gift for you. Seriously, this is the worst form of grace abuse. God has given us *liberty*, but not *license*. We were freed *from* sin, not freed *to* sin. Look at what some of the New Testament writers had to say concerning this issue:

peter

Don't use your freedom as a covering for evil (I Peter 2:16). Or, don't hide your sin behind your salvation. You were freed to enjoy and live for Him, not to sin (2 Corinthians 5:15). You serve a new and wonderful Master now. You weren't freed from jail so you could go out and kill again. Rather, you were set free so you could serve the One who bought you and redeemed you out of slavery.

paul

"For you were called to freedom, brethren; only do not turn your freedom as into an opportunity for the flesh" (Galatians 5:13). Christian liberty is the freedom from self, not the freedom to serve or indulge self. You are now free and able to obey God whereas before you were unable to (see Romans 8:6–7 and Galatians 2:20).

Don't let your liberty cause others to stumble (I Corinthians 8:9). Since being set free, you and I are responsible to live in a way that reflects the character of God to a lost world. Our attitudes and actions should bring honor to the family name. Our liberty does not include the freedom to embarrass the name of Christ or to hinder the progress of the Gospel. We have a responsibility to our brothers and sisters in Christ.

James

"Even so, faith, if it has no works, is dead [faith], being by itself" (James 2:15–20). Our new life in Christ and the resulting spiritual fruit are part of the evidence that we have truly been made new.

As Christians, we shouldn't be asking, *How much can I be like the world and still consider myself a Christian?* We have been bought with a price, and no longer belong to ourselves (I Corinthians 6:19–20). This means that now all your good works, deeds, and obedience to God's commands only *enhance* the experience of salvation you already have. We obey God now for profit and enjoyment, not for merit. So then what's the balance between grace and works in your life? As you obey Scripture and its commands, you now do so on the basis of:

- Your unconditional acceptance by God
- Your freedom to serve Him
- Your desire to obey Him
- Your need for intimacy with Him

So having said that, what have you really been trusting in to get you to heaven? Do you live by a list of dos and don'ts? Is that what the Bible is to you? Do you compare yourself to others in order to make yourself feel good, spiritually? Are you using your freedom in Christ as an excuse to do as you please or are you using it to obey Him? Do you obey God because you're *supposed* to, or because you love Him and are grateful to Him for what he has done for you?

All This For You. Enjoy.

Why is grace such a great motivator for worship? It's because of our deep sin-debt, the daily need for His provision, and the wonder of His love for us. He who has been forgiven much, loves much. Grace puts music to the lyrics of the Gospel. For example, next time you buy a CD, read the words before you play the music. It may be an awesome song with a great message, maybe even very poetic. But it's just a poem until you add the melody. The music is what makes it a song. Try this: Take the words to "Amazing Grace" and sing them to the tune of "Stairway to Heaven," or to the theme song from *The Brady Bunch*. Kinda Different, isn't it? Now take the same song and sing it to the tune of the *Gilligan's Island* theme song. It just doesn't have the same feel, does it? Regardless of whether you're a fan of the original hymn writer's tune, the words to "Amazing Grace" simply don't fit well with a 1960's sitcom. The same is true with the Gospel. The *words* of Scripture apart from the *melody* of grace God composed become cold, hard, rigid, and unattractive. Grace makes the difference. Grace makes the Gospel a song. It's a Gospel of grace. And God never separates the two.

When words are married to the music, they suddenly enter another dimension. They make sense. Similarly, when truth is married to grace, a symphony of praise is ignited. Brothers and sisters, we need more than lifeless knowledge. We need a daily experience of grace. We need the words of Scripture along with Jesus Himself—the Word of God. God meant for them to be inseparable, like two sides to the same coin. And when we see it this way, the ripple effects of grace never cease. The awesome character of God we discussed in the last chapter takes on deeper and more personal meaning as we realize this great God is also our gracious Father.

Worship then becomes an overflow of a relationship and a heart that has been changed.

So if you are a Christian, God is pleased with you because of Christ. Stop worrying. He was completely satisfied at the cross with His Son's payment. You cannot add to it one single bit. He has made you acceptable through Christ. Period. You are holy in His sight. Forever. You stand before Him complete. God is at peace with you. He is not angry with you. You are His child, not His slave (Hebrews 12:4). You are justified, forgiven, adopted as a child of God, redeemed, freed from the law and the power of sin, saved forever from condemnation and judgment, loved, indwelt by the Holy Spirit, accepted, holy, enjoying total access to God, experiencing Abba intimacy, raised up with Christ, possessing God's presence in you, and having a relationship. All this is all a part of the beautiful benefit package you received at the moment of salvation. Therefore, we must see our status as sons, our destiny as heirs. It is impossible to grow in grace while we are still wrestling with our acceptance with God.

Think about it: A relationship with God, your Creator, Savior, Lord, and Friend *should be* the most positive, fulfilling, exciting, liberating, and enjoyable relationship you could possibly have. But often we turn it into a job, a have to. How that must grieve God's heart! He gave His Son for us as His free gift and we have transformed Him into a study, a persuasion, a system of beliefs, a chore, a church, a religion, a weekly meeting inside a multi-million dollar building. Somehow we have lost our way. And to re-enter God's path you must believe this: More than anything, God passionately desires a love relationship with you, initiated and motivated by grace. Stop trying to prove yourself to God. As a believer, rest in the finished work of Christ on the cross as the only basis for your holy standing before God and relationship with Him.

Three cool questions

We have to anticipate and answer three very practical questions that naturally rise to the surface as a result of this grace discussion:

1. How does grace relate to obedience? Or, how do I obey God?

2. How does grace relate to my sin? Or, what do I do when I sin?

3. How does grace relate to my enjoyment of God? Or, is it okay to enjoy Him?

1. How does grace relate to obedience?

True obedience (that is both pure and pleasing to God) is motivated out of a heart of love stemming from grace. We cannot truly love unless we are experiencing grace. Grace maintains the balance between law, love, and liberty, keeping them in a right relationship to one another.

Not long ago a world-renowned speaker addressed the topic of obedience from Jesus' words in John 14:5: "If you love Me, you will keep My commandments." He spent fifty-five minutes talking about the importance of keeping God's commandments without ever mentioning once a love for God as the motivation for that obedience. In this sense, his message was a failure as he ignored the whole foundation of the verse. We have all felt the huge difference between mandatory obedience and joyful obedience, haven't we? Take Keith for example. *Mandatory* obedience was when his dad woke him up at 7 A.M. during summer vacation telling him to get out there and mow that yard. Great feeling, huh? You think Keith was really motivated from the heart? He may have obeyed his dad, but probably did it with a bad attitude. On the other hand, *joyful* obedience was when, a few years later, while working as a server at a swank Orlando restaurant, Michael Jordan stopped in for dinner. *Keith*, his boss said, *get over there and wait on Mr. Jordan.* The wheels in Keith's mind began to turn. *Hmm, let me think. Is this something I really want to do? Should I obey my boss or just quit and go home?* Hello? McFly? Keith willingly and joyfully obeyed his boss that night, receiving a major league slam-dunk tip as a result. Do you see the difference between *having* to do something for someone and *getting* to do something for someone? As a child of God, your greatest honor is that you get to obey God because you have a relationship with Him. Obedience is not a chore. It's a privilege and the greatest one imaginable. But that's precisely why we must embrace grace before obedience and commitment. Grace properly understood naturally leads to obedience. But obedience required apart from grace will always lead to legalism.

So do the commands of God in Scripture seem like more of a burden to you than a blessing?

Are they a source of condemnation when you fail, or do you sense the Spirit producing in you a desire to obey out of love? Are you trying to obey through sheer will and determination, or do you rely on the Holy Spirit to empower and enable you to obey (Galatians 5:16)? Do you view God as a Master who has set before you an impossible code of conduct you couldn't possibly ever live up to? Or do you view Him as your Father who has accepted you and loves you as much at this moment as He did when He sent Christ to die on the cross?

You see, grace changes everything in the Christian life—even your obedience. It transforms obligation into opportunity. Duty into devotion. Performance into relationship. Yes, God has commanded us to obey Him, but He desires that we do it out of a heart of love, not slavery.

2. How does grace relate to my sin?

Temptation is a common experience for all believers. And we all fail and sin. But when you fail, do you feel more drawn to the cross or more condemned by your sin? Do you feel pulled like a magnet to Calvary or pounded like a hammer by your guilt? Some people believe they are only as justified as they are holy and obedient. But it's just the opposite. Our standing before God is not determined by our present performance. Rather, it was determined once and for all by Christ's finished work. There is no longer any legal guilt for us as believers (Ps. 103:12). God's judgment has already taken place at the cross. There is therefore now no condemnation (Romans 5:1; 8:1). None. Jesus paid off our sin debt in full. When we sin, it doesn't get us back in debt again (like it would with a credit card). Grace is our sin eraser. And yet we still sin, don't we? But when we do, the Holy Spirit causes us to feel conviction. Like if you were to accidentally cut yourself, conviction is

The grace factor • 73

the pain receptor telling you to treat the wound. We confess our sin to God in order to *appropriate* and enjoy our forgiveness, not to initially get it. Because God loves you perfectly and persistently, He will correct you as His child, but He won't punish you like a slave. You will sin. We all will. No doubt about it. But know that the blood of Christ already covers it. Confess it to Him as sin. Apply His grace to your mind and emotions and move on in His strength and sufficiency (I John 1:9–2:2).

3. How does grace relate to my enjoyment of God?

The Westminster Confession reads, "The chief end of man is to glorify God and enjoy Him forever." Therefore, it stands to reason that we don't glorify God when we do not enjoy Him.

Contrary to what some might think, God is not committed to your misery, especially now that you are His child (Matthew 7:4–7). He wants your pursuit of Him to be a joyful journey, and an awesome adventure. God is now your Father! Christ is your Savior! You're going to Heaven one day! How much better off could you possibly be? How much better can it get than to be made holy in the eyes of God and be clothed with the very righteousness of Jesus Christ?! Salvation is His *gift* to you! Don't insult Him by not enjoying it! The Christian life is not a burden to carry, but a process to be enjoyed. The Gospel and grace is so much bigger than God simply saving you. He wants us to enjoy His grace today! We tend to forget the grace of the gospel shortly after conversion, but God wants us to look to the supply of that grace daily. If being saved in the past is so great, and being made like Christ in future glory is so great, why would God make the time in between any different? Our present Christian life simply builds on the one (justification) and looks forward to the other (glorification).

The bottom line is that we never outgrow who we are in Christ. Grace is not just how we were saved, but also how we are to live day by day. Did you enjoy being saved? Then enjoy that grace again today, and tomorrow, and the day after that! Remember, if you pay for it or earn it, it's no longer grace. You see, until you rest in the finality of the cross, you will never experience the reality of the resurrection. The Christian life does not depend on your grip on God's hand, but rather His grip on yours (Philippians 1:6; 1 Corinthians 1:7–9). The greatest motivation for worship is the grace of God. Dive into it. Swim in it. Be overwhelmed by it. Get lost in it.

Enjoy it!

CHAPTER 5

Dancing on the Edge
Extreme worship

Every man dies. Not every man really lives.

—william wallace in Braveheart

Live all you can. It's a mistake not to.

—Henry James

The outer Limits

W hat's the wildest thing you have ever done? The most extreme
excursion? The most out-of-the-ordinary activity? And do you
have any battle scars from your adventures? Any special (or perhaps painful)
memories?

Allow us to introduce you to three individuals who were extreme in a
different way. They took their worship over the edge in the eyes of conven-
tional thinking. Refusing to consult the status quo, and without regard for
personal reputation, they bet it all on Jesus by worshipping Him in a way
some considered a bit offensive. Compelled to do something beyond the
realm of the ordinary, they gained the attention of their peers, and more
importantly, God's.

The Bible tells us about several individuals who were a little unorthodox
in their approach to God. They worshipped freestyle, doing things in the

presence of God that few, if any had ever done before. Breaking with tradition they instead chose to blaze new paths through the land of worship. While on these roads less traveled, their unusual expression of adoration brought great honor and glory to God. They marched to the beat of a different drummer. They challenged, even threatened the status quo of their day. Sailing in previously uncharted waters, their curious and uncommon worship tactics raised more than a few eyebrows. Considered too fanatical for some, their worship inspired others to live a more intense faith. In a generation given to extremes, here is some encouragement for you to channel some of that energy into your worship experience.

Boxers or Briefs?

Everybody knows who King David is. We're all familiar with his exploits regarding giants and bathing beauties. But not many people remember the time he publicly danced before the Lord and half of Jerusalem in his underwear. Here's what happened. In 2 Samuel 6, David is excited because the Ark of the Covenant, a symbol of God's presence and blessing, is finally being returned to Jerusalem. As the Ark is being carefully carried back, David is so filled with awe and reverence that he allows the bearers of the Ark to walk only six paces before ordering them to stop. He then slaughters a bull ox and a fattened calf as a sacrifice to the Lord. David can hardly contain his excitement. Following this, a huge processional parade begins making its way into the city of Jerusalem. Leading the parade is David. You would expect him to lead a public parade, right? Nothing weird about that. But David isn't just walking a somber march. He is "dancing before the Lord with all his might" (2 Samuel 6:14).

Now like most ancient peoples, the Hebrews had their sacred dances that they performed on special religious anniversaries and red-letter occasions. But you can be sure David's dance wasn't a country two-step or a ballroom waltz. This was no ballerina routine. David's dance involved leaping, shouting, singing, and raising his hands high in the air. Pluck him out of his time and place him in ours and David would likely be accused of being unholy, drunk, disrespectful, and sacrilegious. Admittedly, his dance would have appeared pretty wild. In his enthusiasm for the glory of God, David was literally wearing himself out leaping before the Lord. His style of worship may seem a bit over the top to us. But in his day, this type of celebration was perfectly legitimate and normal.

However, it really wasn't so much his dancing or celebration that drew criticism; it was his wardrobe, or rather lack thereof. Wearing nothing but a linen ephod, David had shed his kingly garments and effectively disrobed. This ephod was a priestly garment, a close-fitting, sleeveless pullover gown that was about hip length. It was almost like wearing a T-shirt. Perhaps David did this to allow for more freedom of movement to dance and jump around. It's hard to do certain dances wearing a long robe, you know. Perhaps David was so caught up in worship that he momentarily lost sight of social etiquette. Maybe he wanted to worship without his royal wardrobe and be a regular person for a change. Maybe he was tired of being dignified and official. We're not sure of his exact motivation.

But as the procession made its way into the city, David's wife Michal (the former King Saul's daughter) looked out her window and saw her husband dancing in the streets in his underwear. Gazing at his act of worship, Scripture says she despised him in her heart.[28] Raised as a king's daughter, Michal had a concrete mental image of what a king should do and how he should act, especially in public. She was a society woman and after all, he had been a mere shepherd boy. She had come from money and he had come from the pasture. Upon arriving home that night, King David found she had a piece of her mind to give him.

> But when David returned to bless his household, Michal the daughter of Saul came out to meet David and said, "How the king of Israel distinguished himself today! He uncovered himself today in the eyes of his servants' maids as one of the foolish ones shamelessly uncovers himself!" (2 Samuel 6:20)

Imagine David's shock at this remark. He is so excited to share the blessings of the day with his wife. But instead, she blasts him before he ever steps through the front door. There is no *Welcome home, dear. How was your day? Why don't you rest up for a few minutes while I finish making dinner?* Not a chance of that here. She is livid with her husband. Her blood pressure is soaring. In Michal's eyes, David was acting in a way not befitting a King. He had officially become a fanatic in her eyes, taking this worship thing way too far. To her, he was being excessive. Radical. Embarrassing. Not to mention immodest. *How dare you dance around like that in front of those servant girls? You're disgusting!* was the gist of her sentiment. But the King responds to her by defending his actions and informing his wife that his dance was meant for God and not for her. Besides, *it was an act of worship, and therefore neither excessive nor immodest. And by the way,* David adds, *seems to me I remember God choosing me to be the King in place of your father and your family. Allow me to translate for you, Michal. Because of your hatred for my worship, the future King won't be coming from your womb. You've just disqualified yourself.* Scripture tells us Michal later went to her grave childless.[29] Maybe next time she should just keep quiet.

David's delirious dance was not recorded for us in the Bible as a prescription for how to worship. It is, however, an accurate description of how he actually worshipped that day in Jerusalem. Though we are not commanded to imitate his worship style or clothing fashion, we could sure learn tons from observing his fervor, enthusiasm, zeal, and pure delight in the presence of God. So, should you feel the urge to dance before the Lord in your ephod, you might want to consider doing it in the privacy of your own bedroom. But by no means should you quench the spirit of worship David demonstrated that day. Extreme as it was, it remains as an authentic expression of joy in his God.

A party for Doctor Jesus

A second example of extreme worship occurs following one of the most notable conversions in Jesus' ministry. It involves the change of life experienced by a man named Matthew (Levi). Not to be confused with the guy who invented the blue jeans, this Levi was a tax collector by profession. And as you might imagine, being employed by the IRS of his day, Matthew was not exactly the most popular man in town. On the contrary, he, along with his tax collecting cohorts, was generally hated by most people. After all, they made their living by taking people's hard earned money from them. How do you feel after looking at your paycheck and seeing the bite Uncle Sam takes each week? But for those in Matthew's day, they suffered even more from the hands of the tax man. Those first century publicans not only collected the Roman tax, but also tacked on a few additional tariffs of their own. And with these taxes, they lined their own pockets.

As an employee of the Roman government, it was Matthew's job to sit at the tollhouse and collect taxes from each of Capernaum's citizens. The Jews hated the Romans, but they particularly despised the other Jews (like Matthew) who worked for the Romans. These men were viewed as traitors. Turncoats. Benedict Arnolds. Scum. They had not only betrayed their Jewish brethren but in effect stole from them as well. They sold out for a pay raise, placing a career over loyalty to their blood relatives and fellow Hebrews. Tax collectors were typically thought of as greedy, unscrupulous, dishonest, deceitful, unprincipled, corrupt, ruthless, and generally obnoxious. Model citizens, huh?

But all that changed the day Matthew met Jesus Christ. Passing by the tax office as He had no doubt done many times before, Jesus called the crooked tax collector to follow Him.[30] Since it is likely Matthew had seen Christ on other occasions, it wouldn't have been a strange thing for Jesus to speak to Him. Everyone had to pass by Matthew's tax booth, Jesus being no exception. But this day was different. Matthew heard Christ's compelling call, not addressed to a crowd of thousands, but to him alone. Specifically and personally, Jesus called him. Rising up from his comfortable chair, he immediately resigned from his job and resolved to follow Christ. Dr. Luke tells us this publican left all for Jesus.[31]

A little while later, Matthew decided to do something out of the ordinary. He had experienced a change of heart that led to a change of desire and destiny. So he decided to throw a dinner party. But this would not be your normal, run-of-the-mill dinner gathering. This party was unusual because of who was on the guest list that evening. Of course Jesus and His disciples were there, but you would expect that since Matthew was now a disciple. It was the other guests dining at Levi's house that night which made things so interesting. Sitting at the table with the Son of God were many tax-gatherers and sinners.[31] These were Matthew's old drinking buddies. Publican party animals. His frat brothers. These were the men who knew Matthew way back when. They were well acquainted with the old Levi.

There were so many tax gatherers present that evening that the disciples probably kept their hands in their pockets to keep them from being picked. Can you see Matthew's change of heart on display here? Instead of shunning his former friends, pretending to be holier-than-thou, he invited them over to his house. Also joining this rowdy rabble that evening were sinners. These were those people who were not welcome in the Synagogue. When the word sinner was used to describe a woman, it meant an outcast, usually due to her immoral reputation. Translated, there were probably loose women in attendance. It was precisely because of this guest list and other such dinner gatherings that Jesus was branded and labeled as "a drunkard, gluttonous, friend of sinners".[33] He was often accused of receiving and eating with sinners. In those days, to eat with someone signified a desire to have a relationship with him or her. And to this charge, Jesus pleads guilty. He was and still is the friend of sinners. Aren't you glad?

On the other hand, the Pharisees and religious leaders were the enemies and judges of sinners. They purposefully walked on the other side of the street to avoid such people. That's because they thought they were better. And two thousand years later, we *still* think we're better than other people. Time hasn't failed to change the human heart. Religious people still despise sinners, don't they? Jesus scathingly rebuked such people, informing them that the tax gatherers and harlots would get into the kingdom before the Pharisees would (Matthew 12:31–37). That's because those poor people believed in Him. They knew how badly they needed a Savior.

That night at Matthew's house, the Pharisees saw Jesus having a good time with sinners. The windows were open and the sound of laughing and eating were drifting outside and into the street. He actually enjoyed their company, and that made them mad. But Jesus wasn't there that night to show sinners that Christians can have a good time without getting drunk. He wasn't looking for an opportunity to carve another notch in His spiritual belt as He hooked them with the bait of the Gospel. He and Matthew hadn't outlined an evangelistic program for the evening. Following dessert, they had not planned for Jesus to bring a message and Matthew to give a three to five minute testimony, whereupon one of the women would close the night with a song of invitation. Jesus simply came to the party and loved those people, and they loved Him back. He had come to earth for people just like them. Eventually they would place their faith in Him because of this love. But that night, it was a real party, a celebration mixing Jesus and His disciples with tax gatherers, harlots, thieves, and drunkards.

And Matthew was loving every minute of it. He was eager for his friends to see Jesus up close because he was confident that in Him they would find something they had not found in their encounters with other religious people. That something was acceptance. And how did he know this? Because that's exactly how Jesus had treated him. Why would He treat other sinners any differently? So, in response to the mercy and grace shown him, Matthew may have thought, *What can I do that will communicate how awesome Jesus is? I've got it! I'll throw a party for Him! I'll show Him how honored I am to be one of His disciples by introducing my friends to Him. Then everyone will know I am not ashamed of Him. Then they will know I am truly a changed man.* And that's exactly what He did. The event ended up becoming an act of worship disguised as a dinner party. Levi was telling his little world, and particularly Jesus, just how worthy he considered Him to be. But in doing do, he caused a commotion among the Pharisees, who were bystanders at the feast.

Too timid or insecure to put the question directly to Jesus, these religious leaders, perhaps leaning in the window, instead asked His disciples, *Why is your teacher eating with the tax gatherers and sinners?* Or, if we might paraphrase, *Why does your teacher, a Jew who claims to be a faithful follower of Abraham and the Law, fellowship with heathens and unbelievers? Doesn't he realize a man is known by the company he keeps? He must therefore sympathize with their character somehow. He must secretly be like them. That must be why He enjoys their company so much.* Oh good. Now they've stirred up some controversy. Some scandal. They've got some dirt on Jesus. But unfortunately for them, Jesus overheard their murmuring and responded to them.

> But when He heard this, He said, "It is not those who are healthy who need a physician, but those who are sick. But go and learn what this means, 'I desire compassion, and not sacrifice,' for I did not come to call the righteous, but sinners." (Matthew 9:12–13)

The Pharisees thought of themselves as needing nothing. In their own eyes, they were complete. They were spiritual. And it showed in their comments. However, our modern day Pharisees communicate their superiority in more subtle ways, like with a holier-than-thou raised eyebrow, a voice inflection, a facial expression, or simply by silence. Like the look certain people give you when you're slipping in late for church. It's a stare that clearly says, *Tisk, Tisk. You're bad, and we're not. We were on time. You are late for the Lord's service as everyone can plainly see.*

But the Pharisees were never known for their subtlety. They just said what they thought, and rarely did anyone challenge them. Except here, that is. In giving Jesus a piece of their mind they couldn't afford to lose, they opened themselves to a rebuke from the Son of God. Of course, this didn't matter much to them. They were so smug and secure in their self-righteousness that no one was going to verbally out duel them. Besides, they knew the Scriptures from cover to cover (or scroll to scroll). However, they were about to meet their match in Jesus. He not only knew both the contents and context of the Bible, but He actually wrote the entire Book!

Jesus answers their objection with a one-two punch that sends the Pharisees reeling back into the corner on their heels. First, He rebukes their character, letting them know they are not as hot as they think they are. *As the great Physician, Jesus says, I am here for the sick. They are the ones who need me, not the well people, right? And since you're so 'healthy,' and self-righteous in your attitude, I am not here for you. What makes God happy is for you to show compassion, not to work harder and sacrifice more so you can feel better about yourself. Therefore God isn't very pleased with you guys.*

Jesus' response to the sinners was not self-righteous condemnation. Rather, it was mercy and compassion. It wasn't the sinners He criticized, but the self-righteous scribes and Pharisees. And in doing so, Jesus was saying that it doesn't matter how good, obedient, or holy you are if you don't have compassion for people. Avoiding outward contact with sinners isn't what grace is all about. And to show grace you have to first experience it yourself. But to do this you first have to realize your own sinfulness. And therein lies the root of the problem.

Secondly, Jesus not only criticizes the Pharisees' character but also their knowledge of Scripture. They were supposed to be expositional experts, fully able to explain the Bible. But Jesus turns the critical searchlight on them by quoting from memory Hosea 6:6. Like an x-ray machine, Jesus' words revealed what was really on the inside of those hypocrites. He peeled open their chests, exposing their hearts for everyone to see. The Pharisees had never really learned the meaning of this passage, which clearly teaches that a merciful attitude and gracious deeds are more pleasing to God than outward sacrifice and ceremonies. There is a hint of sarcasm in Jesus' words. In essence, *My mission here is to save sinners. And since you're not sinners, I guess I can't save you, now can I?*

We can be fairly confident that Jesus' comments didn't sit very well with the Jewish religious leaders. They didn't like this boy's attitude. Who does he think he is, anyway? And they probably left in a huff, grumbling all the way home. On the contrary, the tax gatherers and sinners present that evening left the house physically full and spiritually healed. Laying his head down that night as he went to bed, Matthew probably thought, *Wow! What a radical time! And gosh, it was great to see all my friends there, too. I'm glad they*

got to meet Jesus. He treated them just like I knew he would . . . just like he treated
me. With mercy and love.

And maybe, just maybe before drifting off into a deep sleep, a smile
broke across Matthew's face. In the dark silence of his bedroom, it might
have occurred to him what a privilege it had been to honor his Lord in this
way. He had stepped out on a limb for God, and it didn't break. Even though
his act of worship was extreme and admirable, in reality Matthew was just
one beggar showing other beggars where to find bread.

Desperately Devoted

The essence of worship is found in telling God just how great He is and then
living out that belief in our daily lives. During His brief three year ministry,
Jesus was approached by thousands of needy people who were frantic to get
close to Him, if by chance His miracle power might look their way. Picture
this scene in your mind. Jesus is facing enormous pressure from the crowds
to heal, feed, and provide for them. They want Him to also assume leader-
ship and deliver the Jews from an oppressive Roman rule. And so, needing
both physical refreshment and time alone with His disciples, Jesus departs to
the region of Tyre and Sidon. Interestingly, God had centuries earlier sent
Elijah to this same area[34] to rest at the home of the widow of Zeraphath,
another Gentile woman. It is fascinating to note that of all the face-to-face
encounters Jesus had with the thousands He met, only twice did He ever
find great faith. It is also interesting to note that both cases involved
Gentiles, not Jews.[35] From this brief meeting, Scripture paints a portrait of a
woman who captured the essence of worship through her off brand faith in
Christ. Through her example, we are encouraged to passionately pursue
our great Savior. Here is what happened:

> Jesus left that place and went to the vicinity of Tyre. He entered a
> house and did not want anyone to know it; yet He could not keep
> His presence secret. In fact, as soon as she heard about Him, a

woman whose little daughter was possessed by an evil spirit came and fell at His feet. The woman was a Greek, born in Syrian Phoenicia. She begged Jesus to drive the demon out of her daughter. "First let the children eat all they want," he told her, "for it is not right to take the children's bread and toss it to their dogs."

"Yes, Lord," she replied, "but even the dogs under the table eat the children's crumbs."

Then He told her, "For such a reply, you may go; the demon has left your daughter." She went home and found her child lying on the bed, and the demon gone.[36]

A simple, relatively brief conversation, right? But pause and take a long look at this woman. What do you see? What do you observe? We can learn a lot about worship from her.

First, she was submissive. Because of His enormous popularity, Jesus' disciples were powerless to keep His presence in town a secret for long. This woman somehow heard that the Healer had come to Tyre. No doubt stories and rumors of Christ had circulated all over the tiny villages that dotted the Galilean countryside. Apparently good news traveled fast in those days. Asking around, she found where Jesus was and no doubt ran to Him. When she arrived, she *fell at His feet*. The Greek word used here—*proskuneo*, which is translated "to fall"—simply means to worship. There was a certain humility about this Greek woman. If what she had heard about Him was true, she figured He would be more than just a man of God, a teacher, or a prophet. She recognized she was in the presence of One much greater than she was. She knew enough about herself and enough about Him that prompted her to take this humble approach to Christ. She bowed down before Him, all the way to His feet because she knew only God would be sufficient to help her in this time of great need.

But what motivated her to come to Christ in this way? Mark tells us it was a family crisis that brought about such a response in her. And can you blame her? It's often during those 911 moments that we find ourselves on a collision course with life's impossible circumstances. And in those times, we often feel like life as we know it is over. Then we smack ourselves in the side of the head as we recognize our need for divine intervention. It may be a crisis of finances, sickness, terminal illness, or maybe even the death of a relative or close friend. It could be a dating or marriage relationship, or like this woman, something involving a son or daughter. But sooner or later, life has a way of landing us right in between the proverbial rock and a hard place. As if caught in a violent thunderstorm, there seems to be no way out. And what makes many of these crises so difficult is that, for the most part, they are beyond our control. Nothing we can do can possibly prevent them from occurring. We find ourselves helpless and hopeless with no control over what will happen next.

For this hurting woman, the crisis involved her daughter. We don't know why or for how long, but her little girl was demon-possessed. We're not talking mentally disturbed or emotionally depressed. This girl's heart and mind were under the control of a satanic entity. Perhaps it was a result of something to do with her family's pagan religion. We're just not told. But we do know that this woman loved her daughter very much . . . even more than her own life. When it comes to your kids, no amount of money, travel, effort, energy, embarrassment, or loss of reputation really matters. All that matters at the moment is that a mom or a dad gets help for their child. And this woman's love for her daughter motivated her to come all the way to Jesus Christ for help.

In fact, she was desperate that day (Mark 7:26). She came as soon as she heard about Him (Mark 7:25). There was a spirit of immediacy, urgency, and priority about her situation. She had probably exhausted every other means of help and hope for her daughter. Being a Canaanite, she may have been a worshipper of Astarte or some other pagan deity that was prevalent among her people. Perhaps disillusioned with her religion's inability to intervene, she turns to Christ as her last hope. Her attention and worship had finally found the right object.

And what an attitude of worship she had! She was saying to Jesus, *God, if You don't do this for us, we're sunk.* Her only hope was Jesus (Mark 7:26). She was convinced that nothing else would do. She literally begged Him. She knew that what faced her was a God-sized task. This demon-possession was, for sure, something unmistakably suited for *His* resources. Her faith in Him was enormous. We often worry too much and trust too little, don't we? We need to come to the end of our rope at the *beginning* of our rope. We tend to exhaust our own resources first, *then* when things get critical, we start trusting God. We make a valiant attempt to fix it ourselves, then we understand that what we have simply isn't enough. Our strength just won't cut it.

Truth is, we wait far too late to get desperate, don't we? In reality, we probably need more desperation in our worship of God. We need to regularly recognize Him as the only source of all we need. Remember Abraham? He trusted against all hope that he would be the father of a great nation (Romans 4:18). Here was a guy who was older than dirt! And yet, he believed as long as there was a God in Heaven, there was hope and a reason to worship Him by faith. And he did. And God gave him Isaac.

What about you? Do you see Jesus as the only hope for your life? What about your relationships? Your family? Ministry? Future? How desperate are you in your prayer life? Do you worship him like He's all you've got? Or do you depend on your own ability, personality, or natural giftedness?

There is a need among this generation to worship God in a way that screams toward heaven, *Father, we'll trust You to do God-size things for us!* This kind of faith worship says we will trust Him for the things only *He* can do. Though this woman's attitude of worship was elementary, almost childlike, there was a certain purity and innocence about her faith. It wasn't yet corrupted by external religion or by man-made formulas. She didn't know the proper protocol for prayer. Though she had limited knowledge of Christ, her act of worship through faith ultimately affected and inspired others (Matthew 15:29–31).

You see, it's not how smart or theologically adept we are that impresses God. It's how much we abandon ourselves to Him that really matters. There must be a passion to pursue God as we cast ourselves before Him in utter desperation. And this woman bridged the gap between head knowledge about God and experiential knowledge about Him. Because her faith wasn't based on that much information about Christ, she was forced to exercise greater trust in Him. She took what little knowledge she had, threw herself at His feet and glorified Him by simply believing. Don't misunderstand. We should be growing in our knowledge of God daily. This ought to be a huge priority for us, because as we grow in our knowledge of God, our faith and worship intensity can grow proportionately. But you don't have to have a degree in theology to worship and honor Him.

However, her act of adoration wouldn't go unchallenged. In some people's eyes, she was taking her worship too far. Surprisingly, she met initial opposition from both Jesus and His disciples. At first, even Christ didn't acknowledge her. Her pleas were met with total silence.

> But He did not answer her a word. And His disciples came to Him and kept asking Him, saying, "Send her away, for she is shouting out after us." But He answered and said, "I was sent only to the lost sheep of the house of Israel." (Matthew 15:23–24)

Now this woman already had three strikes against her:
• Strike one—She was a Gentile.
• Strike two—She was a woman.
• Strike three—She was a descendent of a people God had told Israel to utterly destroy (Deuteronomy 7:2).

Three strikes and you're out, right? Apparently no one had explained the rules of spiritual baseball to this Phoenecian woman. Anyone can come to Christ when there is no risk and when there are automatic results. If it was easy, then everybody would be doing it, right? The question was how bad did she want Christ's power on her behalf? So Jesus first tested her with silence (Matthew 15:23). Here is a woman begging Jesus to deliver her daughter from a demon and she is met by silence from the Savior. Jesus appears to be completely ignoring her. He says nothing. Not a word. Doesn't this sound cold? Uncaring? She was getting no response from Him at all. Though Christ wasn't answering her pleas, she continued in an act of desperate worship by falling down before Him, submitting herself to Him, even calling Him Lord, and Son of David (Matthew 15:22). But it seemed as if Jesus really didn't care to receive her worship. So what's the deal here?

Have you ever had a similar experience with God like that? Have you ever prayed sincerely and passionately about something and yet your prayers went unanswered? It's like your words weren't even rising past the ceiling, like God wasn't even listening. It's as if He didn't really care. Have you ever been blindsided by hard circumstances or by tragedy, only to come before God and hear Him say or do absolutely nothing? Or maybe you have lived like you should but bad things still happened to you. Or maybe it happened to your friends and the ones you loved. God not only did nothing to prevent tragedy, but He seemed as if He would do nothing to change it as well.

That's where this woman was. Jesus wouldn't even speak to her! C'mon! Where was this heart of compassion He had shown others like the tax gatherers and sinners? Where was the "Come unto Me, all you who are weary and heavy laden" (Matthew 11:28–30)? Now honestly, if you had been her, how would you have felt at this moment? Maybe a little hurt? Frustrated? Embarrassed? Perhaps you would have become bitter or resentful toward Jesus. Perhaps you would have stormed away in angry disillusionment and disbelief. This woman could have spread the word that the so-called Savior wasn't all He was made out to be. She could have tried to ruin His reputation. Or she could have just shut up and gone quietly back home. But she didn't.

Strangely enough, this only gave her greater resolve to keep asking Him for what she needed and wanted (cf. Matthew 7:7). She just remained there in submission at His feet. She had no way of knowing that this kind of extreme persistence is what God really values. And fortunately the silence of Heaven does not mean He isn't listening or working. Silence does not always signify inactivity. It only means He isn't answering or responding to us in our way and our timetable. After thousands of years dealing with humanity, His ways are *still* not our ways (Isaiah 55:8–9)! Of course, Jesus' refusal to answer would have stopped others dead in their tracks. But it didn't stop this woman. She hung in there. She somehow knew everything would be okay if she just stayed there with Him.

The disciples, taking what they thought was a cue from the Lord, began hounding Jesus to send this female nuisance away. Apparently, after Jesus' refusal to answer her, she also tried persuading them to get Him to help. Though everything in her circumstances and surroundings said pack it up and go home, her faith just wouldn't die. She had nothing going in her favor except a belief in Him and a love for her daughter. The odds were stacked against her. Her racial heritage was against her. She was the wrong gender and suffered a great disadvantage in a male-dominated society. Satan had control of her little daughter. The disciples and supposedly even Jesus were opposing her. But in spite of all this, she became like a nagging headache—she simply wasn't going away. Her determination to convince Christ only intensified. She believed in Jesus. Her style was extreme, out of the ordinary, unfashionable, and even unacceptable. For Jesus to simply say nothing would have been better than what He said next: "It is not right to take the children's bread and toss it to the dogs" (Mark 7:27).

We don't even have to debate the fact that this is one of those hard sayings of Jesus. What could He possibly have meant by such a statement?

First of all the word *dog* did not refer to a mongrel or scavenger common in that day, but rather it meant a household pet. Jesus was not intentionally being rude to this woman, but rather He was testing her faith. That's because He saw something in her that no one else could see. With all-knowing eyes, Jesus saw a great faith in her that would not go quietly or die easily. She was tenacious. And she teaches us that sometimes in our disappointment with God, we are forced to worship Him *by faith* without any visible confirmation from Heaven. There are times in our lives when there are literally no signs of hope, no visible reasons to carry on. The only assurance you have in those times is the promise of Scripture—the written guarantee of God's Word.

Is that enough for you?

If all you had in your darkest hour was the simple promise of Scripture, could you survive on that? Void of all signs of hope or help, would you still choose to worship Him? This can make us feel a bit like Job, who said, "Though he slay me, yet will I hope in him" (Job 13:15). That's where we sometimes find ourselves, don't we? But will we still worship during those occasions when we hear nothing from God? In the silence, how will we respond? Will we allow it to overtake us or will we fill that silence with our worship of Him? That's precisely where this Canaanite woman was.

So, how did her faith pay off? How does the story end? What did she do?

Knowing that even a tiny portion of His great power would be more than enough for her problem, she persisted. "Yes, Lord," she replied, "but even the dogs under the table eat the children's crumbs."

Wow! What insight! What persistence! What faith! But such was her vision of this Son of David. And that's exactly what extreme worship does for us. It has 20/20 vision. Keep in mind, we don't casually or callously deny the reality of our struggle. We don't ignore our problems. But worshipping God this way accurately sees the enormity of the need as well as the greatness of God. Then it marries the two, bringing them together. It says, this God can do! It is the same kind of glory Joshua and Caleb brought to God. After spying out the Promised Land (Numbers 13), ten of the twelve spies who surveyed the land only saw the size of their enemy. But Joshua and Caleb were focused instead on the size of their God. Ten said, "Our enemies are so big, we can't possibly fight them," while two responded, "No, you're wrong. They're so big, we can't miss 'em!"

In our personal struggles, we have a choice to make. We can focus on our tremendous need or on His tremendous resources. We can become preoccupied with the size of our struggles or on the sufficiency of our God (Matthew 15:27–28; Mark 7:28; Hebrews 17:19). Extreme worship zooms in on Jesus. Let's be honest. Our problems and circumstances really can be enormous can't they? But it is all a matter of perspective. Hold something close to your face and it's huge. Back away and it begins to shrink. Focusing your attention on Christ's sufficiency causes you to back away from your huge circumstances. As we back away to gaze at God, the *greater* He becomes. Stand back and look at Him. He is so great that you will never get all of Him within your scope of view.

For most of us worshippers, it's not a problem of *can* He, but rather *will* He. And will He for me? In this story, the Syrophonecian woman took the very words of Christ, interacted with them and laid them right back down at His feet where she was worshipping. In her faith and worship, she took God at His word in spite of everything she saw and heard. She used His own words to make her case before Him. As a child it may have irritated your parents when you reminded them of what they said or promised to you. "But dad, you promised to take me to the toy store." But it never irritates God when we do this. Instead, it actually delights Him when we do that. He wants to hear us repeat His Word back to Him.

So, what has God said about your particular life situation? Is there a need He has promised to meet but hasn't yet? Are you at his feet reminding Him of His promises? Or have you given up?

This woman's extreme worship and great trust touched His heart and moved His hand (Matthew 15:28; Mark 7:29–30). Check this out: "Then he told her, 'For such a reply, you may go; the demon has left your daughter.' She went home and found her child lying on the bed, and the demon gone."

Something about her faith-filled words struck a chord deep within the heart of Jesus. And He rewarded her by delivering her daughter from this demon. So sovereign is Jesus that He does this simply as an act of His will!

Imagine the celebration in her house that evening. Imagine how her faith must have grown even more as a result of this miracle. Imagine how her heart must have bonded to Jesus because of her experience of faith. Imagine how her worship must have deepened and solidified.

So what about you? What do you need from Jesus at this point in your life? Will you have the kind of worship that won't stop dancing for God and isn't afraid to celebrate? Will you have the kind of worship that won't keep quiet about God? That isn't ashamed? Will you have the kind of worship that won't let go of God, no matter how bad things get? Will you play it safe, or will you go for broke and be an extreme worshipper when it really counts? Will you take that leap and glorify Him in a radical way?

when Little is Much

sacrificial worship

> *If Jesus Christ be God and died for me, then there is no sacrifice too great I can make for Him.*
>
> —c. t. studd

stayin' alive

We live in a misguided world. A planet where morality has been redefined and common sense has vanished somewhere in a maze of political correctness. Leaders are assassinated, governments are overthrown, and wars never cease. Perhaps as a result of the uncertainty of our times and the threat of terrorism, people are now searching for a cause to latch onto, to give their lives purpose. Church membership is down, but spirituality is way up. This is a seeking generation. People are looking inward for some compass within them, or they're searching outwardly to find something great and meaningful to be a part of.

Currently in our world, we are seeing a different kind of sacrifice—not a selfless one, but a selfish sacrifice of the worst kind. Ours is an age where terrorists literally lay down their lives for misguided causes. They sacrifice themselves and many others all in the name of Allah. In light of this kind of dedication, why is it that some Christians seem unwilling to sacrifice even ten minutes a day to worship the true God? Where is the sacrifice for the One who willingly gave Himself for us?

Granted, there are times when worship isn't very easy. But if we only worship when it is convenient, then it isn't worship; it's just a leisure activity. God often calls His people to worship Him during seasons of adversity or suffering. He asks us to give ourselves in worship when we don't feel we have anything to give. And occasionally, He compels us to make great personal sacrifice, the kind that costs something. That sacrifice then becomes our offering of worship to Him. But what might motivate such worship? And is the cost of worship and the challenges that accompany it really worth the price we pay? Is it worth it to worship even when it hurts?

Sacrifice is easy to talk about, but when the pain kicks in, it's a different story. In this chapter we meet two very different people who, in unique ways, displayed acts of worship that cost them something. But what prompted such great offerings from them? What made them want to give so much of themselves to God? And what were the rewards of their sacrifice?

mitey sacrifice

One day as Jesus was spending time with His disciples, He took them to the Temple where they sat and observed the people coming and going. Part of the Temple contained an area known as The Court of the Women, a large open space where worshippers came to pay temple tax and give free will offerings. It was kind of like the tithes and offerings of today, only they didn't pass the plate. Because it was such a public gathering place, this area afforded the self-righteous a golden opportunity to showcase their large financial contributions, which came with immediate recognition from onlookers. Mark picks up the story for us here:

> Jesus sat down opposite the place where the offerings were put and watched the crowd putting their money into the temple

treasury. Many rich people threw in large amounts. But a poor widow came and put in two very small copper coins, worth only a fraction of a penny. Calling his disciples to him, Jesus said, I tell you the truth, this poor widow has put more into the treasury than all the others. They all gave out of their wealth; but she, out of her poverty, put in everything—all she had to live on. (Mark 12:41–44)

Like other places during Bible times, we need to keep in mind the economy was severely depressed. Most people fell under the category of poor peasants. Life really didn't hold much promise for the average person. For them, employment usually meant working a menial trade (usually manual labor) for long hours each day and for minimal wages. And if you were unable to do that, you begged for what you could get. Those who were sick, lame, blind, or unwilling to work, were dependent on the kindness and generosity of others. Unlike our current society where virtually anyone can get a decent-paying job doing something, there wasn't any unemployment office or labor department in those days. If you didn't work, farm, or beg, you didn't eat. And what little you were able to scrape together, you stored, saved, or misered away to help you live another day. Further, should you have the misfortune of being a woman whose husband died, your chief source of income got buried right along with him.

With that as a background, allow us to introduce you to this particular woman. We are not told if she was old or young, recently widowed or if she had been in this state for some time. We only know her husband had died and she had not remarried. She most likely lived alone. She was just this side of destitute, among the lowest of the economic classes. As such, she would be a most unlikely candidate to contribute anything at all to the Temple treasury. But as Jesus and His friends observed that day, she walked over to the wall where thirteen trumpet shaped chests were hung to receive the offerings and donations. Into one of these, she dropped two small copper coins (mites). These were the smallest of Jewish coins, each valued at about one-fourth of a cent or about 1 / 64 of a day's wages, the average daily wage then being sixteen pennies. The mite took its name from its extreme smallness, and was derived from the Greek word *lepton*, meaning "thin." Describing the same scene, Mark adds for his Roman readers an explanation of the word, using a Greek word *kodrantes* (from the Latin *quadrans*, meaning "the fourth part"). So her total offering was the modern day equivalent of about a dollar and fifty cents. A pitiful offering, right? There's not much chance they'd name the new Family Life Center after her. After all, what can a fraction of a penny buy? How important could it be compared to the checks the other big givers were dropping into the offering bucket? Apparently pretty important. Look at Jesus' reaction to her gift: "I tell you the truth, this poor widow has put more into the treasury then all the others."

When you don't have very much to contribute, giving a little means a lot. When you wreck the only car you have, it's a big deal. When your only home burns to the ground, it's a huge loss. When you spend the last thirty dollars in your checking account on groceries and some long distance phone company offers you fifty dollars if you switch to their service, fifty bucks bucks is a lot of money. Some people inherit wealth from family, but for most of us, we get it the old fashioned way—we earn it. What is a lot of money to some is just pocket change to others. An article in a major magazine recently stated that for the average wage-earner in America today, taking a date or a spouse to a movie and getting a snack there, he or she will end up spending about sixteen dollars. That sixteen dollars represents a certain percentage of the average person's overall bank account, right? Most of us don't really miss sixteen dollars. We probably won't lose the farm because we splurged and got butter on the popcorn. But the same article went on to say that for Bill Gates to spend the same percentage of his bank account, he would have to fork out around 1.6 million dollars! Did you get that? sixteen dollars to you is a million and a half to him! He would hardly miss it—just a blip on his financial screen. He probably has that much in the pocket of his jeans hanging on a closet door or sitting out on his dresser. For you to buy a novel down at the bookstore is like him purchasing a company or an island. This demonstrates the fact that money is a relative thing. It's all a matter of perspective . . . and percentages! This particular woman gave 100 percent. She gave all she had to live on. Folded up inside a tattered cloth or kept inside a small jar of pottery, she went and retrieved the sum total of her financial portfolio and simply gave it all away to the Temple treasury. Now she had nothing. Her bank statement was now bare and blank. The deposit column was empty. Her purse was hollow, drained of what little resources she previously called her own. She was officially on empty. She would from this point on potentially be unable to eat until she somehow earned more cash.

But according to Jesus, she had something none of those deep-pocket tithers possessed. She had a sacrificial spirit of worship. In her heart and mind, she was giving it all to God. In stark contrast to the oohs and ahhs others had received upon depositing their huge sums into the Temple coffers, this woman's two coins hardly made a sound (much less a dent) in the collection plate. But they did make quite an impact on the heart of the Son of God. It obviously wasn't the amount of her offering that impressed the Lord as much as it was the proportion of her gift. While others gave out of their wealth, she gave out of her poverty. What was pocket change to them was her entire net worth. And she gave with no desire or expectation of recognition, and with no strings attached. There was no indication that, as a result of her gift, she was expecting special treatment by the Temple officials or to have a heavier vote when the next business meeting was held. And she would also receive no tax deductible government credit for her contribution.

There is also no indication anywhere in Scripture that she was unwilling or hesitant in making such a huge sacrifice. Didn't she know that was all she had, that she wouldn't have anything else to live on? Was this really a wise thing for her to do? Was this being a good steward of her resources? Would a Christian financial counselor have advised her to do this? Wouldn't she risk becoming destitute? Living on the streets? Wouldn't she have to resort to begging? Yes. Yes. Yes. Probably not. Possibly. Maybe. Perhaps. But she seemed to think the sacrifice was worth the risk. And what do her actions tell us about the condition of her heart? About her perspective on money and material possessions? About her view of God? By giving all she had, she was left now with zero resources. She would be forced to depend solely and completely on the very God to whom she had given her last thin bit of money. She now had nothing but her God to live on. But is that really such a bad place to be?

Though she had completely emptied her purse, her heart nevertheless was now full. Full of joy. Full of hope. Full of Him! She had nothing to fall back on but God. No IRA. No investments. No savings. Just a belief that Jehovah was worth her great sacrifice. Through her two little mites, she became mighty in her worship.

Tuna Helper

Celebrity is a funny thing. Think about it. Ordinary people like you and me are taken and, through the magic of airbrushing and photographic technology, they are transformed, literally making them famous. Then their faces are plastered on billboards and movie screens and we are suddenly in awe of them. Many famous people are, to be honest, fairly average looking in person, but thanks to media and marketing, we treat them different in our minds, don't we? Imagine one of your favorite male actors for a moment. Now strip him of his movie roles, mega-stardom and multi-million dollar contracts. Now who is he? Just a person like you and me. Imagine your favorite female star without her three hundred dollar haircuts, thousand dollar outfits, personal trainers, perfectly white-capped teeth, plastic surgery, and implants. Who is she now? She still might win Miss Peach Queen over at the county fair, but for the most part, she's pretty average. Imagine these people still struggling to free themselves from their roots—still waiting tables, living in a car, or working down at the gas station. Imagine Mel Gibson never becoming an actor, but taking up a trade such as carpentry. Instead of bravely swinging a sword as William Wallace, he's swinging a hammer in his late forties, his belly having gone south like most American men his age. Sweaty and perhaps balding, instead of entertaining millions, he's building an entertainment center and bookcase for a young couple somewhere in Sacramento. Instead of cranking out hit movies, he's renting them instead at the local Blockbuster. Just another man in line at the supermarket, that's all. Ordinary hair, teeth, body, and bank account all add up to one thing— an ordinary person. Admit it, for some celebrities, it's the money and public relations campaign that make us pause to look at them, right?

But let's be fair, there are also many famous people who also possess extraordinary talent. The ability to score thirty points in a professional basketball game, throw a football sixty yards, or hit a baseball five hundred feet after connecting with a 95 mph fastball is something the average mortal simply cannot do. The capacity to morph yourself into another character in countless movie roles or television shows is admirable. For most of us, our acting ability never goes past the pitiful fake voice we use when calling in sick for work. Or the performance we give the police officer after he pulls us over for speeding. The confused look on our faces and the astonishment we portray upon discovering we were doing sixty in a 35 mph zone combined with a pretend sorrow all add up to quite an impressive display of thespianism. But though we may have weaseled our way out of a few traffic fines, it's clear that we're not yet up for a big part in the next *Star Wars* movie.

And then there are those famous people who light up the music charts year by year. From the latest one hit wonder group to the established veterans, we sit in wide-eyed amazement as we listen and watch our musical mentors with blistering speed wail on the guitar or astound us with spectacular vocals. We stand on our feet and applaud, jumping and screaming to let them know how much we appreciate their show. And why? Well, because they deserve it, that's why. They are truly great at what they do.

What about you? Have you ever met anyone famous? Maybe you saw a celebrity at a theme park once or at a professional ballgame and got his/her autograph. Or maybe you managed to get a backstage pass before a concert and shook hands with your favorite pop idol. Maybe just being in the audience or the stands is enough for you. Fortunately for our generation, today we have more access and information about our favorite movie stars, sports icons and public figures than at any other time in history. Through television and magazines, we are able to venture into the stars' homes, watch them behind the scenes, and even read about the supposed intimate secrets of their personal lives. And with the added help of the Internet, we can find out almost anything about any one of thousands of famous persons. From web pages to online chatrooms, we can retrieve virtually any information about them. You can buy their signature clothing line or shoes at the mall, or even get an autographed ball or picture through the mail. Because of the time in which we live, if you really want it badly enough, you can see, hear, and maybe even meet your idol or hero.

Not so in Jesus' day.

The Son of God traveled on foot, not in a custom designed tour bus or jet. He had no trainers, makeup artists, or agents. There were no TV commercials, posters, billboards, radio ads, or advance teams to announce the upcoming arrival of the former carpenter from Nazareth. Of course, word did spread from town to town and village to village about the Healer. But unless you had seen Him before with your own eyes, Jesus may as well have been an urban legend to you. With so many teachers, self-proclaimed prophets, and messiahs wandering around Palestine in the first century, for all you knew, the stories about Jesus were fabricated or at best, embellished. But as Jesus' notoriety grew, so did the crowds that followed Him, so much so that He was unable to even enter a town due to the huge throngs of people that constantly pressed around Him (Mark 1:45, 6:33; Luke 8:4, 19:3). In one such encounter, Jesus was surrounded by thousands. It happened shortly after His cousin and friend, John the Baptist, had been beheaded by Herod. John had the guts to tell the King he was in sin for marrying his brother's wife. His non-seeker-friendly approach to evangelism landed him in the dungeon. Eventually he was executed, whereupon Herod was presented with the bloody head of the Baptist. There was no first amendment protection in those days. So anyway, Jesus heard of John's death and sought a private place to go pray and grieve. He got into a boat to escape the crowds, but solitude wasn't possible. With thousands following after Him on foot to see what miraculous sign He would perform next, they eventually sniffed out where He was. Soon it came time to eat, and wouldn't you know it, there wasn't a fast food restaurant around for miles. So Jesus turned to one of His disciples, Philip, and asked him a question:

> "Where shall we buy bread for these people to eat?" He asked this only to test him, for he already had in mind what he was going to do.
>
> Philip answered him, "Eight months' wages would not buy enough bread for each one to have a bite!" (John 6:5–7)

Now Philip isn't blind or dumb. He can see and he can count. Scanning the huge crowd assembled on the hillside that day, he guestimates the size of the multitude, informing Jesus that their ministry budget is a bit shy of covering the cost of this late lunch. Try to get an idea of what the disciples are facing here. Ever had a few friends over to eat? Maybe grilled out some burgers or steaks? Or maybe just a night of chips and dip? Okay, ever fed five thousand men before? Cooked lunch for a small army? We're not talking Sunday dinner at grandma's or even a potluck family reunion. We're talking five thousand men who were famished after following Jesus all over the countryside. Throw in another ten thousand combined women and children and that makes . . . well, you do the math (Matthew 14:21). It's a huge mass of people, bigger than most cities at the time. So you might imagine that Philip's comments are laced with a drop of cynicism. At this point, he's probably pretty tired of all the peasants, thrill-seekers, sick people, and fans. He is ready for some privacy for a change. The disciples even suggest to Jesus that He send the crowds away, so they can go to the villages and buy themselves some food (Matthew 14:15). The disciples' mercy was flowing like a river, wasn't it?

Then another of his disciples, Andrew, Simon Peter's brother, spoke up. "Here is a boy with five small barley loaves and two small fish, but how far will they go among so many?" (John 6:8–9)

Okay, where in the world did this boy come from? Obviously, he was a part of the crowd that was following Jesus, but what was his story? We're not told exactly. He could have been about ten years old, and given the natural curiosity level of little boys, he probably spent most of his time darting in and out of the crowd trying to get an up-close glimpse of the action. Can't you see him nipping at the disciples' heels, no doubt irritating them with his persistent questions? *Hey, watcha doing? Where's Jesus? Can I see Him? Is He gonna do another miracle? What's your name? I'm Timmy. My dad is a fisherman. Are you a fisherman? I'm ten years old. Do you have any boys in your house? Hey, watcha doing . . . ?* Can you picture him, with eyes wide open, watching the Son of God transform lives with a single touch? Perhaps he was fishing with his dad by the Sea of Galilee that day when they heard the buzz of the crowd approaching. His job may have been to hold onto the fish his father had caught. The five loaves may have even been their food for the day.

But regardless of what we don't know about him, we do know he finds himself hanging out with the disciples and most likely eavesdropping on their dialogue with Jesus. And what he hears is the future apostles brainstorming, searching for a solution to the problem of catering lunch for some fifteen to twenty thousand people. Can't you hear his high-pitched, prepubescent voice bursting into the discussion?

I have some food here!

Suddenly the conversation grinds to a screeching halt. Turning to look, they see the little boy holding his stinky, scrawny catch high in the air. In his other hand is some bread. Now scratching their beards instead of their heads, the disciples' dilemma takes a slight turn for the better. Enthusiastically, his small but sacrificial contribution gives Philip and his cohorts a glimmer of hope. Bringing the miniscule portion of food to Jesus, the disciples listened as the Lord gave instructions for the people to sit down in the grass. You can assume the little boy sat as well, watching with wild anticipation to see what Jesus would do with his small gift of worship. Perhaps his father joined him there in the grass. Then Jesus took the few small loaves of bread and two scrawny fish and gave thanks to God. Scripture tells us next that the Lord distributed (the bread) to those who were seated as much as they wanted. He did the same with the fish. When they had all had enough to eat, he said to his disciples, 'Gather the pieces that are left over. Let nothing be wasted.' So they gathered them and filled twelve baskets with the pieces of the five barley loaves left over by those who had eaten. (John 6:11–13)

Now, this boy could not have possibly known Jesus was going to perform this miracle. He also didn't know whether anyone else had food to give. And even if he did, he certainly wouldn't have looked around comparing the amount of his gift to someone else's. He was only focused on what he had to give. Not a part of it, but all of it.

His offering was small, dried up, and crusty. It may have even smelled a little (dead fish have been known to do that, you know). But it wasn't the size or quality of what he offered Christ that mattered so much. It wasn't how fresh or new it was that made a difference to Jesus. It was what it represented to the little boy that made it so significant. It was his food. His sustenance. It was what a poor lad's body required to live for the day. There were no subzero freezers back home full of deer meat and filet mignons. There was no walk in cupboard shelves lined with canned goods. No Y-2K stash in the cellar. It is very likely, that for this impoverished peasant boy and his family, these few loaves and two fish comprised their total daily bread. He was carrying his portable cupboard with him. And now that he had given it all away, he looks down and sees that his backpack is empty. All that remains are a few scattered crumbs at the bottom (can you see them?) and the lingering odor of fish (can you smell it?). There is nothing left. He has bet all he had on Jesus. All he has left is the fulfillment he received from giving to Jesus. His offering wasn't much compared to what you or I can give, but it was his own act of worship. By sacrificing what he had, he was saying,

Jesus, You are worth all I have to give.

What a statement! And make note of what Christ does with his investment. Every man, woman, boy and girl was fed and satisfied that day.

Twelve complete baskets of bread were leftover. Not a single soul left hungry that day. Everyone was filled, their hunger pains having been obliterated by the Son of God. Better than an all-you-can-eat buffet, Jesus' miracle on the mountainside truly satisfied them. Jesus has given them exactly what they needed, what they were starving for. They needed something only He could provide, and He didn't disappoint them.

In reality though, Jesus didn't need the little boy's fish and bread to perform this miracle. He had spoken the universe into being simply by commanding it to be so. He had formed the world by His own word (John 1:1–3). He had created everything out of nothing. No pre-existing materials needed. All He needed to make the universe was Himself. His power enabled Him to speak a solar system into existence. Navigate the downward path of a falling leaf. Multiply bread. Raise the dead. Heal the sick. Transform water into wine. Restore a leper. Make a blind man see. Make a lame man walk. Change a life. Turn fish into more fish. One is no more difficult than the other to the One with infinite power.

And though he didn't need the boy's scrawny fish and hard bread, He used it anyway. But that's part of the mystery of God, isn't it? Though He needs nothing from us, He still graciously receives what we have to offer, no matter how pitiful, and then uses it for His glory. Regardless of how paltry or how priceless, it's what our sacrifice represents that really matters to Him. It was a spur of the moment thing here. This boy hadn't known about this great need before. He just heard, and responded. He saw there was a contribution he could make, and so he just did something about it. He didn't pray or wait until he sensed a peace about it. There was something inside this little guy that just said, do it! Go ahead. Give it to Jesus! Some adults might question the wisdom of giving all you have on a whim like this. You can write it off as boyish immaturity and foolishness if you like. Of course, this is not to say we should make a practice of giving whimsical contributions or making large sacrifices without careful thought. But it is to say that there are times in life when you see a need, and immediately there springs up a desire inside of you just to give something. Your contribution may not be something significant in light of the overall need, but it's still big to you.

Perhaps you hear of a need to house a visiting missionary family for two weeks, and you find yourself volunteering your home on the spot. A fellow college student can't pay his rent this month and you feel an inward desire to reach for your checkbook. You can't pay the full amount, but what you give nevertheless empties your little checkbook. At church they plead for youth leaders and though you have never done it before, you suddenly find yourself the following Friday on a bus with fifty junior highers. You responded by giving away your weekend (and maybe sacrificing your sanity in the process.)

But unknown and unseen by you, God has plans for your relatively small but sacrificial gift. That missionary family you housed went back to the foreign field fully rejuvenated and inspired by their restful stay and time getting to know you. Your gift to that student got him through a very tough month, giving him hope to stay at school. He never forgot what you did for him. That bus full of junior highers included an eighth-grade girl searching for an identity and a friend. From a broken home, she was invited by another girl and had signed up at the last minute. She watched you that weekend, curious to see someone older than her having so much fun as a Christian. Returning to the church that Sunday afternoon, and just before stepping off the bus, she made a private but powerful decision to live for Christ. She's seventeen-years-old now and more passionate for God than ever. In each case, God took a small sacrifice and multiplied it. But why? Because He can of course. But that's not all. He does it because it pleases Him so much when you show Him He is worthy of your sacrifice. To honor Him in this way moves His heart to honor you as well, and He does something great with what you gave to Him.

So when the time comes (and it may come soon), will you be ready to make your sacrifice? When He asks you to look at your checkbook, refrigerator, calendar, talents, or heart, will you gladly give it all? On a moment's notice? Will you drop your last two coins in the box? Will you reach for the bread and fish, gladly handing it over to Him? We dare you to do it, then sit back and watch the master at work.

Just like this little boy, what you do and what you sacrifice never goes unnoticed by Jesus. Perhaps your tiny act of worship will inspire a miracle, influencing and satisfying thousands of hungry lives. Odds are it already has. And of the twenty thousand people there that day, like this little boy, you will end up the most satisfied of them all.

unplugged

simple worship

Our life is frittered away by detail . . . Simplify, simplify!

—HENRY DAVID THOREAU

He has told you, O man, what is good; And what does the Lord require of you But to do justice, to love kindness, And to walk humbly with your God?

—MICAH 6:8

You would have to be an alien from another solar system to not know the name Nike. As a colossal force in the world of sports gear and apparel, the name kind of says it all. A few years back, the company launched a nationwide TV marketing campaign showcasing their strategic genius. In the thirty-second spot ads, there was no dialogue or talking at all. Just athletes doing what they love doing most: running and playing. And at the end of the commercial the infamous Nike swoosh slowly fades into view. Brilliant, huh? Enough said. Today, it's amazing that you can explore the remote mountains of Peru or the jungles of Papua New Guinea and find tribes of people who are unaware man has landed on the moon, but they do have Nike T-shirts. Talk about flooding the market! The Nike empire is literally everywhere. There is almost no place where it doesn't have a presence. But what most people may not know is that the world famous swoosh logo was first created way back in 1971. Company founder Phil Knight met a young woman in those days who was teaching an accounting class. But fortunately for Knight, she also did freelance graphic design work. Knight then asked this woman, Caroline Davidson, to design a logo for his new company, something that would look good on the side of a shoe. Soon afterwards, Davidson produced the now familiar swoosh, for which she was paid a flat fee of thirty-five dollars. Thirty-something years and billions of dollars later, Caroline's design is now the planet's most recognizable sports trademark.

But what makes the swoosh so incredibly successful? And why is the "Just Do It" slogan so easy to remember? It's simple, that's why. Public relations and marketing firms know that the job of advertising is to attract the consumer's interest in the time and space allowed. Don't waste time articulately explaining the product or giving them a history of the company. Don't confuse the customer with needless detail. Get in there, grab his attention, and get out before he changes his mind, presses the remote, or turns the page. The rule is, less is always more.

As Christians, we could learn a valuable lesson or two from this segment of secular society. Instead of engaging in the popular Christian pastime of media-bashing, we should consider calling a truce long enough to peek through our protective curtains to observe the occasional genius found in corporate advertising. You see, it's their sole mission to find endless ways to put their product into the hands of as many consumers as humanly possible. Doing this takes time: brainstorming new methods for marketing their soft drink, car, computer, or shoe. But just ask Phil Knight and the guys at the Nike empire, and they will tell you that apart from having a great product, it all boils down to one thing: simplicity.

The same is true in our walk with God. In the midst of all the necessary activities of our spiritual regimen, what often gets lost in the clutter and fog of Christianity is our actual *relationship* with Christ. To illustrate, consider the true story of what happened recently at a T-League baseball game in a small southern town. The stands were packed with proud parents, intently

watching their little future hall-of-famers battle it out on the baseball diamond. But as typical six-year-olds, the boys' attention spans were lasting
about as long as the time it takes to run from the dugout to their respective
positions. Once there, the boys grew bored and became somewhat dis-
tracted. They were focused on more urgent activities besides engaging in
America's pastime. You know, things like digging in the dirt, chasing butter-
flies, or waving at grandma in the bleachers. One of those little boys was literally out in left field, busying himself with repeatedly tossing his glove high
into the air. His mother anxiously watched, silently hoping her son would
snap out of his dream world and turn his attention back to the action at
home plate. Finally, the tension got the best of her and her last nerve
snapped. Standing to her feet, she walked over to the fence behind home
plate, cupped her hands over her mouth, and screamed at the top of her
lungs loud enough for the entire ballpark to hear,

Tyler! Quit playing around out there! This is not a game!

It was a scene straight out of a movie. Everything went quiet in both
sets of bleachers as every parent's head turned and shockingly stared at the
woman. The batter, whose helmet had fallen down over his eyes, became
startled, pausing from his stance to look. The infield stood motionless like
mannequins, their gum-chewing temporarily halted by the noise. The
pitcher froze, his mouth caught in an open Texas-sized gawk. The umpire
swiveled around on his heels, intently scanning the stands with his eyes.
Both coaches hung their heads, wagging them side-to-side. And just for a
few seconds, everything seemed like it was in super slow motion. Nobody
moved. Then, realizing what she had actually said, the overzealous mom
sheepishly cowered back over to the stands, sat in her seat, and the game
resumed as if nothing had happened.

What this overzealous and competitive mom had temporarily forgotten in her moment of motherly insanity was that there is something even
more important for a six-year-old than to flawlessly flag a fly ball in left field.
Of course, there will come a time when little Tyler will have to grow up and
take the sport (and his position) much more seriously. But what his mom

failed to remember was that for now, baseball is supposed to be fun! It really *is* a game, Mom! After all, isn't that the whole reason he signed up for the team?

Have you ever heard that mom's voice before? No, not from your own mother, but from the Christian culture around you, and maybe even your own conscience. Does it sound familiar? *Hey, get busy out there! The Christian life is not a game. Quit playing around! Stop enjoying yourself and get back to serving!* And the whole reason we signed up for this relationship is lost. Or at least it becomes buried alive. We can become so focused on the disciplines of Bible study, prayer, or witnessing that we forfeit our joy in the process. In the midst of it all, we sometimes spend more time up at the church than we do at home. Christian activities blanket our schedules, keeping us busy for the Lord and His kingdom. Because we are so intent on being the best Christians we can be, we load up our plate, thinking the more gear we have, the better we will become. Like the margins in our Bible, we also fill up the margins in our lives. Our lives become cluttered with great stuff, but they leave room for little else. However, after a while, all the extras get heavy and we grow weary under the strain of keeping up. It's a catch-22 though, because to jettison any of those Christian activities makes us feel a little less spiritual doesn't it?

But what would happen if you got radical and cleared your calendar for three to four months? No meetings. No trips. No additional men's or women's group Bible studies. Nothing extra. No being out two to three nights a week doing the Lord's work. Just for a while, what would it be like to trim down your activities to a bare minimum, to drop a few added, unnecessary pounds in your schedule? Is that even a possibility? What do you suppose would happen? Would you feel guilty? Or do you think you would benefit from such a decision?

something about mary

We're about to go visit a young lady who apparently understood the importance of purity and simplicity in her devotion and relationship with Christ.

Consider the woman known in Scripture as Mary of Bethany. An uncomplicated girl with natural spiritual beauty, we see her just three times in the New Testament, but interestingly every time she is at the feet of Jesus. Each instance tells us something of the purity and simplicity of her relationship to Christ.

"As Jesus and his disciples were on their way, he came to a village where a woman named Martha opened her home to him" (Luke 10:38).

This village here is Bethany, located on the east side of the Mount of Olives, less than two miles from Jerusalem. The house they entered belonged to Martha, who is most likely Mary's older sister. Immediately, the first thing we notice about these two sisters is that they are very, very different from one another. They have strikingly contrasting personalities, which means they tend to value and enjoy different things. And that's okay. God made them that way. And maybe you can identify here because you're very different from your sister or brother. Maybe you thank God every day that you are! But those differences can be the very things that compliment your relationship with your siblings. At the same time they are also what may have driven you over the edge at times. But, in spite of all the conflicts and contrasts, different is still a good thing.

You can probably appreciate Mary and Martha's sibling rivalry then, finding yourself identifying with one or the other. There's Martha, a typical doer. She does things by the book. Task-oriented, she is energized by doing things effectively and efficiently. In short, she gets things done. She has a job to do and she does it well. She probably has a checklist for each day. Organized to the max, she is a planner. Administrative. Competent. Resourceful. Nothing wasted. She spends hours cleaning the house before guests arrive, even in places where they would never see. She is capable, proficient, and professional. Of course, all these are admirable qualities. Everyone should strive for excellence in those areas, as some of the world's most successful people are Marthas. Without people like her, the world (and the church) would be a real mess.

And then there's Mary.

She's probably the younger sister, and that automatically puts her at a slight disadvantage in her older sister's eyes. But the biggest problem Mary has, according to Martha, is that she's not more like her big sister. That would solve everything. Mary is not the task-oriented person Martha is. She doesn't enjoy the household chores as much as Martha. She doesn't wake up early in the morning thinking about all the things she has to do that day. Instead, she probably wakes up gradually. There is no to-do list for her. That would stifle her creativity. She is more free-spirited. Besides, she isn't as much into what *has* to be done, as she is what she *gets* to do. She prefers people to programs. She would rather be talking than taking care of tasks. For her, it's devotion over duty. She loves to be with people because they are alive and responsive. Wherever the action and excitement are, that's where you'll find her. Having a party is more important than rearranging the living room furniture. She is happy when folks are together while Martha is happiest when her world is in order. While Martha's motto is "Let's get it done;" Mary's is "Let's hang out." Enjoy. Have some leisure time. Now again, one is not bad and the other good. We need the Marys to give us spontaneity and creativity. Without them, the world would be boring. But again, these two women are just different. And as you might guess, their differences created a little conflict at times. Christ highlights one of those differences in this passage.

> [Martha] had a sister called Mary, who sat at the Lord's feet listening to what he said. But Martha was distracted by all the preparations that had to be made. She came to him and asked, "Lord, don't you care that my sister has left me to do the work by myself? Tell her to help me!"
> "Martha, Martha," the Lord answered, "you are worried and upset about many things, but only one thing is needed. Mary has chosen what is better, and it will not be taken away from her." (Luke 10:39–42)

Jesus comes to their home, and naturally both sisters respond in diametrically opposite ways. Martha is preparing and working while Mary is sitting on her floor listening. Mary must have been thinking,

Why isn't Martha in here with the Lord? C'mon, it is the greatest possible honor to sit at His feet and hear Him teach us. Why worry about cooking more food at a time like this? She is really missing out on a great experience.

Meanwhile, Martha is thinking,

Why isn't Mary still in here with me preparing for the Lord? C'mon, this is the greatest possible honor to be able to serve the Lord in this way. Why just sit there like a lazy person at a time like this? She is definitely not in God's will.

But, Martha takes her thoughts a step further, marching into the living room and voicing her thoughts to Jesus.

Lord, don't you care that my sister has left me to do the work by myself? Tell her to help me!

It's as if Martha is saying,

The work! The work, Lord! See how I'm serving you? I know how much You love a good work ethic. I've read what You said about the sluggard in Proverbs and I am obeying You by doing something special for You. And all by myself too, now that Mary has left the kitchen. I'm standing alone for what is right, just like Esther and Daniel and all the others who were truly committed to You. Now Mary, on the other hand, is more like the lazy, unbelieving generation that wandered in the desert for 40 years, unwilling to obey You. Anyway, would You just tell her to get back to serving?

Of course, we really don't know all of what Martha was thinking, though Jesus does say there were many things bothering her. It is fairly safe to say that her preference of work over waiting in the Lord's presence caused her to be upset and angry with her sister. The problem is that, in the original Greek text the verse indicates Mary had already been in the kitchen helping and preparing. But in Martha's mind, it just wasn't enough.

> "Martha, Martha, the Lord answered, you are worried and upset about many things, but only one thing is needed. Mary has chosen what is better, and it will not be taken away from her."

Martha is worried and upset. Stressed out. And in need of a life lesson from Christ. Now the flip side is Mary's perspective. She is peaceful and content. Of course, there was nothing wrong with preparing a meal for Jesus.

And everyone would agree, there is nothing wrong with serving God. But Jesus here is clearly saying there is something better. Jesus is not suggesting we all sit cross-legged on the floor reading our Bibles 24/7. This is not a justification for living as a recluse or an excuse for not working hard at school, on the job, or in ministry. But what He is saying is that there is something He values more than *doing* stuff for Him. The only thing we really need, the only real requirement, according to Christ, is to simply *be* with Him. Not that we shouldn't *do*. It's just that there is something greater. It's not as visible or tangible or measurable as doing and serving.

But it is *better*.

Jesus is saying, *Martha, you are complicating things here. There is something I want more than your food right now. I want your fellowship.*

But this isn't an isolated incident. Rather it is a desire and truth Christ echoes elsewhere in Scripture as well. After all, He chose us so that we would be with Him—now and forever. It is a theme He repeated often during His earthly ministry.

> He appointed twelve, that they might **be with him** and that he might send them out to preach. (Mark 3:14)

> Do not let your hearts be troubled. Trust in God; trust also in me. In my Father's house are many rooms; if it were not so, I would have told you. I am going there to prepare a place for you. And if I go and prepare a place for you, I will come back and take you to **be with me** that you also may **be where I am**. (John 14:1–3)

> Father, I want those you have given me to **be with me** where I am, and to see my glory, the glory you have given me because you loved me before the creation of the world. (John 17:24)

> Here I am! I stand at the door and knock. If anyone hears my voice and opens the door, I will **come in and eat with him, and he with me**. (Revelation 3:20)

> To him who overcomes, I will give the right to **sit with me** on my throne, just as I overcame and sat down with my Father on his throne. (Revelation 3:21)

> I saw thrones on which were seated those who had been given authority to judge. And I saw the souls of those who had been beheaded because of their testimony for Jesus and because of the word of God. They had not worshiped the beast or his image and had not received his mark on their foreheads or their hands. They came to life and **reigned with Christ** a thousand years. (Revelation 20:4)

You see, Mary was on to something here. She chose the feet of Jesus to be her place. She had discovered the secret, the one thing God desires. Simple worship. Uncomplicated. Uncluttered. And why is this so important? For at least two reasons. First, it helps us focus on our relationship with the *Person* of Christ. Doing the work of Jesus can never substitute for knowing the Person of Jesus. We don't worship an organization, a faith, the family, the church, or even the Bible. We worship a Person. And when He is in the central spotlight of our lives, it delights His heart like nothing else! After all, that's why we were made. But secondly, this simple and pure devotion to Christ rescues us from the danger of falling prey to religious ritual or even accepting another Gospel. This was one of Paul's many concerns for the Corinthian Christians.

> I wish that you would bear with me in a little foolishness; but indeed you are bearing with me. For I am jealous for you with a godly jealousy; for I betrothed you to one husband, that to Christ I might present you as a pure virgin. But I am afraid, lest as the serpent deceived Eve by his craftiness, your minds should be led astray from the simplicity and purity of devotion to Christ. (2 Corinthians 11:1–4)

So here's Mary, just glad to be there . . . with Jesus. Listening to Him. And as she hears His words she also reads His heart. It comes through His tone of voice and His facial expressions. There is no other way to describe it. She is captivated by the Person of Jesus. While in His presence, she forgets everything else that may trouble her. Nothing else really matters. She is with Him. Simply. And she is satisfied.

Got any clutter in your life that needs to be pushed aside for a higher priority? Have you fallen, becoming unbalanced in your life? Placing too much time and energy on serving? Will you worship at His feet, listening for Him to speak to you? Are you still captivated by the Person of Christ?

dead man walking

The next time we see Mary, we find her once again at the feet of Jesus. However, this occasion is not quite as casual and carefree. Life has taken on a more serious tone now. Lazarus, the brother of Mary and Martha, has died. Scripture tells us he was very sick. Word is sent to Jesus, who is in another town miles away, and He strangely waits until Lazarus is dead before going to Bethany. Upon His arrival there, Lazarus has been dead in the tomb for four days. There is a huge wake still in progress with many friends coming to express their condolences. A thick, heavy cloud of grief now smothers the little home where Jesus once dined. However, before Jesus ever reaches Bethany, Martha hears He is on His way and goes out to meet Him. She has no interest in preparing a meal for Him this time. Far greater than her need to serve is her heart's need to be with Him. Martha has learned her lesson. She understands what that one thing is now. Her priorities are in order. Wearing not a kitchen apron but a mourning shawl this time, she runs to Him.

"Lord," Martha said to Jesus, "if you had been here, my brother would not have died. But I know that even now God will give you whatever you ask."

Jesus said to her, "Your brother will rise again."

Martha answered, "I know he will rise again in the resurrection at the last day."

Jesus said to her, "I am the resurrection and the life. He who believes in me will live, even though he dies; and whoever lives and believes in me will never die. Do you believe this?"

"Yes, Lord," she told him, "I believe that you are the Christ, the Son of God, who was to come into the world." (John 11:21–27)

Martha confesses her belief in Jesus as the Messiah. But she goes beyond that in declaring her faith in Him as the Son of God. She may not have yet pieced together the truth or mystery of the Trinity, but she knew Jesus was divine. She even goes further by highlighting the fact that this Son of God has come into the world, as if to vaguely hint that since He is here, He might bring their dead brother back to life. There may have either been some unrecorded dialogue or at least a look from Jesus which indicated that He was going to do something. Regardless, Martha finally discovered what her baby sister had experienced. This total family tragedy had caused her to pause long enough to look unflinchingly into the face of Jesus. And she fell in love with what she saw. At this point, Jesus asks her to go get her sister Mary. Upon hearing that Jesus is calling for her, Mary rises quickly and sprints out to meet the Lord, who has yet to even make the city limits, probably due to the crowd hemming Him in. In fact, He hadn't yet moved from the spot where He and Martha had met. The group of friends who were attempting to comfort Mary think she is heading out to the tomb, so they follow right on her heels.

Running out to meet her Savior, Mary peers through a haze of tears until she spots the throng surrounding Jesus. As we might expect, her eyes are puffy from countless hours of weeping. She probably hasn't eaten very much or slept. She is exhausted, weary from wailing over her lost brother. Upon reaching Jesus, she falls at His feet, repeating word-for-word what her sister had said,

Lord, if you had been here, my brother would not have died.

Apparently the two sisters have something in common after all! Jesus pauses and takes a moment to look around. He sees the mourners who have followed along. Then He gazes down at Mary, who is still weeping at His feet. But He sees beyond those tears. With X-ray vision, He peers deep into her heart. He sees the hurt, the pain, and the grief. He sees darkness of the soul she and her sister were experiencing. And He understands it. Jesus loved this family very much (John 11:3,5) and the sisters' sorrow gripped His spirit, deeply moving Him within. Inquiring as to where Lazarus' tomb was, they begin the short journey to the graveyard. This is now the second funeral procession for Lazarus she has participated in this week. And the crowd this time is a bit larger due to Jesus' presence. It's a sad day in Bethany.

Jesus wept.

Two words. One in the Greek. An amazing phenomenon, not because tears flowed from the Carpenter's eyes. He had been moved within like this before when encountering a poor leper (Mark 1:41). And He would later weep over Jerusalem (Luke 19:41). But this time Jesus wasn't weeping over them. He was crying *with* them. A wave of emotion swept over the Son of God. His eyes filled with tears, brimming to the edge then spilling over, flowing down His cheeks. And this was not like a small tear escaping unnoticed. No, Jesus was really crying, so much so that He was noticeably and visibly moved, for those standing there that day commented on how much He must have loved Lazarus (John 11:36). And just like the ocean's tide, when they reached the tomb another wave of emotion hit Him and He wept again.

Does the Savior you worship weep with you when you hurt?

It wouldn't hurt any of us to be a little more like Mary here. We need an attitude that allows us to approach this awesome God, feeling the freedom to fall at His feet at any time, especially when we are confused and crushed by the knockout punches life throws at us.

Jesus then gives orders for the stone to be rolled away from the tomb. Martha expresses her concern to the Lord that this might be a bad idea considering the stench of the rotting corpse. Lazarus assumed room temperature four days previous and just might part the crowd with his ensuing smell. Jesus responds by reassuring her, no doubt communicating with a look that says, simply trust Me.

When he had said this, Jesus called in a loud voice, Lazarus, come out!

Jesus was specifically calling out for His friend. After rolling the huge stone away from the tomb's entrance, out comes Lazarus, wrapped tightly from head to toe with strips of linen. Hopping out of the grave (or at least taking very small steps), Lazarus is unwrapped and let go, smelling as sweet as spring. No doubt the first thing he feels is the combined embrace of his sisters. Mary and Martha are crying once again, but for a different reason this time. And there is a good chance Jesus shed a few more tears just watching the reunion. Now look at what happens next: "Therefore many of the Jews who had come to visit Mary, and had seen what Jesus did, put their faith in him" (John 11:45).

But for Mary, there was something about her worship that enabled her to trust in Christ to do something great for her. In her simplicity, there was the innocence of a child. She knew Jesus had come to her and because He was there somehow everything would be all right. Will you worship at His feet, trusting Him to do something great for you? Is there some great need you have that only He can meet? Will you let Him feel your pain? Will you worship until He rolls away the stone?

The smell of worship

The last time we see Mary in Scripture, we find her once again at Jesus' feet. When we first met her worshipping at His feet, she was sitting there because she wanted to *know* Him (Luke 10:38–42). Then we see her caught up in the embrace of worship because she wanted to *believe* in Him (John 11:31–32). Finally, we last see Mary anointing His feet out of devotion to *serve* Him (John 12:1–8). Each is an act of worship, but perhaps this third scene is more compelling than all the rest. It's Wednesday, just two days before Jesus is crucified. Simon the Leper gives a party, presumably in Jesus' honor. Lazarus is also there, along with his sisters, Mary and Martha, and the disciples. Can you imagine what that must have been like? Jesus is having dinner with a group of people whose lives He has forever changed. There's James and John, who used to be called the Sons of Thunder, not because they were the local weathermen or suffered from some strange gastrointestinal disorder. They were called that because they were hot-tempered and maybe even prone to violence. But not any more! Then there's Simon the Zealot, who used to be a political assassin. Talk about changing your behavior! Of course Simon used to have leprosy and Lazarus used to be dead! They were all a bunch of used-to-be's. And when you think about it, in reality, all of us are.

> Do you not know that the wicked will not inherit the kingdom of God? Do not be deceived: Neither the sexually immoral nor idolaters nor adulterers nor male prostitutes nor homosexual offenders nor thieves nor the greedy nor drunkards nor slanderers nor swindlers will inherit the kingdom of God. **And that is what some of you were**. But you were washed, you were sanctified, you were justified in the name of the Lord Jesus Christ and by the Spirit of our God. (I Corinthians 6:9–11)

Can you see the guys at this party trying to top one another on how much Jesus had changed them? Since the dinner was probably in His honor, perhaps they took turns around the table, with each of them telling their own story of what Jesus had done for them, of how He had made them now. Martha serves dinner (naturally), and Mary . . . well Mary has found yet another way to demonstrate how worthy she thinks Jesus is. She may have not had the sinful or radical sort of testimonies the others were retelling that night, but she steps forward and honors Him in her own special way.

She takes a jar of very expensive perfume, costing three hundred denarii, which is equal to about a year's wage for a rural worker. She takes this fragrance and pours it over Jesus' head and feet. The word used to describe this perfume (costly) is the same word used to describe the precious blood of Christ (I Peter 1:18–19) and the precious character of a godly woman (I Peter 3:4). She then begins wiping His feet with her hair (Mark 14:3; John 12:3), spreading the fragrance so that it fills the entire room. This perfume measures about a pint and is made of pure nard. This particular perfume was imported from India, and contained extracted oil from a plant native to that region. Keep in mind, there were no malls, department stores, or mail order catalogs back then. We don't know how Mary obtained the perfume or how long she had waited for it. We do know that she had saved up her money for quite some time. And she didn't have to use this perfume on Jesus either. But she chose to pour it out—all of it—on Jesus. It was a worship gift that represented her unique love for Him.

But it also cost Mary her reputation as well. When she undid her hair, that was something nice Jewish women didn't do in public. In doing so, she laid her glory at His feet (1 Corinthians 11:15). The disciples began scolding her for this kind of lavish worship, objecting that the perfume should have been sold and the money given to the poor (Mark 14:4–5). But this was a bogus protest for several reasons. First, it was none of their business what Mary did with her money, especially concerning how she chose to give to God. Second, we don't see any of them honoring Jesus in such a lavish manner. Third, if Jesus wasn't correcting her, why should they? They were assuming the place of Christ by opening their mouths. And fourth, it was a false spirituality on Judas' part to object since he, as treasurer, used to steal money from the ministry account. But instead of Mary, Jesus sternly rebukes the disciples. He then turns to commend Mary for her simple yet profound act of worship.

You see, Mary possessed a unique insight into the person and work of Christ. She saw something even the disciples failed to see about Him and His mission. She understood that His death was approaching and so she anointed Him for His burial. And how did she know this? Because of her simple and passionate devotion to Him. She knew that *Messiah* meant "anointed one." All that time at His feet, she had been listening. Soaking in His every word, she had believed what He said. And part of His teaching had been regarding His impending crucifixion. So Mary wanted to do something that would demonstrate her love for her Savior. It wasn't a forced pious act meant to impress others. It was just an overflow of her love for Him. It was the natural thing for her to do.

But Jesus also commends her for recognizing the urgency of her worship. She knew the Lord wasn't always going to physically be with her, so she took advantage of the short time she had with Him. The disciples are no doubt shocked as Jesus tells them to leave her alone. He considered what she had done to be a beautiful thing. He then honors her by saying that wherever the Gospel is preached, what she has done would be mentioned. Okay, what a legacy!

And what did her sacrifice do (Mark 14:6–7)? It became an example to the disciples—a mild rebuke. It became a fragrance in the house (John 12:3), filling the whole place. And you can be sure that every time they smelled that brand of perfume they thought of Mary and her worship of Jesus. But it also became an enduring witness to the world. Everyone now knows of her devotion to Jesus. Do they know about yours? She left her mark for Jesus. What will yours be?

To be honest, sometimes in our Christian culture simplicity is seen as shallow, elementary, or needless. We like our worship polished, slick, orderly, and planned. But often we need to unplug and just make it simple. It was considered a waste of time for Mary to sit at Jesus' feet when she should have been serving Him. It was a waste of hope to ask Him to help her dead brother when she should have been moving on with her life. And it was a waste of money to pour that perfume all over Jesus. But for Mary, her simple devotion paid off each time. Nothing is ever wasted when poured out on Jesus—not your time, your money, or your perfume.

You think Mary knows something we don't? Maybe what her worship tells us is that when you are hopelessly in love with someone, you tend to lose track of time. When you're in love, you can hope against all hope, and you don't really think about cost. Those things just don't matter (Luke

18:29–30). Jesus was simply worth it to her. When was the last time you blew an afternoon on Jesus? When did you last sacrifice something precious and valuable just for Him? Are you willing to risk your reputation for Jesus? Mary just wanted to be with Jesus. Is your relationship with Him like that? Or has it become cluttered with things? Do you tend to complicate what God desires you to keep simple?

Dude, where's my worship?

So do you think Mary would even recognize our brand of Christianity today? Ever since she first sat at His feet, she was in love with Him. She just couldn't get enough of Jesus. Sometimes we act as though we've had enough of Jesus. We just show up to get a little dose on Sunday. We've heard it all before. We've already learned about Him, read that story, memorized that verse. But Christ is not a collection of facts you learn. He's a Savior you love. Our problem is that we begin the Christian life with all the enthusiasm of a rabid football fan, but we soon get over it, don't we?

The church at Ephesus was that way. It had been a strong, vibrant lighthouse in that dark city. But something had happened since their first being introduced to Christ. Thirty years earlier Paul had commended them for their overflowing love (Ephesians 1:15–16). In fact, he mentioned love at least twenty times in his letter to them. But something happened. Something changed. The second generation of Christians simply didn't have the same passion for Christ that their natural and spiritual parents had. They had the:

- doctrine, not desire
- rules, not reasons
- religion, not relationship
- purity, not passion
- service, not simplicity

The *form* was passed down, but not the *substance*. They had lost their first love. It's like the honeymoon love of a husband and wife. A loss of first love means the honeymoon is over between you and Jesus. They may not have intentionally left Him, but they had still left Him. They had everything but the one thing. They had failed to keep the main thing the main thing.

So what if you have lost that simplicity in your relationship with Christ. How can you get it back? Here's how to recapture that first love. Jesus gives us three words in Revelation 2.

Remember (2:5)

First, slow down. Then worship—Psalm 46:10. Think about the way it used to be, the way your heart felt during those first months and years of knowing Christ. The newness. The freshness. The way you marked up your Bible. The way you carried it with you. The way you prayed. The way you studied. The way you worshipped. The way you witnessed. The way your heart was so teachable. The way each day was an adventure. Remember the books you read? Why not read them again? Find your old marked up Bible. Rummage through those old study notes in the attic. Look again at your pictures and slides. Listen to that old tape or CD. Don't you miss the way you used to love Jesus?

Repent (2:5)

To repent in this context means that you make a decision to change your priorities. It means to make the changes necessary to fall in love with Christ once again. For example:

- You may need to give up Letterman or Leno so you can spend thirty minutes in the Word before going to bed.
- You may need to put down John Grisham for a while and pick up the apostle John.
- You may need to confess some sins and take practical steps to avoid them.
- You might want to get out your daily planner and plan some simple time alone with Him.

- It's all about being getting back to that one thing.

Repentance is a daily decision.

Return (2:5)

Return and *do the deeds you did at first*. What made your Christian life so vibrant and exciting in the beginning? What simple devotion did you have then that you need to return to? Who was inspiring you in your walk with Him? Do you need them again? What about time alone with God? Prayer? Obedience? Fellowship? Meditation? Worship? Ever go back to the place where you asked Christ into your life? Ever call the person who led you to Christ just to say thanks one more time? Jesus says that in order to go forward, you must first go back.

History tells us that Ephesus was the sight of a major church council in the fourth century, but after that time both the church and city began to deteriorate. Today, this city is nothing more than a big pile of rocks. Don't let that happen to your life.

So have you grown cold toward God? Oh, you're not hostile towards Him. In fact, you may be very active for Him. But are you in love with Him? Have you ever been more devoted to Christ at any other time in your life? Has there ever been a time when you were more in love with Him than you are right now? If so, then you have left your first love.

- When's the last time you told Jesus that you love Him?
- When's the last time you told Him how much you love Him?
- How long has it been since you thought of the cross in amazement?
- How long has it been since you felt deep emotion over His love for you?

Remember. Repent. Return.

Or maybe you don't have a first love to return to. Maybe you need to meet the Savior for the first time. If so, then put down this book right now and trust Him to forgive your sins and to come be your Savior. Remember back at the beginning of this chapter, the story of the little boy who was scolded for playing around in the outfield? Maybe we could learn something from him, too. The game of baseball wasn't complex to him. It was just fun. Simplify, friend. And keep it that way.

Go toss your glove in the air a while.

CHAPTER 8

Be Yourself

personal worship

To be yourself in a world full of counterfeit character is not only honorable, but also honest.

— Anonymous

A Time for Everything

A llow us to introduce you to Dave. Dave is a friend of ours, and leads people in worship like we do. However, we think he's much better at it than we are. Well-liked by everyone we know, most people would never guess he is actually a man of many moods. This is particularly seen in his relationship with the Lord. For example, we have sometimes known him to be in the depths of despair, even wanting to die. The next day he's dancing and singing again. At times, he gets so angry he asks God to destroy those who are against him. He can boast in the Lord one day and the next he's crawling to God on his knees in humble confession and repentance. He celebrates victory one day and laments his failures the next. He is a great Bible teacher, instructing others in the right way. And he eloquently declares the greatness of God in his many hit songs. Then without warning he changes moods; his emotions seem to change more than the weather. So what's wrong with our friend Dave? Do you think he is emotionally healthy? Sane? Schizophrenic? In need of serious counseling? Does he need to be medicated? Institutionalized? Locked up? Sentenced to five years hard labor working with seventh-grade boys?

Not at all. Don't panic. Our friend Dave is just fine. No need to worry about him. So how then do we explain the many moods of Dave? We've got one word for you. God. Yep, the Almighty made Dave just the way he is. The portrait we just painted is not one of a mentally unstable man in the music industry. It's just a description of the only man in all of Scripture whom the Lord said was a man after God's own heart. David was a prolific writer and a gifted musician. But he was also 100 percent human. Read through the Psalms and you will eventually find the mood you're feeling. Celebration. Sadness. Hope. Repentance. It's all there. Sometimes King David felt like staying in bed all day. During those times he just wished the world would go away. Other days he felt like standing on a mountaintop and shouting praises to God at the top of his lungs. His soul's temperatures seemed to fluctuate according to his circumstances. Go figure.

David was a true individual, and he vividly illustrates through the inspired book he wrote that you can't nail down worship into a succinct how-to manual. For him, worship was an unpredictable thing. It was impulsive. Free. Open.

And honest.

Scripture is right. There really is a time for everything. There is a time appropriate to laugh out loud and for so long that you have trouble drawing in another breath. Then there's also a time to cry, to feel deep hurt and pain in the soul. And there's a time to jump up and down and party. Perhaps you're more reserved in your emotions, less expressive. That's cool too. The point is that there is a time for everything and a place for every kind of person and personality in the body of Christ. And this is especially true when it comes to expressing our worship. Our times of praise can be extended or brief. Private or public. Loud or quiet. Spontaneous or planned. Conscious or unconscious. Expressive or contemplative. There is a time for awe-filled fear as well as a time to cry out Abba Father. Our worship of God includes times when, like Isaiah, we find ourselves pinned against the wall by the blinding holiness of God. We bow in humility, confession, and submission. Like Abraham, we fall on our faces before Him, recognizing we are merely dust. Like Moses, we remove our sandals, realizing we are standing on holy ground.

one of a kind

It's important to recognize that it actually is God who has made us. Despite what misinformed philosophers and scientists might have us to think, we were not the random collision of particles, resulting from billions of years of evolution. After over a hundred years of evolutionary debate, education and research, the archeologist's spade has yet to unearth the infamous missing link, or even anything close to it. There still isn't the slightest conclusive evidence to support evolutionists' claims. Where are the portions of fossilized bones from the millions of transitionary species evolution claims once existed? But don't believe it just because it's written in this book. Go and study the evidence for yourself.

The truth is that you were made by God, every part of you. In fact, He was involved in specifically and uniquely creating you while still in your mother's womb. Look at Psalm 139:13–16:

> For you created my inmost being; you knit me together in my mother's womb. I praise you because I am fearfully and wonderfully made; your works are wonderful, I know that full well. My frame was not hidden from you when I was made in the secret place. When I was woven together in the depths of the earth, your eyes saw my unformed body. All the days ordained for me were written in your book before one of them came to be.

Like a skilled surgeon, God stayed with you throughout the entire operation of your creation. As a result, His fingerprints are all over you. Paul writes that we are His workmanship, created in Christ Jesus for good works (Ephesians 2:10). The word "workmanship" is from the Greek word *poiema*, from which we derive our word "poem." You are His work. His poem. Handcrafted. An original. A priceless work of art. God's magnum opus. A masterpiece!

God's handiwork extends to you physically, mentally, and temperamentally. The Father doesn't just make you, then cast you aside or set you on a shelf to gather dust. He is constantly thinking about you. He's still working in you.

> How precious concerning me are your thoughts, O God! How vast is the sum of them!
>
> Were I to count them, they would outnumber the grains of sand. When I awake, I am still with you. (Psalm 139:17–18)

Next time you're at the beach, pick up a handful of sand. Then take a pinch out of that and try to count the number of them. You might get frustrated in the process, or you may begin to appreciate how much and often God thinks of you. He made you an individual—you are unique.

sounds like a plan

Consider the prophet Jeremiah for a moment. As we observe from Jeremiah 1:1–19, we learn something of God's creative work in us as well as His design for our lives. Eavesdropping on His conversation with him we, like Jeremiah, can discover our own special design and calling.

God called you before you were born (1:5).

God's call to Jeremiah came *before he was even born*. As incomprehensible as it sounds, God set His heart on Jeremiah before the foundation of the world was even laid. This is God's sovereignty in action, as we saw before in Chapter 3—His prerogative to do what He pleases (Psalm 115:3). As adopted sons and daughters, we are called to salvation the same sovereign way (Ephesians 1:3–4). Have you ever wondered, *What was God doing before He made the world and the universe?* While we aren't exactly sure about everything He was up to, this much we do know: He was setting His heart upon individuals whom He would graciously call to Himself. Paul also informs us that he too was set apart from his mother's womb (Galatians 1:5). And so were you.

god called you personally (1:5).

Before I formed you in the womb I knew you The Hebrew word for "know" here is the word *yada*, which refers to a deep, intimate knowledge and relationship with someone. Depending on the particular context in which it is used, it can have different meanings. For example, it is the word used in Genesis 4:1 to refer to Adam's sexual relations with his wife. But the theme of intimacy is brought out in another way in Genesis 18:19 where it is translated chosen (referring to God's choice of Abraham) as well as Amos 3:2 (referring to God's choice of Israel). God does not make a cold, aloof, indifferent, and impersonal decision when He chooses us. Rather, in communicating this truth to us, He selects a word which describes the most intimate and loving of relationships. Again, "In love He predestined us to adoption as sons . . ." (Eph. 1:5). God's choice of Jeremiah (and of you) was an individual, personal, intimate, and loving one.

god has given your life purpose (1:5).

. . . before you were born I consecrated you. To be consecrated means to be set apart. It means to be created for a specific and unique purpose. The word was used in the Old Testament to refer to the vessels in the Tabernacle and its special furnishings. These were ordinary vessels designed for an extraordinary purpose. The God who fearfully and wonderfully made Jeremiah, the God who knew Jeremiah, is also the God who set apart Jeremiah for a purpose in life. Later in the same book, Jeremiah quotes God's declaration to Israel: " 'For I know the plans I have for you', says the Lord, 'plans to prosper you and not to harm you, plans to give you a future

and a hope'" (29:11). You see, God really does love you and have a wonderful plan for your life!

god has given you a mission (1:5)

I appointed you as a prophet to the nations. While the term *consecrated* refers to God setting Jeremiah apart for a purpose, the term *appointed* specifically identifies what that purpose is. Jeremiah is to be God's prophet, His mouthpiece. The office of prophet was not through election by majority vote. Nor was it earned through education. Rather, it was by divine appointment only. Jeremiah could have no more made himself a prophet than he could have chosen the place and date of his birth. It was a high and holy office. But the sense of the verb here goes beyond just the appointment of Jeremiah to this office. The verb implies that God also *installed* him as a prophet as well. In other words, God *called* him to be a prophet *and then made* him one! He didn't just appoint him to a mission. He also equipped him for it. Jeremiah would spend the bulk of his life primarily ministering and speaking to Judah. But as a prophet to the *nations*, he would also pronounce judgment against other countries as well. He would be the voice of his day. Being a prophet and speaking to the nations would be Jeremiah's unique and personal way to worship God. But it would also be his *best* way. By becoming the prophet God made him to be, this would also be the greatest possible way he could bring honor and praise to God. By obeying God's call for his life, Jeremiah was saying, *Lord, Your plan and design for me is the best imaginable thing for me. I will therefore declare your worth by being a prophet. By doing so, I affirm that your wisdom is supreme and Your plan cannot be improved upon.*

For Jeremiah to have become a priest, king, or a shepherd would not only have been sin, but a step down as well, because God's perfect will is just that—perfect. Being a prophet was his highest calling. Living to the max for Jeremiah meant prophesying in God's name and power. In doing so, God would be praised.

Sometimes people think that to *really* bring praise to God, they have to become a preacher or a missionary. They have to surrender to ministry, like it's slavery or something. Because of the huge gap often created between the clergy (the professional ministers) and the laity, the idea is that somehow, the work of those in full-time Christian service is more valuable to God than the service of the common man. And we should certainly admire and respect those gifted professionals who preach, teach, sing, and play for God. That's okay. We need heroes and people we can look up to. But we can take it a step too far by elevating them to celebrity-like status, envying their calling and giftedness. After all what could be better than being a big time prophet for God?

Here is what's better than that. Here is a way to bring the greatest possible honor and glory to the name of Jesus Christ: Just be yourself and fulfill your own calling from God. If He calls you to preach, then by all means do so. If He calls you to sing or play guitar for Him for a living, then pack up the car and get after it. If he calls you to be a nurse, firefighter, salesperson, physical therapist, school teacher, computer programmer, or to work in a coffee shop, then do that with all your might, too! Besides, all of us are full-time ministers anyway. It's just that some are also called to do it vocationally. It's all about following your God-given passion. It's not what kind of *parson* you are, but what kind of *person* you are that matters to Him. And in doing so, you will bring unbelievable praise to God by being the best *you* can be!!

It's all about discovering and becoming, as Paul reminded his friends in Philippi: Therefore, my dear friends . . . continue to **work out your salvation** with fear and trembling, for it is God who works in you to will and to act according to his good purpose (Philippians 2:12–13).

To work out here has the meaning of bringing something to completion. Maturing in Christ, growing in your relationship with Him, understanding all God did for you at the cross and how you worship Him on a daily basis—all this is a process. A progressive work. And they were to work out their own salvation, not someone else's. It's an individual thing. And to a certain degree, everyone works out their salvation differently, according to how God has uniquely designed them.

IT's MY pleasure

In 1924, the Summer Olympics were held in Paris, France. Eric Liddel, a young Scotsman, was due to represent England in the one hundred meter sprint in which he was the favorite to win. You may remember his story as immortalized in the hit movie *Chariots of Fire*. Eric truly possessed a gift, a gift to run like the wind. But in Paris, he found out that his desire to honor God through winning his race was not to be. He discovered that the heats for the 100m fell on Sunday, and Eric simply refused to run on the Sabbath day. Tremendous pressure came upon him from all the race officials and from all the British coaches. But Eric's mind was made up—God was his highest priority. He flatly refused to run on Sunday. His convictions were stronger than the Olympic committee. So Eric gave up his spot in the one hundred meter and another teammate gave him his place in another race. But in an effort not to waste the sprinter's talent, eventually Liddell was entered into the two hundred meter and four hundred meter events, both of which he had never run before. In the two hundred meter race, he surprised many by taking the bronze medal, but it was in the four hundred meter event that he really displayed his prowess. Eric had drawn the worst starting position in the race, way out on the rim of the curve. His would be the last spot to hear the starter's gun and with no visible competitor it would be difficult for him to judge his own progress throughout the race. The gun sounded and Eric shot out of the blocks like a gazelle. He led from the start of the race. The race announcer began to get excited: "They've cleared the last curve. Liddel is still leading! He's increasing his lead! Increasing and increasing! Oh, what a race!" He could speak no more, being choked with excitement. Against all odds, Eric won the gold medal in the four hundred meter. But not only did he win it, he broke the world record with his time. It was not the gold medal that honored God, but Eric's putting God before everything else.

However, that wasn't the most important message of the film or of Eric's life. Liddel was also called to be a missionary to China. His sister shared his zeal for God but felt like Eric's track and field pursuits got in the way of his calling to ministry. She felt he was compromising by competing in the Olympic games. In one of the most memorable scenes in the movie, Liddel and his sister are walking together in a field, debating about his calling and his competition. Turning to his beloved sister, Eric declares with passion,

> God made me for a purpose—for China—but He also made me fast. And when I run . . . I feel His pleasure!

What a declaration! And it was evident when Liddel ran. He always seemed to find a hidden reserve of power and speed in the last one hundred meters of each race, bursting past his opponents at the finish line. Throwing his head back as he ran, which became his trademark style, Liddel finished each race with a look of ecstasy beaming from his face. Ian Charleston, who played the role of Eric Liddel in the film, had to learn to run with his head tilted back in the style of the Olympic champion. On the sixth day of filming, Charleston concluded that Eric's unconventional running style was inspired by trust. He trusted to get there, said Charleston. He ran with faith. He didn't even look where he was going. It was this same trust that carried over into Eric's spiritual life. It was this trust that took him to China as a missionary. Head up, trusting his Savior, he died young in a Japanese concentration camp during World War II, still faithfully serving God. He finished his race strong.

Have you ever felt His pleasure? And what does that mean? Feeling God's pleasure is the confident assurance of knowing God is delighted through seeing His perfect plan unfold in your life. It is the joy and satisfaction that fills His heart when we are true to the original blueprint. And it's more than just obeying Him, or going to college and choosing the right career, or marrying the right person. It's more than being morally pure or teaching a Bible study, as important as those things are. It's also about being true to yourself, and being in harmony with your God-given temperament and personality. It's about being comfortable with the you He made and the you He wants you to be. It's about feeling okay with playing your specific role in the world and in the body of Christ. Many people who are unhappy with their life and career are that way because they're stuck in a job they don't enjoy. Like how you may have felt when your parents forced you to play baseball, take dance or piano lessons. They dragged you to practice. Like enduring medieval torture, you persevered and survived. You managed to tolerate the torment. Hopefully, you're even a better person for the experience.

But it probably wasn't long afterwards that you discovered something you *really* enjoyed. Maybe it was computers or technology. Perhaps it was a foreign language, or playing a different instrument or sport. That's when you began to actually *enjoy* for a change, to anticipate the activity, to practice without being asked. Maybe you loved it, not because you were an instant all-star or virtuoso, but because it just fit you better.

Isn't it so cool that God grants us permission to just be ourselves? And He sets us free to be that person even within the context of something bigger than us. We retain our individual identities when we are involved in a larger setting, such as the Church. Like a body has many parts with different but complimentary functions, God has placed each one here for a purpose. You have an irreplaceable contribution to make. Nobody can take your place. There are no subs on the bench. The team needs you. You may have been gifted and equipped to be the quarterback, wide receiver, or lineman. You may be on the offense or defense. You may throw the ball, run with it, catch it, or never touch it. Or you may be wired to play more than one position well. But regardless of where you fit, be energized by that role, knowing that as you perform it, God will feel pleasure and share it with you.

Eric Liddel was one of those special individuals who discovered who he was and took great delight in pursuing that identity. For him, that identity unfolded in three parts. Part one was to be an Olympian. He gave everything he had to this role, and without compromising his integrity, he brought great glory to God, enjoying the process. The second part of Eric's life was spent as a missionary to China, and he devoted himself to that work with the same passion and fervor he had done on the track. But the third and final part of Eric's life was spent as a prisoner during World War II, locked up because of his faith in Christ and work for Him. Eric Liddel died in that prison. His path and offering of worship was unique. How many people get the opportunity to be a witness to the entire world through winning an Olympic gold medal? How many of them go on to serve on the foreign mission field, teaching others to be worshippers of God? And how many also have the great privilege of being a true martyr for their faith in Jesus Christ? Those three worship offerings were Eric's contribution to showcasing the glory of God. And though He doesn't call all of us to be Olympians or missionaries or martyrs, God does call each of us to work out **our** own salvation. He wants us to use who we are to ascribe honor, worth, value, and glory to our great God.

custom-made praise

So why is it that some people love to stand and lift hands in praise to God while others are content to remain still and seated? Why are some rejoiceful while others more contemplative? Because worship is both a multi-faceted and very personal encounter. Our individual experience ranges from awe to intimacy, from reverential fear of the King to the comfort of an Abba Father. The range of the worship experience in the body of Christ is as broad as that body itself. It is no respecter of denomination, race, culture, or country. It doesn't matter if you're Pentecostal or Presbyterian, born a Baptist, bred in the Bible belt, taught tradition, or converted under a contemporary ministry. The Lord gives you the freedom to worship in the way that best suits your divinely designed personality and temperament. That certainly doesn't mean that we exercise that freedom anytime we please. There are times when we show restraint out of regard for others. But be encouraged to know that the Father is most glorified when you simply worship Him the way *you* were made to.

You are one of a kind. Resist the temptation to be a cheap imitation of someone else. There is only one you. Discover your uniqueness. Recognize it as having come from God. Then, under His Lordship, just enjoy being you! By doing this, you will automatically be giving God glory. You will be worshipping just by becoming the person God made you to be. And as He reveals to you what the next chapter of your life contains, pursue it with everything that is within you! Keep in mind the words of Solomon: "Whatever your hand finds to do, do it with all your might, for in the grave, where you are going, there is neither working nor planning nor knowledge nor wisdom" (Ecclesiastes 9:10).

Give it all you've got! Fire on all the pistons! Go for it! Live life full throttle! Seize the day! *This* day! Before death comes and takes away your opportunities to do so, enjoy and give Him praise! So what is it for you? Have you discovered it yet? How would you complete the following sentence:

When I _____, I feel His pleasure.

If you're not yet sure of what that is, consider asking those who know you best to give you input. Take a personality test. Seek godly counsel. Pray. As you delight yourself in God daily, listen to your heart's desires. What are they saying to you? Is there a reoccurring theme? Of course, they are not infallible, and ought to be checked in the light of Scripture and godly wisdom. But at the same time, don't dismiss the inner promptings and passions of your heart, especially when you experience so much joy from them.

The Magi Mystery Tour

In the New Testament, there are many examples of people who worshipped God uniquely. One of those stories occurred in the events surrounding the birth and early years of Christ. Do you remember the Magi, the men who came to worship Christ after His birth? Though tradition states there were three of them (hence the Three Wise Men), Scripture doesn't actually tell us their number, names, origin, or even how they got to Palestine. But we do know that Magi is a term which designates an order of priests and philosophers who originally belonged to Persia. As such, they were extensively distributed over the region of the Euphrates. In fact, the astrologers and magicians in the book of Daniel belonged to this order. But for these New Testament Magi, we can only guess that they journeyed from the valley of the Euphrates. We know they were skilled in astronomy and astrology and even had some sort of sacrificial system in their religion. Many Magi interpreted dreams and were involved in various occult practices. Our English words magic and magician are derivatives of the word magi.

Most Bible scholars think the Magi believed in one God, and were possibly a part of what Scripture refers to as the God-fearing Gentiles (Acts 10:1–2; 16:14). They had extensive knowledge of agriculture, science, mathematics, history, and the occult. And because of their proficiency, they became a powerful force of political advisors in the Medo-Persian and Babylonian Empires. The laws of the Medes and Persians were founded upon their teachings. We also know that they usually traveled in huge entourages. But we don't know exactly how God told them the King of the Jews would be born. Regardless, they were spiritually minded enough men to follow the Christmas Star (probably the glory of the Lord), which eventually led them to Bethlehem.

But one obstacle stood in their path. It was the ruthless King Herod, whom the Magi stopped by to visit when they arrived in Jerusalem, probably to pay homage to the ruler of the land and to see if he had any info on this new King. However, Herod apparently feared their political influence as much as he did the threat of this so-called King. For all he knew, they were coming to Jerusalem to start a revolution. Herod was known for being a bit on the paranoid side. The people of Jerusalem became afraid because when Herod got upset, people started dying. Heads rolled . . . literally. And though he was skeptical about these Magi, he still wanted to use them to find the King of the Jews. However, these spiritually-minded men had developed the ability to see what others could not. They read Herod like a book with a little help from God speaking to them in a dream. After all, that was their job.

sign, sign, everywhere a sign

As modern-day God-seekers, we often miss the signs God sends our way because we don't know they're there and because we're not looking for them. We are often too preoccupied with other things. But God *is* working in the world. And He is at work in your city, your school, your church, and in your life. Can you see what He is doing? Do you know what He is up to? Do you see the signs? To see them, you have to develop a different perspective on reality. You have to see through another grid, another lens. You have to put on another pair of glasses, one that will change the way you perceive the world, life, and reality. You have to get another perspective . . . *His* perspective. So how do you get this perspective?

first, get a look at the plan

What is your plan to improve your eyesight? How can you begin seeing more of what God is doing, just like the Magi did? Here's one suggestion: Study Scripture. It's God's written revelation to you. His mind, but more importantly His *heart*, is contained within its pages. The Bible records God's perspective on just about everything. Life. Sin. Love. Heaven. Relationships. Family. Sex. Joy. Problems. Finances. So what about your Bible? Do you read it? Do you know it? Use it? Memorize it? *Scripture is the primary lens through which we see the ways God speaks to us.* So if you haven't already, go buy a Bible, one you can understand. Get into the Word and let the Word get into you. The Magi followed God's way of communicating to them (the star and a dream), and you can do the same through the Scripture today.

second, get on with the pursuit

Contrary to folklore and church Christmas plays nationwide, it took this caravan of Magi around two years to find Jesus. Whether they traveled the entire two years or initially studied the phenomenon of this star before embarking on their journey is not known. But by the time they arrived, Joseph and Mary were living in a house (Matthew 2:11). The Magi caravan had traveled from the east, which was a very long journey (perhaps over two thousand miles), as caravans tend to move very slowly. How slowly? Imagine taking about ten families to the Grand Canyon for a vacation. Now imagine making that same trip on the backs of camels. No video games, no Cracker Barrel restaurants and no roadside bathrooms. Just lots and lots of sun and sand. It was a very slow trip. We know it took them about two years from the time they first saw the star until finally arriving (Matthew 1:7,16). We also know this because Herod executed all children two years old and younger. Remember he did this hoping he would kill the Jewish Messiah, thus preventing him from growing up and becoming a threat to Rome. So based on the Magi's calculations, they would be searching for a boy about two years of age or younger. They must have wanted to see Jesus pretty badly because they never gave up pursuing the promised Son of God. They had more than just *perseverance,* they had a holy *hunger.* They asked everyone they met about where the Christ was (Matthew 2:2). The Magi were so excited to finally find the house where He was that Matthew was at a loss for words, saying simply that they rejoiced exceedingly with great joy (Matthew 2:10). These guys were true seekers (Jeremiah 29:13). And when they finally got there, what did they do? Check into a hotel? Crash on the couch? Unpack? Ask for food? Inquire as to where the bathroom was? Tend to their saddle sores? No, instead . . .

. . . they worshipped Jesus.

Then they opened their treasures. They had brought these all the way from the East as an offering to this new King of the Jews. And they believed Him to be a King, too. Bowing down before Him, they presented Him with gifts such as were offered to royalty by ambassadors or vassals. These regal gifts consisted of gold, frankincense, and myrrh. Of course, gold was a usual offering to kings. And it was not unusual for a child to be crowned King in those days. But these Magi knew this child-king was the Ruler of another kind of Kingdom. Secondly, they offered him frankincense. This was an aromatic, costly, and fragrant gum distilled from a tree in India and Arabia, used in sacrificial offerings. And then finally, myrrh, which was an aromatic gum produced from a thorn bush that grew in Arabia and Ethiopia, used in perfuming ointments. Some have suggested that each gift represented a different aspect of the Person and work of Christ.

- Gold—precious metal, because He would be King.
- Frankincense—incense for Him as our High Priest.
- Myrrh—perfume, to prepare for his death and burial as our Savior.

These opulent gifts indicate that these Magi were persons of some affluence. Joseph and Mary may have used these gifts to finance their trip to Egypt and to sustain them in their subsequent stay there. It would have taken some resources to fund a family's prolonged visit to a foreign land. Bottom line: Their gifts were individual, unique expressions of worship, given out of an overflow of grateful hearts. Theirs was not the journey of a nearby shepherd or the offering of a fisherman. They just naturally gave what wealthy and influential Magi would give. Their worship of Christ was reflective of their distinct identities. And as they worshipped Him in their own individual way, their hearts were transformed, filled with joy.

You may not be a modern-day Magi, but you still have a worship offering to give your Messiah, your King. Just for a moment, place yourself on the back of one of those camels. Moseying and meandering along at the speed of a turtle, you slowly make your way towards the home of Christ. Camped in the Persian wilderness night after night, you've had much time to think as you've gazed up at the stars. You've had time to contemplate what gift you'll present to Him. It has to be a gift that uniquely reflects you. Something only you can give. Something that will tell Him how worthy you believe He is. Maybe you would like to honor Him as Savior with your gift. Recognize His right to rule as King with your offering. Or maybe you should ask yourself these questions: From what earthly activity do I gain the most pleasure? What do I enjoy doing more than anything? The answer to those questions is something only you know. Is it a sport? A talent? A skill? Whatever it is, wrap it up. And do it now. Your caravan has just arrived at Jesus' house. Are you ready to worship this king? Ready to bow before the Messiah with your frankincense? Dismount that camel and go inside. He's waiting for you.

god moments

unexplainable worship

There are two ways to live your life. One is as though nothing is a miracle. The other is as though everything is a miracle.

—albert einstein

If God is small enough for us to understand, He isn't big enough for us to worship.

—anonymous

the Rest of god

Question: What does God have in common with your VCR?

Answer: Try as you might, it's impossible to program either.

With all we know about God, we must still confess that our knowledge is limited and finite. Like Abraham, there are times when, in reverence, we fall on our face in humility before Him. Like Isaiah, we recognize our smallness. Though we may become educated in biblical interpretation and theology, there is yet a vast ocean of truth and experience concerning God that still evades us. We would agree that the Lord never acts in ways contradictory to His Word, yet we often cannot track His movements by pointing to a specific chapter and verse. There are times when He surprises us by taking an unexpected, intangible, and untraceable path. He does many things we just don't understand, right? God occasionally throws a wicked curveball just to remind us that He is God and we are not. He wants us to never forget what He told Isaiah:

> For My thoughts are not your thoughts, neither are your ways
> My ways, declares the Lord.
> For as the heavens are higher than the earth, So are My ways
> higher than your ways, And My thoughts than your thoughts.
> (Isaiah 55:8–9)

God's methods and ways intersect on a level far beyond human understanding. You may somehow, through superior intellect or utter determination, figure out how to program your VCR. But you will never completely figure out God. It is as if you come to a point in your spiritual journey where the road ends at an impassable chasm. You stand motionless, staring across an impossible bottomless abyss. On the other side resides the rest of the knowledge of God. Between the two sides is a sheer drop-off leading straight down to nothingness. Your toes inch over the precipice where your human ability ends, where your capacity to understand officially terminates. Peering in the distance, it's really impossible to see through the thick billowing smoke that seems to engulf the other side. It's the edge of reason and learning, a place where the credits roll, announcing the film of our knowledge has officially ended this side of Heaven. From that location, there is not much left to do but drop to your knees and worship this God. Is it any wonder Paul wrote:

> Oh, the depth of the riches both of the wisdom and knowledge
> of God! How unsearchable are His judgments and unfathomable
> His ways! For who has known the mind of the Lord, or who
> became his counselor? Or who has first given to him that it
> might be paid back to him again? For from Him and through
> Him and to Him are all things. To Him be the glory forever.
> Amen. (Romans 11:33–36)

Perhaps you have personally visited this place before. Maybe you have returned to the edge in your walk with God. Or maybe He has led you there, to give you a snapshot of His glory. We're not talking about some missionary person who experienced something supernatural. This isn't some Christianized urban legend—not like the story of the couple picking up a hippie hitchhiker, who subsequently warns of Jesus' soon return, then unexplainably disappears from the back seat of the car. These aren't camp-fire stories. We're talking about real experiences that happen in real time to real people. Has God ever done that for you, bringing you to a moment that was far beyond your expectations and understanding? Have you ever known an instant when the only explanation possible was that it was a God thing? A cancerous lump disappears with no medical explanation. A fatal accident is narrowly avoided. The friend or relative you thought would never become a Christian suddenly surrenders to Jesus. A bizarre string of coinci-dences happens to you, leading up to a huge, unexpected blessing. You wit-ness a service where a man preaches, an outpouring of God's grace occurs, and huge numbers respond to the Gospel. You take part in a mission trip and see the Good News of Christ taken to a place where it has never gone before. A desperate need is met just in the nick of time, at the very last moment. You pray, and . . . Bang! It happens. A check for a large sum of money appears in your mailbox just when you needed it, and right to the penny. There is an almost mysterious, even comic element to it at times. You try and explain it, but you cannot. You put it down on paper, but it doesn't add up. It puzzles you. All of a sudden other mysteries seem trivial. It becomes inconsequential how those statues got on Easter Island, or how they built the Pyramids, or who shot JFK. Those things pale in light of the fact that God did something and you witnessed it! He showed up!

But lest we become too preoccupied with the spectacular, we must rec-ognize that these God-moments are not limited to supernatural divine inter-ventions. They can also come in the quiet solitude of our soul—like lying in a sleeping bag under a cool, cloudless Colorado night sky; galaxy-gazing on your back—the stars are crisp, almost touchable, brighter than ever before against a velvet backdrop. You stare into space, spotting constellations you've never seen before. And in the chill of the Rocky mountain air, you lock on like a laser-guided missile to the wonder of it all. God is spreading His canopy for you, showing you but a tiny fraction of His grandeur. Or maybe it comes to you through witnessing the birth of a child, capturing with your mind's camera the indelible image of a newborn taking its first breath of earth's air. The miracle of new life captivates you, and the only explanation is the Creator. Or perhaps in the midst of a difficult time, such as a severe personal loss or deep depression, you hear Him whisper softly with a voice of compassion, *I still love you*. It's a voice only you can hear, and one only you need to hear.

It is during those times that God parts the curtain of normal and natural living for a brief instant, just for you. You see God in a way you have never seen Him before. Your perception of Him and perspective of things changes. He's bigger, more awesome than you had ever realized. And it is for events such as these that a special kind of worship is in order. It's worship inspired by the unexplainable, a worship that uniquely reminds you that He alone is God. Can you recall events, experiences, or moments of biblical enlightenment that have marked you? They're things you never forget—like where you were on September 11th, 2001.

Scripture abounds with such impressionable moments. In a sense, all of Scripture is a God-moment—one huge fifteen hundred-year era filled with incredible, unexplainable accounts where God chose to crash the party. If God were working in our world, there would be some occasional Wow! episodes. And there are. Each one occurring for a purpose, sometimes on behalf of a person, family, or even a nation's benefit. But each time, it communicates something about Him as well. And it always demands a response. Imagine being the proverbial fly on the wall as an eyewitness to the following four scenes:

scene one: outnumbered but not outlived

The nation of Israel found herself greatly disadvantaged in a war against a formidable Assyrian enemy camped outside Jerusalem. This was the same pagan army who, in a matter of a few hours, would certainly level the Jewish capital city and turn it into a parking lot. But the good news for Israel was that God had promised He would not let that happen, vowing, "I will defend this city to save it for My own sake and for My servant David's sake" (Isaiah 37:33–35). The tension mounted as evening fell on Palestine. And while the soldiers of Israel were making sure that their last will and testaments were in order, their Assyrian counterparts settled in for a good night's sleep. Israel had reason to be nervous. Assyria had laid waste to all their enemies, and due to this, they were a dreaded foe. Those whom the Assyrians didn't kill, they conquered, often leading the defeated people away by tying ropes to rings bored through their noses. But that night, God decided to give both Israel and Assyria a fight they would never forget. For Israel, this would be one for the highlight reel—a scene soon to find its way into the scrapbook archives. For Assyria, it would be a devastating loss, making it extremely difficult to recruit soldiers for next season.

That night God sent the angel of the Lord, who promptly slaughtered 185,000 Assyrian soldiers while they slept (Isaiah 37:36). They went to bed confident and cocky. They woke up very dead. Many believe this angel was a pre-incarnate visit from the second member of the Godhead: Jesus. And how did He slaughter such a mass of military in such a short time? As documented by secular records, one Greek historian suggested their destruction was the result of a fast-acting bubonic plague. Others say it had to do with bad food. In that case they should have definitely fired the camp cook. And if so, the deadly illness had great timing as far as Israel was concerned. The truth is that it was a supernatural slaughter. Pleasant? No. Gruesome? Possibly. Smelly? Most definitely, especially as 185,000 bodies began decomposing. While we have no idea as to the Lord's methods in this matter, we know He did it in a way that unmistakably said, God was here. Of course, if you're Sennacherib, the King of the Assyrian army, this would have been a real downer for you, putting a major crimp in your invasion plans. So he did what any King with half a brain would do—he packed up and went home. But his bad fortune got even worse when he got there. While worshipping his god, his sons promptly came in and murdered him (Isaiah 37:35–38). Now if you're Israel, you have to believe the Lord is on your side, right? While you were sleeping and snoring, He was out slaughtering your enemies. That ought to inspire some real worship, don't you think? Surely the soldiers and citizens of Israel didn't yawn at this miracle. This was a God-moment for the purpose of Israel's protection.

scene two: rebel forces go south

Okay, rewind several hundred years. Moses had led the people of God out of Egypt through an incredible series of supernatural events popularly known as the Ten Plagues. But in spite of these and other events, such as a pillar of fire and miraculous manna from Heaven, some of those redeemed out of bondage still refused to get the point. If you can't see God in all of that, you need to sell all you have and buy a clue. One of these Einsteins was a man named Korah. Grumpy and discontent, he began a nationwide complaining campaign against Moses. His basic gripe went something like this: *Moses, you think you're hot stuff, don't you? You're so high and mighty, you and that stick of yours, not to mention your wimpy little brother. Well, you're no better than any one of us. Besides, where is this new land you promised us? All I see is desert and sand. In case you haven't noticed, nothing grows in sand. We were better off back in Egypt! So you can go back up on that mountain and play God all you want, but just leave us out of it. We're going back home!* So persuasive was Korah that he convinced 250 influential leaders to follow his little rebellion. Little did he know that Moses' desire was never to control the people, but to serve and obey God. Unfortunately, it was too late for explanations at this point. This uprising would have to be dealt with quickly and severely. Moses' response to this attempted coup d'etat was to simply inform all of Israel to stand back from the tents of Korah and his merry band of malcontents. Then Moses responded to their allegations, declaring to the people, *Okay then. Let's see who is really from the Lord, them or me. If it is God who has led us out of Egypt and if I am His chosen instrument, then let the earth open up and swallow these men.* But before Korah could say, *Hey Moses, could we use a slightly different if-then scenario?*, God showed up in a big way:

> Then it came about as he finished speaking all these words, that the ground that was under them split open; and the earth opened its mouth and swallowed them up, and their households, and all the men who belonged to Korah, with their possessions. So they and all that belonged to them went down alive to Sheol; and the earth closed over them, and they perished from the midst of the assembly. And all Israel who were around them fled at their outcry, for they said, The earth may swallow us up! Fire also came forth from the Lord and consumed the two hundred and fifty men who were offering the incense. (Numbers 16:31–35)

Okay, there was quite a bit of mass hysteria going on here among the Israelites. Can you blame them? The earth just split apart and engulfed a large group of their friends, while fire was shooting out of the Tabernacle killing another 250 of them! You can be sure the image of those rebels sliding into the earth was indelibly imprinted on many minds for a long time.

But keep in mind, the people of God were still learning what it meant to worship this God. This was all a new experience for them. They didn't always know the right response to God's acts. Most of them were probably thinking, *Hey, the ground just opened up and swallowed a bunch of people! Let's get outta here!!* They had been without a leader for about four hundred years, so it would take some time for the people of God to catch onto the idea again. And yet, even with this clear display of God's judgment, the people refused to acknowledge God or bow down to worship Him. Amazingly, the very next day after witnessing this terrifying scene, another complaint rose against Moses. *You killed the Lord's people,* they said. This second rebellion prompted the Lord to show up in a cloud, telling Moses, "Get away from among this congregation, that I may consume them in a moment" (Numbers 16:45). God was visibly angry because the people had stubbornly

resisted His plan and provision. They had learned nothing from the example He set with Korah. His terrible judgment was about to fall on a few hundred thousand of them when Moses and Aaron fell on their faces before
God in intercession for the people. By the time Aaron had made atonement,
14,700 had already died from an awful plague.

Here was a God-moment given for the purpose of judgment of God's
people. They eventually understood the fear and reverence necessary when
approaching God, and submitted to God's chosen leaders (Numbers 17:12–13).

scene Three: will the Real god please show up?

In this unforgettable episode, the prophet Elijah made a gutsy and dangerous decision. He confronted evil King Ahab of Israel concerning his worship
of false gods. As you might expect, the King did not appreciate Elijah's cri-
tique of his religion one bit. But Elijah had to confront the King who was
supposed to be spiritually leading Israel into God's ways instead of leading
them into apostasy. So Elijah proposed an idea to settle once and for all who
the real God was: a contest of sorts between the two Gods up on Mount
Carmel. *And just to sweeten the pot a bit,* Elijah offered, *you can bring 450
prophets of Baal and 400 prophets of the Asherah. I alone will represent Yahweh.*
So King Ahab, thinking this would be a cakewalk, bought the idea. Word
spread about the event, and on the morning of game day, the stands were
packed with thousands who had come to see which God would take home
the championship trophy. To make things fair, both Elijah and the prophets
of Baal got to lay an ox on an altar of wood. Then they would have the
opportunity to call on their respective Gods to see who would answer. The
God who responded with fire would prove Himself to be the real God.
Everyone present thought this was a good idea since both parties believed
their God to be responsible for thunder, lightning, and storms. The Baal
boys won the coin toss, so they got to go first.

Taking their place center stage around the altar, they began to pray, *O
Baal, answer us. O Baal, answer us.* But there was no reply. So they prayed a

little louder, but still were met by silence. Hmm. Maybe Baal liked more movement. So they began wildly leaping around the altar. Still no answer. Crickets were chirping. This went on for several hours. Elijah, who had no doubt been watching all this trying to hide the satisfactory grin on his face, began mocking the prophets, "Cry aloud, for he is a god; either he is meditating, occupied or gone aside, he is busy or he is on a journey, or perhaps he is sleeping and must be awakened" (1 Kings 18:27).

Talk about sarcasm! In the original Hebrew, the phrase "he is busy" sometimes referred to relieving one's self. Elijah was saying, *Hey, maybe your god has gone to the bathroom. In that case, you better knock harder on the door.* Can't you hear his cynicism? *Oh boys, maybe Baal is on vacation. Maybe you should leave him a voice mail and call it a day, huh?*

Elijah's taunts only infuriated the Baal prophets, and they responded by screaming out to their god, even gashing their bodies with swords and lances until the blood literally gushed out of them. They were convinced Baal would see how serious and dedicated they were to him and have pity and send fire. But Baal didn't send so much as a spark. Scripture records that they raved until about 3:00 p.m., but there was no voice, no one answered, and no one paid attention (1 Kings 18:29). *Give it a rest*, Elijah told the prophets. Then he invited all the people of Israel to scoot their chairs up real close to him. *Watch this*, he said. Then he rebuilt the dismantled altar of the Lord with twelve stones, after which he dug a trench around it. After this, he instructed the people to drench the altar and fill the trench with water . . . lots and lots of water. Twelve pitchers to be exact. What's the big deal about that? you say. Not much, really until you remember that Israel was suffering through a major drought—three-and-a-half years with no rain. There was no running water, no faucets, no drink machines, no sno-cones, no iced cappuccinos, and no bottled water. So you can imagine how water must have been a pretty scarce commodity. Yet in spite of this, Elijah dumped all this water on the altar, soaking the wood. The people must have thought him crazy, but it was all a part of Elijah's master plan. If God really did answer with fire, Elijah wanted no one to attribute it to dry wood, or a spark, or to spontaneous combustion. He didn't want anyone to accuse him of using trickery or illusion. If that wood, thoroughly marinated in water, caught fire, there could be only one explanation—God.

The stage was now set. There was tension in the air as the crowd moved from the edge of their seats to their feet. The prophets of Baal were wiping the sweat off their brows and tending to their bloody cuts. They were still breathing heavily from all their frantic activity. Their mouths were parched, as there was no water to quench their thirst. Elijah then called out to the Lord, begging Him to show up and prove He was God and God alone. If He did this, it just might turn the hearts of His people back to Him. Look what happened: "Then the fire of the Lord fell, and consumed the burnt offering and the wood and the stones and the dust, and licked up the water that was in the trench" (1 Kings 18:38).

Don't you love the image of the fire of God licking up the offering and the water? There was to be no mistake Who was answering Elijah's prayer. This phenomenon wasn't going to be explained away by a lightning bolt or some spontaneous combustion from a piece of dry wood. Nobody could claim Elijah had a box of matches hidden somewhere in his tunic. This was no ordinary fire that incinerated the ox, the wood, the stones, the dust, and the water. What a heat blast those people must have felt! Imagine the temperature on that mountain soaring several hundred degrees in a millisecond's time. The fire visibly came from the sky for all to see, striking precisely on the altar the man of God had built. There was only one explanation for this phenomenon.

God. Unmistakably. Unequivocally. Undeniably. God.

And every eyewitness to the event was fully persuaded. All the people fell down on their faces and began chanting repeatedly, "The Lord, He is God; the Lord, He is God" (1 Kings 18:39).

They couldn't even look toward the altar. Instead, they pressed their singed beards and faces into the still warm terrain. The only thing cold there that day was the chill running down each spine. Nobody was high-fiving Elijah. This wasn't about him. The people weren't flat on their faces in fearful praise to the prophet. Whatever clout or presence Elijah enjoyed as spokesman for God was instantly overshadowed by the spectacular display of God's power. By showing up there that day, Yahweh proved He was the only true God and that Baal was impotent. Ahab's pagan deity was not real. Non-existent. And certainly not worth worshipping. God also filled Mount Carmel with His presence, hands down demonstrating that He alone was worthy of praise. It was a God-moment meant to restore His people back to Himself.

Okay, now, be honest. Haven't you ever secretly wished God would do something just like that today? Wouldn't that be cool? Maybe something like this: On Tuesday, when all the cults and religious groups are passing out magazines and pamphlets, a huge debate forms near the fountain located in the middle of campus. You challenge all the representatives of all other faiths to a contest. They pray, nothing happens, and the crowd yawns. They call on God, using every name but His true name. They pray to Allah, but nothing happens. They call on Confucius, but he doesn't respond. They cry out to the Mormon god, but he must be busy. They scream to Krishna, but he is silent. Then you, along with a few of your Christian friends, stand on the edge of the fountain wall and call on the Lord of Heaven. Suddenly the fire of God falls from the sky, consuming the water in the fountain, and the crowd stands stunned in an eerie silence, their eyebrows singed from the intense heavenly heat. You and your friends spend the rest of that afternoon and evening individually leading hundreds to faith in Christ. Seriously, haven't you ever wished God would do something like that? Wouldn't it be great if He did something spectacular at the United Nations, for representatives of all countries to see? Do you ever become righteously angry with some of those liberal talk shows where the rest of the guest panel (joined by the audience) is bashing a fellow Christian to death on national television? There is probably a little Elijah in all of us. A bit of sarcasm. A touch of boldness. A desire for God to show the world how real He really is. It's passion to give the world a true God-moment. Don't feel guilty for feeling that way. It just means you want God to be praised among the nations.

scene four: forty winks and twelve wimps

Had you been one of the twelve disciples traveling with Jesus, you would have had more than your share of divine experiences. Hanging out with Jesus every day for three years, you would have accumulated a ton of amazing stories to one day share with your friends. You would have filled a notebook with God-moments. A few of the disciples did just that, writing their experiences down in the four Gospels for us. Of course, because He was also 100 percent man, Jesus no doubt did many ordinary things with His disciples. He ate with them, walked with them, had normal conversations, and in some ways was no different than they were. But still, they were His disciples, and as such were privileged to hear private messages and see miracles the rest of the general population never saw. One such miracle is recorded in chapter four of Mark's gospel. It took place in a boat one night on the Sea of Galilee. Jesus and His disciples were making their way across the sea, as they had done numerous times before, when a fierce gale of wind arose suddenly. Such violent storms were not uncommon on the Sea of Galilee. At 670 feet below sea level, winds rushed down from the surrounding nine-thousand-foot mountains, creating an instant storm which caused dangerous and life-threatening conditions for boats on the water. In this case, the disciples' boat was being tossed around like a paper cup in the Atlantic. Waves began crashing over the sides of the small vessel, causing it to fill with water. Realizing they were in imminent danger, they began bailing as fast as they could. Mark tells us that in spite of all this, Jesus was sound asleep in the front of the boat on a cushion. But wait a minute—why would He be asleep? And how could He be? How does a person sleep through a storm like this? Was He narcoleptic? Did He hit His head and black out? Was He only pretending to be asleep?

Negative on all three counts. A simple explanation clarifies why Jesus was unaffected and undisturbed by the wind, water, and storm.

He was tired.

We're not talking a mid-day power nap tired. It wasn't even a bedtime tired. It was a weariness that goes past having achy muscles and sore feet. It was the kind of tired that extends from the top of your head to the soles of your feet. That's where Jesus was. Worn out. Beat. Bushed. Done in. Dead on His feet. Drained. Down for the count. Fatigue had filled every cell in His body. He could no longer hold His eyes open. And why? Consider what kind of day Jesus had been through. He began the day beside the Sea of Galilee, the crowd being so big He was forced to climb into a boat to keep from being overcome by them. Keep in mind this was the same crowd mentioned in Mark 3:7–9, a day or so earlier:

> But Jesus withdrew with His disciples to the sea. And a great multitude from Galilee followed Him; and from Judea, and Jerusalem, and Idumea and beyond the Jordan; and these from Tyre and Sidon, a great multitude, when they heard how many things He was doing, came to Him.
>
> **So He told His disciples that a small boat should be kept ready for Him because of the multitude, lest that they should crush Him.**

Picture this massive crowd pressing in on Jesus. In a heartbeat, they could easily turn from a mild-mannered multitude into a malicious mob. More than once, they would attempt to force Him to be their King. He knew He could incite a riot or a revolt with just a matter of a few words. So Jesus was careful to put Himself at a safe distance during such times. Just one day earlier, Jesus had spent literally every waking hour healing the sick and casting out demons. Then, He was up the following morning back at it again. And on that day He spent every waking hour teaching them many parables, all the while standing or sitting in that same boat (Mark 4:1–34). Even when He managed to free himself from the mass of people, He continued teaching a smaller crowd of disciples. If it's true what doctors say—that an hour's worth of public speaking is equivalent to an eight hour workday—then Jesus put in about a week's work in just that one day! His body was shot. His energy level depleted. His physical and emotional tank was bone dry. And as a man, He desperately needed rest.

Now back to the boat and the night of the storm. The disciples meanwhile were brainstorming, but could find no reason in their minds how or why the Lord could have been so sleepy during such a violent storm. Of course, being the levelheaded, spiritually in touch men that they were, they did what any group of future apostles would do in a situation like this: They panicked. No. On second thought, make that they *freaked*. ". . . they awoke Him and said to Him, 'Teacher, do You not care that we are perishing?'" (Mark 4:38)

Keep rolling the film of this scene in your mind. It was pitch dark out there. The wind was blowing. The sea was raging. Waves were crashing over the side of the boat as it was rocked back and forth. The rain was falling in horizontal sheets, pelting them like needles. Grown men were holding on for dear life, clinging to the sides of the boat, hugging the mast like a two-year-old clinging to his mother's leg. Anything to keep them from being thrown overboard. They could hardly see five feet in front of them. They were soaked from head to toe. And in the chaos of the moment, one of them must have shouted, "Somebody wake the Master!" The other eleven responded in unison to the call. Can you see them scrambling to the front of the boat? Considering how loud the storm was, they had to physically crawl to where Jesus was in order make enough noise to wake Him.

They managed to wake Him up, shaking Him out of His deep slumber. The first thing they did was accuse Jesus of not caring about them. *We're dying over here, Lord! And You're sleeping on the job. We thought You cared. Why are You allowing this storm? Where were You when we needed You? We gave up everything to follow You, and look what happened? Save us, Lord!* Don't you find it interesting that as soon as the storm hit, their first thought was that God didn't care about them? In their distress, they equated problems and difficult circumstances with God not caring. Have you ever felt like that? Truthfully, most of us have at one time or another. Ever wondered where God was in your storm? Has it ever seemed like He was asleep, unaware of what you were suffering? Maybe there have been times when you called on Him, and like the prophets of Baal, no one answered. Perhaps it was during a tragedy or sudden personal catastrophe, and you immediately assumed that God had given up on you. You felt alone. Forgotten. Maybe it happened your first night away at college. In a new and somewhat unfriendly environment with few or no friends at all. Or perhaps it was in high school when your steady pulled the plug on your relationship. Your heart sank down the drain as you read the letter or hung up the phone that afternoon. And the next two weeks were fourteen days of depression like you had never known before. You wondered why God would allow this to happen to you. Or maybe your storm involved something more painful and serious than that. And as the wind and rain howled in your soul, you shook your head in disbelief, crying out, *God, do You care that I am perishing?*

That's where the disciples were that night. If Peter could step out of that boat and off the pages of Scripture, he just might put his hand on your shoulder, look you straight in the eyes and confess, "We all know how you feel." But what Peter and his frightened friends didn't yet realize was that this storm was actually a pop quiz in disguise, given to test their faith. The black night and raging sea were merely part of a backdrop against which God was about to display Himself. Like a master artist, God had already painted the background and was on the verge of brush-stroking a God-moment in the foreground of that portrait.

After having been awoken, Jesus immediately issued two strong rebukes: One to the wind and waves, and the other to the disciples. "And being aroused, He rebuked the wind and said to the sea, Hush, be still. And the wind died down and it became perfectly calm" (Mark 4:39).

The Greek word translated into "be still" is the same word that Jesus used when He told the demon to "be quiet!" in Mark 1:25. Here, Jesus was effectively commanding the gale force wind and the huge waves to shut up. But merely stopping the wind alone wouldn't have caused the sudden calm, for the waves would have continued to rock the boat. That's why Jesus' words went out to both the wind *and* the waves. And they did exactly what

He commanded them to do. In an instant, the weather pattern changed. This was not the eye of the hurricane kind of calm. Jesus commanded the very molecules to stop moving. The elements of nature itself were under His control. He had created those mountains as well as the Sea of Galilee. He knew the composition and history of every drop of water in that Sea. The wind speed was at His command. This was not one to blame on the devil. These were wind gusts from God. And as God in the flesh, Jesus had authority to do the things only God could do, like forgive sins (Matthew 9:6), teach the truth of God (Mark 1:27), have authority over unclean spirits (Luke 4:36), execute judgment (John 5:27), and exercise all authority in heaven and earth (Matthew 28:18). That pretty much covered it. Jesus suspended the laws of nature for His own purposes. That's what we call a miracle. And it happened in the split second He rebuked the storm.

But secondly, He also rebuked His disciples: "And He said to them, Why are you so timid? How is it that you have no faith?" (Mark 4:40).

Upon first glance, Jesus' reaction sounds a little harsh, doesn't it? After all, his friends were petrified, right? They needed Him to be there for them. Isn't that what He was there for? Didn't the Lord understand that? Was He being a bit too tough on them? Or was He just grumpy from being awakened from His nap?

Okay, one question at a time. The disciples were afraid, and that's a natural reaction when you're in a potentially life-threatening situation, such as the one they were facing. So we can see why they initially panicked. But consider for a minute just Who it was in that boat with them. This wasn't the captain of the sailing club, or some Galilean lifeguard. It was God in human flesh—the Creator, the King of the Universe in that fishing boat. So the obvious question then becomes, should the disciples have known this already?

Answer? Yep.

But why? Why should they have had the kind of faith that would have kept them from freaking out? Several reasons: First, they had been eyewitnesses to His other miracles that clearly illustrated to them that He was more than just a teacher. They may have compartmentalized all His previous miracles into another category of their minds, reasoning, *He may be able to heal a leper, but this is a full-fledged storm here, fellas!* Or maybe they all suffered from some form of short-term memory loss. Or maybe they just didn't yet have confidence in Him. Secondly, they had heard Jesus say, *Let us go to the other side.* He didn't say, *Let us now all take a voyage to the bottom of the Sea.* He had already promised them safe arrival. They should have believed Him. Thirdly, Jesus Himself was in their boat with them. Did they think He was going to allow Himself to drown? As mentioned before, this storm experience was a pop quiz, testing them on what they had learned so far. And according to Jesus, these poor guys all flunked with flying colors.

Enough about them, though. What about you? How would you have responded to Jesus in the same situation? Had you been in the boat that night and witnessed this God-moment, would you have exhibited that deer in the headlights look? Would you have shouted, *Wow, Jesus! That was so cool! How'd You do that?* Would you have given Him a thumbs up from the back of the boat? Nah. Don't think so. Sure, Jesus is our friend and we take great comfort from knowing He identifies with us in our humanity. But seeing and experiencing this kind of event up close and in person should produce a radically different response in all of us. You wouldn't be thinking about wind any more. It would be insignificant to you that from head to toe you looked like a human sponge dripping with seawater. The reality of what just took place would have shaken you visibly, as it did the disciples. A wave of a different kind now came crashing into that boat. It was a wave of fear. A surge of reverential awe. A scary swell washing over them. Their fear was much greater now than it had ever been in the storm. Turning to one another, ". . . they became very much afraid and said to one another, 'Who then is this, that even the wind and the sea obey Him?'" (Mark 4:41).

Dr. Luke tells us they were fearful and amazed. Perhaps for the very first time they realized they were in the very presence of Deity. God was in their boat.

The sea was calm now. Hardly a breeze was blowing in the coolness of the night. The humidity level in the air had dropped drastically. Can you see one of the Twelve carefully picking up an oar and beginning slowly to row? This was not a time for chitchat or meaningless conversation. Odds are they were all speechless, rendered mute by Jesus' marvelous miracle. They were astonished. Bewildered. Fear and amazement had gripped them. It all seemed surreal to them. Had it not happened to them all, each man might have wondered if it was a dream. But what had occurred was undeniably very real. As they neared the other side of the sea, some of the disciples were looking down, stroking their wet beards (or ringing them out!) while silently contemplating this thing that had just happened to them. Others were intently looking at Jesus, who perhaps had turned to look towards the approaching shore. He knew something they didn't—that another miracle was about to occur when they once again set foot on solid ground. Still others tried to put the pieces of the puzzle together, processing in their minds what this event might mean. What should they do with this new revelation Jesus had given them concerning Himself?

From this point on, the disciples would look at Jesus through a brand new set of lenses. They would interpret subsequent events and experiences through a whole new grid. Their perspective had changed. *They* had changed. Everything had changed because God punched a hole through the wall of the natural world, allowing the blinding light of His deity to come bursting through. He had showed them God in human flesh.

Aren't you sometimes jealous that the disciples got to see and experience so many God-moments? Or do you ever grow impatient with them because they failed to get it? That Jesus had to tell them things over and over again before it finally sank in? What was wrong with these guys? Intellectually challenged? Slow? Dull? Keep in mind, the original disciples didn't have the luxury of leather-bound updated translations of the Scripture, complete with study notes, maps, concordance, cross references, summaries, and outlines of each book in Scripture. Even so, Jesus still expected them to apply certain principles to their life experiences. But to their credit, they wouldn't always flunk the test. They may have been slow, but they sure were determined in their faith. After a few more

God-moments (including the resurrection and ascension), they finally got it, taking the truth about Christ to their world, and suffering horribly for it. Some were crucified, while others were beaten, banished, boiled in oil, butchered, and beheaded. And you can bank on this: Every one of those disciples used their last breath to worship this One who commanded the wind and the waves.

The Benefit Package

Sometimes our God-moments come in ways that are undeniable, unavoidable, and unmistakable. His presence and power are put on display before us in such a manner that to try and explain it any other way would just be plain dumb. You would have to be blind not to see it. There is a measurable, concrete, tangible result. The overwhelming evidence points to God. He did it. He showed up and moved, changing both the circumstances and us. But there are also times when our God-moments come more subtly, gradually, almost in an inaudible whisper. In those cases, it takes a person with spiritual eyes and ears to recognize them. Often they occur when a Scripture just seems to leap off the pages of your Bible right into your heart and mind. Though you may have read the same passage hundreds of times, you somehow are able to see it in a way you never have before. Or it happens in a worship service where a pastor or teacher explains a passage in a way that opens your understanding in a fresh, life-changing way. That's the Holy Spirit creating a very special God-moment for you.

Spotting some of those special gifts from God sometimes requires a certain level of discernment on our part. But this discernment is not limited to those who are older or more mature in the faith. A childlike innocence can detect the hand of God at times when a seasoned Christian misses it. Again, they can come unexpectedly, easily unnoticed except by the eyes of faith. They are sometimes indirect and sometimes over the top. Yet they are always glorious because of what they do for our worship. But no matter how they are presented, we should never walk away from them unchanged.

There is always a reason God manifests Himself to us. What do these God-moment experiences do for us?

First, they reveal something about God. They tell us He is there. He is real. Powerful. That He is listening. That He cares. That He is still invading our time and space. It gives us great hope to know that God is alive in our world. Face it. God doesn't always reveal Himself in the same way and with the same intensity every time. So when He does, we should be comforted knowing He has not left Himself without a witness. As great Christian thinker Francis Schaeffer put it, *He is there and He is not silent.*

Second, they reveal a lot about us and our level of faith. Like an x-ray machine, these experiences uncover things about us not easily seen from the outside. When God does something unusual, that encounter can uncover shallowness, weakness, impatience, fear, immaturity, and hidden pride that lives within us. It can purge us. But that cleansing also releases a joy within us. As we see our weaknesses brought to the surface, we shouldn't be discouraged. Rather, this should cause us to realize how much we need Him. It should motivate us to keep growing in intimacy with Him each day.

Third, they often come during (or just after) a life storm. It is in the crucible of pain that God often delights to visit us. In fact, the greatest yet most powerful unexplainable experiences with God come through our pain. It's then that we are usually most vulnerable and dependent. As John Hercus has said, we must *trust God even when the pieces don't fit.* And in difficult times, the pieces rarely seem to fit. In the blinding rain of real life, when we are at our weakest point, His strength becomes our greatest sufficiency (2 Corinthians 12:9). It is during those times when we sense a peace and strength not our own which holds us up. And a massive dose of the grace of God is poured out, often in a moment's time . . . just for us. Don't fear the storm, fellow believer. Know that He is right there with you in your boat.

Fourth, they erase preconceived ideas about God. Though we can know God personally, we can never completely figure out all His ways.

There are times when God simply exercises His prerogative and right to be God in history and in our lives. They may occur on the mission field or in any situation where our faith and expectation level is peaking. When we're risking, giving, trusting—that's when He shows up. These God-moments keep us from stuffing the Almighty into a neat little box in our minds. They tell us we will never figure out all the ways He works. And He *really does* work in mysterious ways. His will and His ways are still not ours. The disciples were forced to realize this in their boat experience (Luke 8:22–25). They thought Jesus would rescue them from the storm. The storm didn't quite fit their theology and their image of God and His ways. They were forced to jettison their preconceived ideas about Him, and so must we. We must allow His Word to mold our thinking regarding who He is. And when He does things or allows things to happen which are contrary to how we think He should act, we have to surrender our wills to His. God-moments are there to teach us that while His ways cannot always be traced, His heart can always be trusted.

Finally, God-moments exalt God. As we respond to these awesome displays of God in and around our lives, we will be moved to worship in various ways. Sometimes the best thing to do is just be silent and still (like the disciples probably did after Jesus calmed the storm). Other times we will be impressed with a need to submit our lives in a fresh or deeper way to Him (like the people of God at Mount Carmel). Or we may be inspired to rise up and do something great for God in strength (like the army of Israel after God made the sun stand still). We may even desire to memorialize the experience (like the stone memorial Joshua built after God showed up at the defeat of Jericho). We might also choose to make or establish something in His honor to remember in the months and years to come. But the best thing about our God-moments is that He gets all the credit. The glory is His. The praise is His. You know without a doubt that it was God. Only God. All God. And in your heart, you worship Him that way.

It's really not about explaining all the things God does, is it? It's really more about responding to what He does, whether we understand it or not.

So during your next God-moment, think of what you might be learning about God. Take care to see if there is something about yourself that is being revealed. Jot down what you learn in your notebook. Share it with your Christian friends. But above all, beyond everything else, be sure to worship the One who slays armies, swallows up rebels, singes altars, and silences storms. It's not about figuring Him out. It's about falling on your face.

CHAPTER 10

we cannot say enough

Heavenly worship

Ascribe to the Lord the glory due His name; Bring an offering, and come before Him; Worship the Lord in holy array.

—1 chronicles 16:29

Surrounded by your glory, what will my heart feel?

—i can only imagine

Destination: Dream vacation

Pack your bags; we're taking a trip. It's a trip to a very special place. It's a secluded spot, far from the rat race of work, classes, and life in general. It's a place where palm trees sway in an ever-present gentle breeze. It's a place of pristine sugar-white beaches, where aqua blue Caribbean waters await you with their soothing warmth. It's a secluded getaway, removed from the fast-paced, stress-filled routine that tends to tighten like a noose around your neck. Upon arriving at your destination, your biggest hassle is deciding whether to relax in a swinging hammock in the shade, soak up some rays on the beach, or go for a swim. In this tropical paradise, there are no traffic jams, no air pollution and no stoplights. There are no high-rise condominiums or cheap T-shirt shops. No long lines in which to wait and no tourist traps. It's undiscovered and undisturbed by modernism. You wake up every morning to the alluring aroma of fresh-roasted, native-grown coffee. Then, for your breakfast appetizer, there's fresh mango, cantaloupe, pineapple, and watermelon. This is followed by your choice of hot banana pancakes, French toast, or an omelet of your own design. Name your favorite morning fruit juice. It's there. For lunch and dinner, venture into a nearby village for some of the best authentic tropical food your palate has ever sampled. Explore ancient ruins or hang out back at your cabana, which is decorated with sapphire blue walls, handcrafted furniture and floors embedded with stones and mosaic patterns. There is no need for air-conditioning here, for the cool Caribbean breeze keeps the temperature just right. It's a private beach, and at night if the moon is full you can take a swim in water so clear you can count your toes on the ocean floor. It's a place you can relax, rest, and play. And, it's a no-work zone. No homework. No research papers. No phone. No e-mail. It's a back to nature adventure where you are free to simply be.

Don't you want to go there?

To be honest, all of us at one time or another want to (make that *need* to) get away from it all. But in the event we can't quite come up with the cash to hop a flight to our fantasy dream vacation, we can still escape for a few hours at the movies or go for a drive in the country. At the very least, we can go to this paradise in our minds. But suppose for a moment you were promised a trip to this wonderful place. Would you be excited? Wouldn't you count down the days leading up to your departure?

Now let me tell you about another place. It too is a far away destination, removed from the trials and troubles of this life. It's a place where your cares melt away because of the spectacular scenery—a place unspoiled and relatively undiscovered by man. But you can't get there by car, boat, or plane. Of course we're talking about Heaven. Unlike our Caribbean tropical paradise, you can confirm your reservations immediately. This is one trip your travel agent can't help you with. And if you have gotten this far in the book, we hope you've made your reservations by now. To be honest, most people don't really know that much about this place called Heaven. Oh sure, they know bits and pieces, but much of what they believe about Heaven has come from movies or their own imaginations. But haven't you ever wondered what Heaven is really like?

jesus—your travel agent

Had you been one of the twelve disciples, you would have no doubt been curious about Heaven. After all, Jesus came from Heaven and talked a lot about going there. In John 14, the Lord gave them (and us) a few simple, yet revealing facts about this place called Heaven:

> "Let not your heart be troubled; believe in God, believe also in Me. In My Father's house are many dwelling places; if it were not so, I would have told you; for I go to prepare a place for you. And if I go and prepare a place for you, I will come again, and receive you to Myself; that where I am, there you may be also." (John 14:1–3).

first, Heaven is a real place (verse 2)— Jesus promised He would soon go to an actual place He called His Father's house. Because of this we can know that Heaven is not a state of mind or a philosophical concept. It's not a happy thought or some fairy tale Jesus made up to temporarily soothe our grief. It is a real place, as real as the chair you are sitting in. As real as your own home or city. It's a place you can see, feel, and touch. Heaven exists. Aren't you glad?

But second, Heaven is a prepared place (verse 2)—In first century Palestine, there was a custom that engaged couples practiced. After the engagement, during what they called the betrothal period, the man returned to his father's house where he would begin construction of an additional room where he and his bride would live after the wedding. When the room was complete and furnished, the groom would often return unexpectedly and sweep away his bride to their wedding. After the ceremony and celebration, they would then go live together in the place the husband had prepared beforehand. Knowing these men were aware of this practice, Jesus drew upon this familiar custom. In doing so, Jesus conjured up these images in the disciples' minds to help them have an idea of what Heaven was like. Then, He promised to spend the time between His ascension and second visit to planet earth preparing a place in heaven for all those who know Him. When you consider the vastness of creation—the majestic mountains, the immense oceans, the beauty of the skies, and the magnitude of the universe, how great will Heaven be? It took Him just seven days to make the earth. But He has spent the past two thousand years preparing Heaven. Think of it! Jesus, the Christ and Master Carpenter, is building a place *for* *you*! It is a place beyond your greatest imagination.

Third, Heaven is a place of hope (verse 3)—Consider the context of Jesus' words. He spoke to them on what would prove to be His last night with His best friends. He was about to leave them and go to Heaven. That would mean loss, separation, and the painful ache of not being together anymore. And so, wishing them to be comforted, Jesus tells them He is not only preparing a place for them, but that He will also come back and take them to Heaven one day. And that gave them hope.

Finally, Heaven is the place where God is (verse 3)—We will learn many things about heaven in this chapter, but more than anything the greatest joy in heaven is simply being with Christ.

There's More in the Brochure

Those facts really help us understand a bit more about the place Jesus is preparing for us. But there is much more to know. So, here are a few more of the most common questions people ask and how Scripture answers them.

Question: Will we know each other in Heaven?

Answer: Yes. In fact, we won't really know each other *until* we get to Heaven. Our capacity for knowledge and relationships is hindered now because of sin, but it will be unbelievably enhanced in Heaven. Yes, we will definitely know each other. Peter recognized Moses and Elijah when they came from Heaven down to earth for a short visit (Matthew 17:1–14) and Jesus indicated we will all retain our individual identities in Heaven (Matthew 8:11). We will immediately know everyone in the afterlife, including not only friends and family who have gone before us, but also all the great saints of the Bible and throughout history. Won't it be great to ask Noah about his boat ride? Or Elijah about his chariot ride? Or Moses about parting the Red Sea? There will be lots of reunions and incredible discussions when we get there.

Question: What will our bodies be like in Heaven?

Answer: Just like Jesus' glorified body. There will be no floating spirits there. And we will not look like fat, naked, little babies playing harps. Our heavenly bodies are much better than that. Once there, we will never get sick, tired, wrinkled, bruised, or hurt (I Corinthians 15:42–43). We will receive special bodies made to withstand the intense glory of Heaven. With these new bodies, we will be able to walk through walls (John 20:19), travel through space (Acts 1:9–11), and appear or disappear (Luke 24:31). And yet we will still have the capacity and ability in these physical bodies to talk, walk, eat, and drink (Luke 24:39–43). In fact, Jesus even promised He would eat and drink with us at a very special upcoming wedding feast (Luke 22:18; Matthew 8:11; Revelation 19:9). Pretty cool, huh?

Question: Will we be married in Heaven?

Answer: Negatory. But this is one of those good news/bad news things. The bad news is that we won't be married. Marriage as we know it is an earthly relationship only, and one which will pass away (I Corinthians 7:31; Matthew 22:24–30). But the good news is that Jesus does have a planned wedding ceremony for us as His bride. In addition, our current relationships with our spouses will experience a very special change once we arrive in Heaven. They will, for the first time, be *perfect*!

Question: Will we ever be sad in Heaven?

Answer: Not a chance. There are absolutely no lasting tears or unhappiness (Revelation 21:4). There may be some initial tears of joy, but God has promised to wipe them all away. In Heaven, we will have the perfect mind of Christ, able to see all things from His perspective. Our joy will never again be threatened.

Question: What else will *not* be in Heaven?

Answer: Lots of stuff. Things you will never see in Heaven include: suffering, death, grief, pain, cancer, AIDS, abuse, murder, abortion, divorce, racial prejudice, stress, war, fighting, hurt feelings, disappointment, worry, emptiness, boredom, or any other product of sin (Revelation 21:8, 27). Sound good so far?

Question: What will we do in Heaven?

Answer: Despite what you thought or have been led to believe, Heaven will never be boring. Since God is the Creator of all fun and enjoyment (Ecclesiastes 2:25), you can be sure nobody will be yawning up there. We don't know all of what we'll do, but among the many things we will do are the following: We will reign with Christ (Revelation 22:5), including overseeing cities (Luke 19:17–19), judging angels (I Corinthians 6:30), and governing nations (Matthew 19:28). We will also serve Christ in ways He has yet to reveal to us (Revelation 22:3). We will experience the greatest level of friendship and fellowship possible (Mattew 8:11; I Thessalonians 4:17). We will rest (Revelation 14:13). And we will spend forever in a never-ending joyous adventure discovering about God and His universe. And keep this in mind: all of our senses will be heightened to the max with a constant and perfect fulfillment. In fact, Heaven is going to be so great that Scripture says all of mankind's imagination cannot even come close to how awesome it's going to be (I Corinthians 2:9)! Take your happiest and most exciting thought and multiply it by a billion, and you will have just scratched the surface of what Heaven will be like. No wonder we'll have to have new bodies, we'll need them just to withstand the experience!

Don't you want to go there?

Are you ready to pack your suitcase? Are you ready to go? Oh, but wait a second. In all the excitement, it almost slipped our minds. There is one more very important thing we will do in Heaven.

We will worship.

Not like we worship here on earth. Up there, it's worship of another kind. Worship from another dimension and in a different language. It's worship on a totally different level. It's worship that transcends our current understanding and capacity. But rather than just try and describe it to you, why don't we just go there for a few minutes? Throw a few things in an overnight bag and let's take a mental field trip to Paradise. You don't have to watch the Matrix to free your mind. Just look through the lens of Scripture and view Heaven from right where you sit.

passport to paradise

Through the vision given him by Christ, the apostle John is catapulted in his spirit to Heaven. Once there, he is shown things the human eye has never seen before. In fact, some things are so incredibly beyond him that he has to use symbolic language in an attempt to describe them to us. Let's look at what he sees in Revelation 4.

> Immediately I was in the Spirit; and behold, a throne was standing in heaven, and One sitting on the throne. And He who was sitting was like a jasper stone and a sardius in appearance; and there was a rainbow around the throne, like an emerald in appearance. And around the throne were twenty-four thrones; and upon the thrones I saw twenty-four elders sitting, clothed in white garments, and golden crowns on their heads. And from the throne proceeded flashes of lightning and sounds and peals of thunder. And there were seven lamps of fire burning before the throne, which are the seven Spirits of God; and before the throne there was, as it were, a sea of glass like crystal; and in the center and around the throne, four living creatures full of eyes in front and behind. And the first creature was like a lion, and the second creature like a calf, and the third creature had a face like that of a man, and the fourth creature was like a flying eagle. And the four

living creatures, each one of them having six wings, are full of eyes around and within; and day and night they do not cease to say, holy, holy, holy, is the Lord God, the Almighty, who was and who is and who is to come.

A Throne

And what do we see there? The very first thing John notices is not pearly gates or streets of gold. He doesn't immediately encounter angels or clouds. And He definitely doesn't see St. Peter at the gate with a reservation list. What first captures John's attention instead is a throne (Revelation 4:2). But this is not just any old throne. This particular throne has Someone seated on it. Whenever in history an earthly monarch or dictator dies or is overthrown by a coup, there is usually another person waiting anxiously in the wings to take his or her place. In the event no one is readily available, then there is typically a scramble to find somebody and crown him as soon as possible. Find an heir. Appoint a military figure. But just get someone on that throne! And why? Because the throne symbolizes the stability of a nation or kingdom. An unoccupied throne is an invitation for insecurity, uncertainty, and even anarchy.

At about lunchtime on November 22, 1963, President John F. Kennedy was assassinated in Dallas, Texas. Riding in an open limousine, and in full view of his wife Jacqueline, the Commander-in-Chief was struck several times by bullets fired from at least one high-powered rifle. The last proved to be a fatal gunshot wound to the head. Bleeding profusely, the president was rushed just a few miles away to Parkland Hospital, where doctors frantically worked to save the dying leader. It was a courageous and valiant effort, but it proved to be futile. The wound was simply too severe. At 1:00 P.M. that Thursday, President John F. Kennedy was officially pronounced dead. Immediately, like a Texas brush fire, word began to spread all across the country and the world that the President had been murdered. In an instant, our country was cast into a sudden and unexpected state of shock. Millions held their breath as rumors began circulating that the assassination was only the preface to an all out attack by the Russians, who at the time were our Cold War archenemies. Some Americans headed for the fallout shelters preparing themselves for a nuclear strike. Others sat in their homes, glued to their television sets. Schools dismissed early in light of the tragedy. It was one of the darkest days in our country's history, certainly one of the most tragic of the century. But within ninety minutes of Kennedy being declared dead in Trauma Room One of Parkland Hospital, Vice President Lyndon Johnson was hurriedly sworn in as the new President. Standing in a rear cabin of Air Force One, flanked by his wife and the widowed Mrs. Kennedy, and surrounded by politicians and reporters, Johnson became the new leader of the United States. And an entire nation exhaled. Though we would remain grief stricken and in mourning for many months to come, Lyndon Johnson's unexpected occupation of the Oval Office was proof the government would survive after all. There had been a smooth transfer of authority. He was now at the controls. Somebody was on the throne.

As the beloved disciple John sets foot on Heaven's shore, his attention is riveted on this throne of God. Far beyond an earthly office, this throne dwarfed all others John had ever seen. The throne of Roman emperors and self-proclaimed gods were never this majestic. This is a throne that is established. Unmovable. He describes God the Father's appearance as glimmering jewels—like jasper and sardius (Revelation 4:3). Jasper has a diamond-like crystal clear appearance, possessing the ability to reflect and refract all the other stones in brilliant hues and colors. Sardius, on the other hand is like a bright, blood-red ruby stone color. These formed the base of the throne. Around this throne is a circular multi-colored rainbow with an emerald tint to it. This is wild, isn't it? Sounds more like a 60's psychedelic painting than a scene from Heaven, doesn't it? It's hard to picture it in our minds. In some ways, John must have felt overwhelmed as what he sees is virtually beyond human description. But though we can't fully appreciate or understand John's verbal portrait of this celestial throne, there is one thing we can appreciate. It's the fact that this throne is occupied. Someone is sitting on that throne. God himself is seated in this celestial chair. On His throne, God is the Supervisor. He's in charge. Being there on His throne tells us someone is in the cockpit, at the controls of the ship. It means that everything is under control and that all is well. And because God *is* in control, this means when your world is falling apart, you don't have to. If God isn't panicking, then neither should you. Because He is in control, this means there is no circumstance, problem, person or feeling that can steal your joy and peace. As Jesus put it, "In the world you have tribulation, but take courage, I have overcome the world" (John 16:33). Don't worry. He's steering this universe, the planet and your life with ease. Leave the driving to Him.

But John also sees a lot of activity around this throne. First, he observes twenty-four other thrones with twenty-four elders seated on them (Revelation 4:4). These elders are most likely representatives of redeemed humanity who have been crowned and rewarded for their faithfulness and service. From God's throne also come flashes of lightning and thunder (Revelation 4:5), probably signaling the awesome judgment about to be released from Heaven upon the earth during the Great Tribulation. Now John's senses are heightened as he begins experiencing Heaven audio-visually! It's like a giant IMAX theater, only he's really there! Loud thunderclaps and blinding flashes of light fill the throne room of heaven. Before God's throne John sees a sea of crystal-like glass (Revelation 4:5). Around the throne are four of the strangest-looking creatures you could possibly imagine (Revelation 4:6–8). They look like something out of a *Star Wars* movie rather than a scene out of the Bible. These super intelligent angelic beings have eyes all around their heads. Close your eyes and picture that! They also each have six wings. Is this vision weird or what? All four seem to be preoccupied with one thing. This one thing consumes them 24 hours a day, 7 days a week, *365* days a year. Without ceasing they proclaim,

"*Holy, holy, holy, is the Lord God, the Almighty, who was and who is and who is to come.*"

These angels are fascinated with the holiness of God. They have been created for one purpose—to declare the holiness of God. We first saw these six winged creatures when Isaiah introduced us to them way back in Isaiah 6:2. Each one of these angels uses two wings to cover his face, two to cover his feet and two with which to fly. With two of their six wings, they hover like giant hummingbirds in mid-air. Perhaps because they are in such close proximity to Him, the radiance of His glory is too great for them to bear, and so they have to shield their eyes from the blinding brilliance emanating from the throne. With their bottom two wings they cover their feet, perhaps to indicate their unworthiness or a sense of reverence. And finally, with their mouths they incessantly proclaim the holiness of God. But wait a second. Why holiness? Why not love? Or power? Or even glory? Why would God choose this particular attribute to be perpetually proclaimed in His presence?

To answer this, we need to understand a little more about what holiness actually means. Normally when we picture God as holy, our minds immediately think about God being without sin. And that would be correct. God is without sin in any form. His very nature forbids Him to think, say or act in any way that could possibly come close to sin. He is pure. His name is holy (Psalm 30:4). His commandments are holy (Romans 7:12). Jesus is holy (Acts 4:30). His eyes cannot look on evil or sin with approval (Habakkuk 1:13). God has never sinned or imagined a sinful thought. Sometimes a skeptic may ask, Is there anything God can't do? And the answer is yes. God can't sin. It's impossible. Out of the question. Can't happen. Never has. Never will. Why? Because He is holy. Contemplating this aspect of God's nature, Job posed the question centuries ago, *Can mankind be just before God? Can a man be pure before his Maker?* (Job 4:17). Job looked at God's holiness and it caused him to see his own sin more clearly. But the answer to his question is, absolutely! Through Christ, we are holy in His sight (2 Corinthians 5:21). And as a result of our holy position in Him, God also calls us to be holy in our daily behavior as well (1 Peter 1:15). We are to live lives of purity and holiness. After all, we do have the *Holy* Spirit living within us, right?

So God is holy and without sin. Got it? And that's part of what these six-winged angels are communicating through their perpetual vigil around God's throne. But there is another even more basic and fundamental aspect of God's holiness that we often overlook. It's actually found in the root meaning of the word itself. To be *holy* literally means "to be set apart." In other words, these angels are primarily proclaiming the fact that God is set apart. Different. Distinctive. Unique. Not like us. We are poles apart. He is separate. Something else. God is not a man or like man (Numbers 23:19). And though we do bear His image, He is a completely separate essence altogether. His perfect righteousness, His holiness, is so high above us. Aha! So that's one major reason why we have such a problem understanding Him, identifying with Him and relating to Him, right?

Just think for a moment how difficult it can be to relate to someone of another gender. Not to stir up a gender war here, but we all know guys and girls are worlds apart. Forget that Guys are from Mars, Girls are from Venus thing. Some girls are from Pluto and some guys we know are from another solar system! But any way you look at it, no guy living on the planet completely understands his woman, and no girl has totally figured out her man. Agreed? That's simply because we're so different. And even though we can complement one another in relationships, we still have to recognize we are distinct and separate. We always will be. That's why it seems odd for a man to have too much femininity and a woman to have too much masculinity. We're meant to have those clear differences. Or take someone of another race. Many of our racial prejudices and struggles have resulted from an inability to understand, or at least accept, our many differences. What a shame! Or what about a person from another country? Take someone who speaks another language, dresses differently, and who practices a totally different set of customs. Now transplant that person into your hometown. Don't you think there will be some adjustments for him/her to make?

So now that we can understand a little bit of the tension felt when trying to relate to someone completely different from us, let's apply that to God's holiness. Put in human terms, God is from another race. His native tongue is not English. He is from another city, state, country, continent, and planet from us. He has always existed. We were born sometime in the twentieth century. His knowledge and wisdom are infinite. Ours is . . . well, you know. He is a

Spirit. We primarily relate to the physical world. He communicates in His own unique way. He is independent and totally free. We are dependent and limited. He controls all things. We can't seem to get our checkbook to balance. He is not, despite what some may claim, locked in a toe-to-toe struggle with the devil. We battle with evil daily. He does not have to wonder. We do a lot of that. And He doesn't ever *wander* either, while we earn PhD's in the subject. He never worries. We get ulcers. He never panics. We head for the exits in a crisis. He does not break promises like politicians do. He does not disappoint like heroes do. He is neither Democrat nor Republican. He does not attend one particular church or preside in one denomination. And boy, aren't you glad? He does not cheer for one college team over another (even though both may pray to Him prior to the game). In His essence, He is not human.

So can you hear those angels now? Are you listening with different ears now when you hear them cry out holy, holy, holy is the Lord God Almighty? Is their announcement more audible to you now? Can you translate and hear them saying, *He is different, different, different. So totally different in His love. So totally different in His power. Different in His knowledge. Different in His ways. So totally different in His plans. So completely different in His essence and character. No one is like Him. He is separate. He is set apart. He is holy, holy, holy.*

This two-part meaning of holiness was the idea Peter communicated in his first letter. He first exhorts us to be holy in all our behavior, meaning we should maintain purity in our lifestyle. But then, just a few verses later, he uses the flip-side meaning of the same word, reminding us that we are a chosen race, a royal priesthood, a holy nation, a people for *God's* own possession (1 Peter 2:9). In other words, we are to be different and unique because we belong to a unique God. God has always desired His people to be different. Leviticus 20:26 says, "Thus you are to be holy to Me, for I the Lord am holy; and I have set you apart from the peoples to be Mine." Combined with this emphasis on His holiness, these heavenly angels also refer to this holy God as the "Lord God, the Almighty (*El Shaddai*), who was, who is and who is to come." Our God is Lord (*kurios*), the One who is eternal. What a revelation! And John is overwhelmed.

His amazement is reminiscent of the story concerning the 1940's Kansas farmer who won a trip for the whole family to New York City. Having never been outside of his own state, he wasn't quite sure what to expect once he got there. He had never seen anything taller than a grain silo before. Upon arriving at Grand Central Station, the old farmer, along with his wife and teenage son, stepped out onto the bustling streets of the Big Apple and immediately dropped their jaws in amazement and disbelief. Dwarfed by buildings that seemed to reach up into the clouds, the farmer stared straight up with mouth wide-open until finally getting a muscle cramp in his neck. Soon his wife strolled across the busy boulevard to look in a clothing store, so the farmer and his teenage son, both clad in overalls, decided they would see the inside of one of these so-called skyscrapers. Passing through the huge glass revolving doors the first thing they noticed was an elevator, but since they had never seen one before, they didn't quite know what they were looking at. The boy and his dad stood to the side and watched with curiosity as an elderly, unattractive woman with a walking stick slowly made her way inside the brass doors that opened to each side. After the doors closed, a bell sounded and the two Kansans watched as a series of lights began illuminating. At first the lights moved to the right, then they paused and began moving back to the left. Following this, there was another bell. The double doors slowly opened again, and out walked the most beautiful young woman either of them had ever seen. As she walked past the farmer and his son, it suddenly dawned on them that they definitely weren't in Kansas anymore. More curious than ever, the man stroked his chin for a moment while looking intently at that elevator. Then turning to his teenage boy, the old farmer eagerly said, *Son, go run across the street and fetch your mama. We're gonna run her through this contraption and see what happens!*

You can only imagine John's similar feelings of astonishment as he stepped into the throne room of God. To the aged apostle, now probably in his nineties, the things he saw certainly weren't like anything he had ever seen before in Palestine or on Patmos, his island of exile. The thunderclaps he heard were greater and louder than any he had ever experienced in those storms on the Sea of Galilee. He was blown away by what he saw and heard. But hang on. His orientation to heaven has only just begun.

crown me with many crowns

> And when the living creatures give glory and honor and thanks to Him who sits on the throne, to Him who lives forever and ever, the twenty-four elders will fall down before Him who sits on the throne, and will worship Him who lives forever and ever, and will cast their crowns before the throne. (Revelation 4:9–10)

As was mentioned before, these elders represent redeemed humanity from the Old and New Testaments – perhaps half of them symbolizing the twelve Tribes of Israel and the other half symbolic of the twelve apostles. Regardless of their symbolism, John watches in awe as the elders literally fall down before the throne of God. But they haven't come to God's throne empty-handed. As a part of their worship they bring golden crowns. Just a few verses earlier, they were wearing these same crowns on their heads. Now they are removed and placed at the base of the throne. But these are not the crowns of kings and rulers. The crowns described here are not diadems, but rather *stephanos* (literally "wreaths"). This word was typically used to describe a garland of intertwined olive branches bestowed at the Greek national games. At this forerunner to our modern Olympic games, those who won their events in wrestling or track and field would receive such a crown. But the biblical crowns are rewarded for a different kind of race. They are given to those believers who persevered in faithful service to Christ while on earth. There are five of these crowns we find mentioned in Scripture: the Crown of Life (James 1:12)—awarded to those who persevere under trials; the Imperishable Crown (I Corinthians 9:24–27)—awarded to those who fix their eyes on Jesus, placing their lives on the altar; the Crown of Exaltation (I Thessalonians 2:19–20)—given to individuals who win souls to Christ; the Crown of Righteousness (2 Timothy 4:5–8)—given to those who look to the appearing of Jesus at His Second Coming, leading holy and blameless lives; and the Crown of Glory (1 Peter 5:2–4)—the reward for those obedient pastors who shepherded the flock of God faithfully.

Would you like to receive any of these crowns? Do any of them sound appealing? Well consider this: God's Word also affirms that whoever encourages, supports and ministers to those who ultimately win these crowns, the same will also share in their reward. Look at what Jesus said:

> "He who receives a prophet in the name of a prophet shall receive a prophet's reward; and he who receives a righteous man in the name of a righteous man shall receive a righteous man's reward." (Matthew 10:41)

> "And whoever in the name of a disciple gives to one of these little ones even a cup of cold water to drink, truly I say to you he shall not lose his reward." (Matthew 10:42)

> "For whoever gives you a cup of water to drink because of your name as followers of Christ, truly I say to you, he shall not lose his reward." (Mark 9:41)

Keep in mind that there is a huge difference between *accepting* salvation and *earning* rewards. Salvation is a free gift that we are unable to work for (Ephesians 2:8–9). However, there will definitely be an awards ceremony at the Bema or judgment seat of Christ (2 Corinthians 5:10). At stake here is not your salvation. It's not a Heaven or Hell thing. That issue was forever settled the second you trusted Christ. Your destiny was sealed at the cross because of His work there on your behalf. However, this other judgment is based on your service to Him *after* becoming a Christian. The basis for these crowns and rewards is whether we built on the foundation of Christ alone. And according to I Corinthians 3:10–15, our works for Christ will be tested for their quality (not quantity) as well as for our motivations (why we did it). Once we get to Heaven, we will want to receive these crowns so that we can offer a greater sacrifice of praise to Him who sits on the throne.

Think of earthly blessings and Heavenly crowns like mirrors. You can use a mirror to reflect your own image or you can use it to refract the light from another source, diverting its light somewhere else. Blessings and crowns are bestowed so we can ultimately turn that glory back towards Him. When people compliment MercyMe because of songs we have written or awards we have won, we humbly just say thank you. We don't have to always verbally say thanks. Praise the Lord, though at times we do. But whether we do or not outwardly, we all know where our talents come from. We know Who is responsible for our voices and our abilities to play instruments. We know Who is behind any success we might achieve or blessing we may experience. Every CD we record is cast at His feet like a crown. Besides, He made it all happen anyway. That way, the focus is not the earthly accomplishment. Those things are simply means to a greater end. They are tools. The focus is Him. Of course, the key to all this really is our motivation. If receiving blessings and crowns means we have more to cast at the feet of Jesus in that day, resulting in greater praise to Him, then we'd be fools not to work for them. Again, it's all about Him. It's not about us.

That's what these heavenly elders realized. Having served Him faithfully on earth, they had been abundantly rewarded with crowns in Heaven. They had heard Him say, *Well done, good and faithful servants.* Much of their reward was simply knowing they had brought glory to Him. And it was all because of His grace. So what else could they do but declare His worth by removing those golden crowns and laying them before the One seated on the throne? It's like this: If you were on a team and had the choice between helping your team win one game in the season or win the league championship, which would you choose? Which would bring more honor and recognition to the team? Or if God gave you the opportunity to lead one person to Christ or to lead a hundred, which would you choose? If you had the choice between changing the color of your church's carpet or changing the hearts a generation of young people, which would you choose? Which do you think would bring greater honor and recognition to the name of Christ? It makes more sense to bring much honor to God than just to bring some honor to Him. And why? Keep reading. The clue is found in what the elders are saying.

> "Worthy art Thou, our Lord and our God, to receive glory
> and honor and power; for Thou didst create all things, and because
> of Thy will they existed, and were created." (Revelation 4:11)

Why are they so filled with praise for God? Why are they so motivated to remove the crowns from their heads and place them at His throne? Why are they are moved within to fall down and worship? One reason: Because He is worthy. That means that all this praise given to Him is an appropriate gift. It's the kind of praise worthy of a King. God is worthy to receive honor, because He is honorable. Worthy to receive power, because He is powerful. Worthy for all creation to praise Him, because He created all things. He is worthy for all created things to find their ultimate purpose and meaning in Him, because He created them for Himself and for His perfect plan. We were created for His pleasure. And so Heaven worships God simply because He deserves it!

so great a salvation

John's attention shifts once again as he looks up at God the Father seated on the throne. He sees in His hand a scroll. He then hears a strong angel proclaiming with a loud voice, *Who is worthy to open the book and to break its seals?* But no one is found worthy enough in Heaven, earth or under the earth. This greatly upsets John, who begins to weep. His spirit is grieved because no one was found worthy enough to break open the book of God. Then one of the elders who had been worshipping at the base of the throne comforts the apostle, telling him the Lion from the tribe of Judah has overcome so as to open the book. Standing in the midst of the company around that throne is Jesus Christ. No longer a humble carpenter, He is now exalted and glorified. And yet He still bears the scars He received from His brutal death at the cross. He takes the book out of the hand of the Father and, in doing so, ignites a new round of praise from the twenty-four elders and the four living creatures. Each of them grabs a guitar (harp), and golden bowls full of incense, which represent the prayers of the saints (Revelation 5:8).

> And they sang a new song, saying, Worthy art Thou to take the book, and to break its seals; for Thou wast slain, and didst purchase for God with Thy blood men from every tribe and tongue and people and nation. And Thou hast made them to be a kingdom and priests to our God; and they will reign upon the earth. (Revelation 5:9–10)

Why do they now engage in this song of praise? First, because of the price Jesus paid for us. The word slain denotes a violent death here, and reminds us we should never get over the sacrifice He made for our benefit. But secondly, they praise Him because of the scope of His redemptive work (Revelation 5:9). They praise Him for saving souls. Have you ever wondered who will be in Heaven when you get there? Jonathan Edwards, the great preacher and theologian of the eighteenth century, once said, *There are three things that will amaze me about Heaven. One, is all the people there I didn't think would be there. Second, all the people not there I thought would be there, And third, the fact that I am there.* And yet, while we don't exactly know the names of every person who will ultimately populate Heaven, we do know this: There will be at least one person from every nation, every people group, every language and every tribe. These verses tell us that salvation literally reaches to the ends of the earth. That's how great and deep the grace of God is. God is saving people each day from all over the world.

This song of heavenly praise is enhanced by yet another mind-blowing fact. John looks and rubs his eyes, because he sees more angels than he can possibly count. In fact, in his attempt to describe the number, he simply runs out of words. Imagine a concert held at a huge football stadium jam-packed with fans. One hundred thousand strong, they wait in anticipation for the artist to take the stage. But hold on. Scratch that. It's not big enough. Let's expand our vision a bit. Imagine instead a vast green meadow two hundred miles wide and 200 miles long. Now into this area, use your mind to digitally fill it up with angels and redeemed Christians from the beginning of time. Thousands. Millions. Billions. Even more. It's a sea of worshippers. A mega-mass of redeemed humanity and angelic beings. As far as the eye can see. There appears to be no end to them. Can you see it?

One of the things that will surprise us when we arrive in Heaven will be the sheer number of worshippers already there. *Hang on a second*, you might be thinking. *Didn't Jesus say that narrow is the road that leads to life, and few there be that find it?* Yes, He did say that. But passages like this one in Revelation tells us two very important things about Jesus. First, it tells us that His few and our few are two totally different numbers. That's good news! It is true that in relation to every human who has ever lived or who will ever live, a relatively small percentage of them will end up seeing Heaven. But guess what? A whole lot of people have lived on the earth. Over five billion currently inhabit this round mound of dirt spinning in space. If only 10 percent ended up in Heaven, there would still be five hundred million people in heaven. Add several hundred thousand (or more) angels and you have quite a crowd! But the second thing this passage in Revelation teaches us is that God really is working in people's lives a lot more than we might think. Truth is, we have no idea how many people God is saving all across the world every day. Thousands die every day. And while many of them die without Christ, that death toll also includes those who have trusted Him for salvation.

Your Attention, please

Now keep that scenario in your mind for a few more minutes. Can you see the massive gathering? All at once John tells us this huge multitude begins to shout. A cry. A declaration. Almost a chant. And they're all saying the same thing. Together. In unison. With one voice. There is incredible unity in Heaven as this mass congregation bursts into a chorus of praise.

> . . . saying with a loud voice, Worthy is the Lamb that was slain to receive power and riches and wisdom and might and honor and glory and blessing. And every created thing that is in heaven and on the earth and under the earth and on the sea, and all things in them, I heard saying, To Him who sits on the throne, and to the Lamb, be blessing and honor and glory and dominion forever and ever. And the four living creatures kept saying, Amen. And the elders fell down and worshipped. (Revelation 5:12–14)

One thing is clear here: All of Heaven's attention is focused on the Lamb of God, the Lord Jesus Christ. He is the centerpiece of Heaven, the point at which every syllable of praise intersects. He is worthy to be praised because He was slain. He is worthy to be the recipient of all power, riches, wisdom, might, honor, glory, and blessing. That's how precious the Lamb is. He is worthy enough for you to submit the power of your will to Him. If there is any authority that you have (on the job, at school, on the team, etc.), then He is worthy for you to submit that authority to be under His control. He is worthy for you to relinquish ownership of your riches and possessions to Him. This goes way beyond the wallet, purse, or checking account. It involves everything from the car to the guitar. From your clothes to your CD collection. The expensive things and the cheap things. The big things and the small. Your cell phone. His. Your watch. His. Your computer. His. Your fishing pole. His. That change on your dresser. His. It includes every-thing else you might call your own. All His. After all, isn't He worthy to receive your riches? Heaven seems to think so, and we can be sure that their perspective on reality is clear. And how clear is that?

Crystal.

Joining this celestial praise festival is every created thing. It's now a universal choir of creation. This song of adoration that originally began with the living creatures and elders, and then spread to the angels, now swells itself throughout the whole created universe. It includes every person in heaven as well as those on the earth. Every land and water animal is included; wild beasts, fish, dogs, birds, beavers, and barracudas will all join in this worship service. In their own way, they will give honor to Christ. The departed spirits in Hell must also recognize the greatness and glory of the One who is the Alpha and Omega. In the midst of their torment, their minds are still lucid. They know the truth now better than at any other time while on earth. They know exactly who Jesus is, and they are compelled by His worth to declare the greatness of His name (Philippians 2:9–11). Wow! Is this God so great that literally every living thing shouts in praise to Him? How great must He be if He deserves this kind of honor? There has to be a sense of awe that fills our hearts when we think of a truth like this. While you're hanging out down here, up in Heaven they're exalting a God who is worthy. But the worship service isn't nearly over. The billions present in heaven, hell, and the earth begin ascribing blessing and honor and glory and dominion forever and ever to the Son and the Father. "But where is the Spirit in all this?" you may be wondering. He's right there in the midst of it all. In fact, He's the One responsible for all this incredible commotion of worship. You see, it's His role in the Godhead to motivate and move others to praise the Father and Son. He doesn't desire to glorify Himself, but rather diverts all praise to the Son (John 16:14). The Father is glorified when the Son is exalted. And the Spirit is glorified through His role of leading you to glorify Christ. It's His office, and also His passion. In the mystery of our Triune God, there is perfect harmony and balance between the Father, Son, and Spirit.

The last thing John notices about this memorable scene is that "the four living creatures kept saying, 'Amen.' And the elders fell down and worshipped." The word amen simply means, yes, I agree, let it be, or may it be so. These angelic beings begin another repeating chant before the throne, in effect saying, *May this worship of God be so forever. Yes, Lord. May it ever be true.* Simultaneously, as if choreographed, the elders fall down once again to worship. By this point, John must be mentally and emotionally exhausted. He has run the entire gamut of emotions. He has been exposed to frightening thunder and flashes of blinding light. He has broken down in tears. He has fallen like a dead man at the feet of Christ. And he has witnessed the greatest display of reverential and celebrative praise ever displayed. Imagine the combined energy as billions alternately shout in praise and bow before this awesome God.

plug it in and turn it up!

What a breathtaking experience! So what can we learn from what John saw and heard? Here are a few observations: Knowing this is how Heaven does worship enhances our worship experience down here. It's also great practice for what we will experience later! Following are some other things we can learn.

First, worship intensifies when we come together (Revelation 5:11). If there had only been ten people around the throne, the dynamics would have been totally different. It's like being in that one hundred thousand seat stadium and only fifty people showing up. It's just not the same. Part of John's amazement was the utter number of those gathered to worship this fantastic God! The size of the crowd stunned him. Though God is certainly praised when we individually worship Him or when we gather in small groups, there is still something special about being with a big crowd of people who are all celebrating the same God. It's that big God experience we all need and crave—just to look around to see hundreds or even thousands of worshippers giving Him glory. What a great feeling for us, but even better than that, it makes us glad for *God*. It causes us to rejoice that He is receiving so much glory. It's just a fact that when the people of God come together in church, at a concert, revival, conference, or some other large gathering, there is a certain dynamic of praise not duplicated at any other time.

Secondly, it would appear God likes His worship loud (Revelation 5:12). Why is it we don't think twice about shredding our vocal chords at a basketball game or a concert, but when it comes to worship, we often develop an acute case of laryngitis? C'mon people! Lift up your voices. Make a joyful noise! And make it loud. Turn the amps up. Crank up the sound system. Turn the volume up on your CD player. Plug in the headphones and feel the bass blasting in your inner ear. When was the last time you came home from church with a hoarse voice? When is the last time you were literally exhausted from praising God? Has anyone ever stared at you while stopped at a red light because you were singing or shouting to the Lord? When is the last time you woke up your roommate from shouting *yesss*! after reading something in your Bible? God is worthy to shout about! In fact, it can't be loud *enough*. Though we may have limits on our ears' ability to withstand certain sound and decibel levels now, the same is not true about Heaven. Let's get used to the idea. In heaven, the worship is loud. And God likes it that way!

Third, worship is directed towards the Lamb (Revelation 5:12). Every eyeball is riveted on the Lamb of God, the One who is, who was, and who is to come. In Heaven, it's not about the band or the performers. It's not about the worship leader, the preacher, or the sermon. It's not about looking around to see who is raising hands or jumping up and down or closing their eyes. It's not about the audience, but rather about the Object. Worship is a simple concept, really. We praise God and Him alone. How hard is that? Sure, it's okay to appreciate and be grateful for our musicians and preachers. But worship is *not* about them. As we discussed in Chapter Three, *we* are not the point. He is. We need to be careful not to fall into the Christian celebrity trap. We have to keep our perspective and avoid exalting man too much. Jesus is our focus of worship.

Finally, we learn from this scene in Heaven that worship is not a spectator sport (Revelation 5:12–13). Football coaching legend Bud Wilkinson described a pro football game as eleven men desperately needing rest playing before fifty-five thousand fans desperately needing exercise! But in Heaven, the sidelines are empty. In fact, the grandstands are also silent. Everybody is on the field. Everybody is in the game. The sight they behold on the throne completely captivates their concentration. In other words, there is no attention deficit disorder in Heaven.

Did you get that? There is no need for medication or motivation to help those in Heaven concentrate. That's because they are all taking in a view that defies their wildest imagination. The mere sight of the glorified, exalted, enthroned Christ lays hold of them, seizing every individual like a vice-grip. Every one of the five senses is heightened. Like at no other time before, their total person is entirely alive. From head to toe. Inside and out. And perfect praise begins naturally running through them like an electrical current. Everything they had thought about or experienced concerning worship prior to this moment will fade into nothingness along with the rest of their earthly memories. In its place is the reality of being in the physical presence of the great I am. He fills every thought and every word. Every breath utters praise to Him. Every facial expression is a direct and outward overflow of a heart bursting with adoration. Crying out in praise to Him will be like taking our first breath of air. We will finally know what it's like to really be alive. Our purpose for being will be realized.

now boarding. gate seven.

Take a breath and think about this: What we lost way back there in the Garden is finally restored in Heaven. And everybody knows it. The paradise we lost in the beginning is regained in that place. It is a new day, the dawning of a new era. A new beginning. There is no longer any curse. No sin or temptation or sin nature. No devil or demons. Suffering and pain are a thing of the past (Revelation 21:4). There is no need to turn the lights on at night, because the whole concept of nighttime has been rendered obsolete. He himself is the Light (Revelation 21:23). There is no death. No separations. No goodbyes. Every relationship is perfected. Nobody is thirsty there, for He quenches every desire with Himself.

You know, in light of eternity, our lives here on earth are nothing more than a blip on the screen. We are here but for a few minutes, relatively speaking. Our lives are like a breath (Psalm 39:5) and a shadow (I Chronicles 29:15). In just a few ticks on eternity's clock, we'll be in Heaven joining this very worship service. Or as Gospel music pioneer Andre Crouch put it, "Soon and very soon, we are going to see the King." Fellow believer, everything this world has to offer is a cheap imitation of the real thing that awaits us in Heaven. Even our worship here is muted and pale in comparison to what it will be like then. And here is a thought: The sight of Jesus will be so wonderful; we will never tire of worshipping Him. The best thing of all about Heaven is that we will see His face (Revelation 22:4). It is there we can drink the water of life without cost (Revelation 22:17). God's conclusion after all this is to invite us to come to this place called Heaven. *Come away with Me,* He says. *Come to Heaven.*

Don't you want to go there?

CHAPTER 11

Royal Want Ads

god is seeking worshippers

For the eyes of the Lord move to and fro throughout the earth that He may strongly support those whose heart is completely His.

—2 chronicles 16:9

shiver me timbers!

As a child, perhaps you read books or saw movies of pirate ships and lost treasure. Tales of swashbuckling adventures on the high seas evoke images of one-eyed bandits and wooden-legged buccaneers. Maybe you read *Treasure Island* by Robert Lewis Stevenson or heard the legends of infamous pirates like Blackbeard or Diamond Jim. But long before they became mascots for professional sports teams, pirates were rough, foul-talking, rank-smelling, disgusting, and filthy scalawags (when's the last time you heard a word like that?). These sea-faring sailors of yesteryear turned thievery into an art form, plundering merchant ships and passenger ships for their booty (now there's another great word). After ransacking a ship, they would often set fire to her, drinking and laughing as she slipped into the darkness of the deep. Following a night of looting and pillaging, they would divide up the spoils of their conquest, with the head pirate usually keeping a larger portion for himself. But often, these pirates failed in their mission. Unable to locate the valuables they were looking for, they settled for stealing food, ammunition, dry goods, and personal items. Sometimes they were simply unaware of the real treasure hidden below the decks. For centuries, merchant and cargo vessels were used to transport gold currency from one port to the next. In fact, it was rumored there was a large amount of gold and jewelry on board the Titanic, stored in the Purser's safe. Like that doomed ocean liner, many of these ancient ships failed to reach their intended destinations. Lying undisturbed on the ocean floor for hundreds of years, they are now being systematically discovered due to the efforts of a new breed of explorer. These teams of aquatic archeologists (heavily funded, of course) are willing to go to any lengths, test any extreme, cross any ocean, dive to any depth, and pay any price to find these sunken vessels. It's the ultimate scavenger hunt. They study history, oceanic maps, and nautical records, tracking down leads and rumors in order to detect the general area where a particular ship may have sunk. Sometimes a ship sunk in a fierce gale-storm, other times it was due to a cannonball fired from another clipper. Often a search yields nothing, or it reveals a wreck so scattered and broken up that nothing can be salvaged. But every now and then, the legend proves to be true. After diving and exploring these sunken wrecks, what these modern-day treasure hunters are bringing back to the surface is mind-boggling. Dishes, weapons, artifacts, and you guessed it—gold! We're talking millions of dollars in two-hundred-year-old Spanish doubloons and crowns from England. After a little cleaning and polishing, the gold shine is restored to the coins, making them look virtually new. Then they are returned to the mainland where archeologists and gold brokers can determine their current worth and market value. Afterwards they are sold or auctioned off, yielding a fortune of profit to the treasure hunting investors. Called modern-day pirates by some, all that matters to these treasure hunters is that the search pays off.

ᴛʜe seekeʀ sensitive ɢod

Maybe you have dug for treasure at the beach, looking for that special shell, conch, starfish, or shark tooth to add to your collection. Or perhaps you enjoy a different kind of expedition, like finding a deal in a flea market or at the mall. Or your family may have vacationed out west, where you got to pan for gold in a canyon stream. And it's entirely possible (especially if you're a guy) that you have snuck out into the backyard to dig up your pet parakeet after a year's internment, just to see what he looks like. Though it may manifest itself in various ways, there is a little bit of that explorer's spirit in all of us. But have you ever thought of God in that way? Ever pictured Him searching for something? Can you imagine Him looking, exploring, seeking? And if so, what would He be looking for? What would He be seeking today? What is His treasure, something for which He is willing to search the whole earth? Is it sunken ships? Egyptian mummies? Buried bullion? The Holy Grail? As you rummage through Scripture, at times you'll find God looking for something. For example, in Ezekiel 22:30 God was searching for someone who would "stand in the gap before Me for the land, that I should not destroy it," but He found no one. The prophet Jeremiah was instructed by God to "Roam to and fro through the streets of Jerusalem, And look now, and take note. And seek in her open squares, If you can find a man, If there is one who does justice, who seeks truth, Then I will pardon her" (Jeremiah 5:1). Again, not a single person was found. Then there's the prophet Hanani who revealed a principle to King Asa of Judah regarding something else God was looking for. "For the eyes of the Lord move to and fro throughout the earth that He may strongly support those whose heart is completely His" (2 Chronicles 16:9).

There is another major pursuit that resides in the heart of our God. It's something that supercedes every other previous search of His. Buried within the sea of humanity is a treasure like no other. It's more valuable than silver coins. More precious than gold bouillon. It's something more dear to His heart than planets, kingdoms, and angels. It's something so cherished, so close to Him that He even refers to it as the apple of His eye (Zechariah 2:8; Deuteronomy 32:10). Would you like to know what it is? Want to know what it is that's so priceless to Yahweh? Are you ready for this? *People.* That's it. People. Humans. The pinnacle of His creation. But it's not just any person He's looking for. God isn't looking for just any old sunken ship. He is searching for a special kind of person . . .

. . . the *worshipping* kind.

More specifically, He has a certain type of worshipper in mind. This kind of person is not just a garden-variety worshipper. He or she is serious about worship. This is the only kind of worshipper that really touches the heart of God. On His treasure map, X marks the spot where this special kind of worshipper dwells. And fortunately for you, there is a carbon copy of that map found in your Bible. In John 4, Jesus drops anchor and begins submerging in His hunt for a particular person. Strap on your air tanks and let's join Him.

wonderful stranger

Here's the true story of one of those treasure hunt expeditions. Jesus had recently finished enduring (and overcoming) forty days of being tempted by the devil in the wilderness. During that time, He hadn't eaten a thing. Instead, He had focused all His physical and spiritual energies on fulfilling the Father's will. He resisted temptation so He could qualify to die as a sinless substitute for you and me. Shortly after this experience, John the Baptist was arrested by Herod, and because of this, the religious landscape heated up a bit. So to avoid unnecessary persecution, which at that early stage would have greatly hindered His ministry, Jesus decided to head north into Galilee. Now to get there, He and the disciples could have chosen from three possible routes. The first was west along the Mediterranean Sea while the other lay east and followed the Jordan River. Both of these would have meant taking the long way. But Jesus instead chose a third travel option, which meant walking a straight path north to Galilee—a path that would take them right through the heart of Samaria. No big deal, right? After all, the shortest distance between two points is a straight line, right? True, and due to the fact that Jesus was never one to needlessly waste time, this choice made perfect sense. He was well aware that His stay on earth was limited and rapidly approaching an end. So it would have seemed a prudent thing for Him to lead them that way. Only there is one slight problem. Traveling that route would take them right through, shall we say, the bad part of town. The region of Samaria was considered off limits to Jews because that's where the Samaritans lived. Ordinarily that would be no biggie, except for the fact that Jews hated Samaritans! We're not talking *I hate you because your dog turned my sidewalk into a public restroom* kind of hatred. We're also not talking the cross-town rival kind of animosity either. No, this is a deep-rooted hatred that dated back hundreds of years. Jews detested Samaritans. And here's why:

The Samaritans were a mixed race: half Jew and half Gentile. It all began back about seven hundred years before Christ when the Assyrians held Israel captive. While in that captivity, Jewish men took Assyrian women as their wives and, well . . . there you have it. But in addition to being a racially mixed people, they also were a religious mix as well. Because of their half-Jewish heritage, they combined Jewish and pagan religions to form sort of a hybrid faith. Though it contained basic elements of God's truth, it wasn't an orthodox faith in the true God. The Samaritans had their own temple and their own special holy place to worship. For these reasons and many others, Jews hated the Samaritans. And they invented ways to demonstrate their hatred. When a Jew wanted to insult or degrade you, he called you a Samaritan (Jesus was even called a demon-possessed Samaritan in John 8:48). This hatred was so bad that some Pharisees prayed that no Samaritan would be raised in the resurrection! And though it wasn't out of hatred, Jesus Himself at first forbid His disciples to take the Gospel to Samaria, but only to go to the lost sheep of Israel (Matthew 10:5). But when the Holy Spirit came into the world at Pentecost, God commanded us to proclaim the Good News in Judea, Samaria, and the uttermost parts of the earth (Acts 1:8).

So Jesus decided to take His disciples to the other side of the tracks to visit this forbidden region of Samaria. They hiked about twenty-five to thirty miles until they reached a city called Sychar—"Sychar, near the parcel of ground that Jacob gave to his son Joseph; and Jacob's well was there. Jesus therefore, being wearied from His journey, was sitting thus by the well. It was about the sixth hour."

Now think about this for a minute. Jesus had just walked a marathon—not in a pair of $120 cross-trainers either, but in first-century leather-bound sandals. And those things didn't keep the dirt off your feet very well. No moisture-absorbing running socks back then. It was a looong walk. Try it sometime. So they arrive about 6 P.M. in Sychar. Jesus, understandably tired from the journey, sits down by a well while the disciples go off into town to try and rustle up some dinner. But while He is sitting there, a woman walks up carrying a water pot. Because His lips were no doubt parched and His throat dry, and because He had no way of drawing water out of the well, Jesus requests a drink to quench His thirst. Startled, the women replied to Him,

> How is it that You, being a Jew, ask me for a drink since I am a Samaritan woman?

Now here was one savvy woman. From her question, we can discern that she recognized Jesus as a Jew, probably from His dress and dialect. We don't normally think of Jesus having an accent, but He did. He spoke like every other Jewish man from Nazareth. But beyond His accent, this woman also recognized the difference between Jews and Samaritans. She knew all too well what Jewish men thought of her race. Beyond that, she was aware it was taboo for a Hebrew man to speak to a strange woman like this in public. Unfortunately, women were very second-class citizens in those days, forbidden to vote or hold public office. However, that would soon change. Not only were women the chief financial supporters of Christ's ministry (Luke 8:3), they were also some of His most devoted followers (Luke 10:35–42). Women were the ones honored to be the first witnesses of the resurrected Christ at the tomb, and privileged to be the first to tell the world He was alive (Mark 16:9–10). For these and many other reasons, the female gender found a true friend in Jesus. But this particular gal wasn't

really thinking of Jesus in this way just yet. She was too busy being astonished and amazed that He had spoken to her in the first place. Perhaps she
is also wondering what this man's real motives were in striking up a conversation with her.

oops, she did it again

Suddenly, Jesus changed the subject. Laying aside His own deep physical
thirst, He instead concentrated on the woman's own spiritual need. He
threw her a curve ball by turning the topic to spiritual things. This wasn't
the time to merely allow lifestyle evangelism to take effect. He didn't have
the luxury of building a friendship or allowing her to see His life and
become convinced of who He was and attracted to God. There wasn't time
for that. Jesus saw into this woman's heart like no mortal could do. He
observed a lifetime of sin, hurt, and disappointment. Peering into her soul,
He saw an unfulfilled woman locked in a desperate search for love and satisfaction. She was caught in a depressing cycle of unfulfilling relationships,
looking for love in all the wrong faces. And so, knowing her situation, Jesus
goes right for the jugular.

> Jesus answered and said to her, "If you knew the gift of God,
> and who it is who says to you, 'Give Me a drink,' you would have
> asked Him, and He would have given you living water."
> She said to Him, "Sir, You have nothing to draw with and the
> well is deep; where then do You get that living water? You are not
> greater than our father Jacob, are You, who gave us the well, and
> drank of it himself, and his sons, and his cattle?"
> Jesus answered and said to her, "Everyone who drinks of this
> water shall thirst again; but whoever drinks of the water that I
> shall give him shall never thirst; but the water that I shall give
> him shall become in him a well of water springing up to eternal
> life." (John 4:10–14)

Were it not so true, it would almost be funny. Here is a man, covered with dust from his knees down, his robe and undergarments damp from a full day's sweat, and He no doubt smells like it too. The arid Palestinian desert has scorched His lips. His throat is dry and His body is craving rest and desperate for a drink. And yet He's talking about giving her water! What a paradox. He lays aside the familiar gratification of that first sip of cool well water for something that is infinitely more important to Him. You see Jesus, using His spiritual sonar, has just located the exact spot of a sunken wreckage. It's the scattered debris and remains of a life without hope. Instead of dropping that water pot down into the well, He's dropping an anchor instead, preparing to dive. Sure, He speaks to her about water, but not about the water she can give Him. Rather, Jesus turns the conversation around and her world upside down by offering her spiritual water that forever satisfies the thirst of the human soul. Suddenly, it's her lips that seem parched. Her throat is dry. Her soul is weary and thirsting for something more. This water of which Jesus speaks sounds like what she has been looking for all these years. Swallowing hard, she turns the tables right back around by asking Jesus for a drink of this wonderful water. But Jesus doesn't respond in a way we might expect. Instead of inviting her into the ocean of satisfaction that awaits her in Christ, He throws yet another pitch, this time a ninety-five mph fast ball. Strangely, He tells her to go get her husband. Now why would He say something like that? Was He tired of talking to her? Did He suddenly realize He was breaking social etiquette by speaking with her? Was He being rude or racist?

None of the above. Far from being an unkind or sexist comment, Jesus knows that before she can receive the pure water He offers, she must first recognize something about herself. Look what happens next:

> "The woman answered and said, 'I have no husband.' Jesus said to her, You have well said, 'I have no husband'; for you have had five husbands, and the one whom you now have is not your husband; this you have said truly." (John 4:17–18)

This poor woman had been married five times and now lived with a sixth one (and she wasn't even from Hollywood!). Here's a helpful hint: If you have been married five times, it just might be you're missing something along the way. That something may be the key to a successful relationship. And this woman wasn't even close to finding it. She had jumped from one relationship to the next, having been passed around from man to man. And each one had failed to give her what she really longed for. Oh, they had fed her plenty of lines, telling her time and again the things she wanted to hear. But never had a man told her what she really needed to hear, or even cared to. That is, until now. That's because this particular Man was different. Very different. Jesus wasn't after a romantic or physical relationship with her. He wasn't just one more guy who wanted to take something from her. His motives were pure. But all this woman knew so far was that He was not like all the others. Of course, there was no way Jesus could have known these things about her, that is unless He had access to information out of the reach of most mortals. That's why she responded to Him by saying, "Sir, I perceive that You are a prophet." So believing Him to now be a prophet (and obviously a Jewish one), she engaged Him in a conversation about race and religion. Specifically, the topic was who's right? The Jews or Samaritans regarding the proper place to worship God? Jesus responded to her statement by telling her it's not where you worship that is the ultimate issue. Rather it's *who* you worship that really counts. And incidentally, Jesus said, you Samaritans have totally missed the truth regarding the worship of God. We worship the true God, for God has revealed Himself to the Jews. The Messiah will come from the Jews as well. And He was right of course. Salvation did come first to the Jews as God's covenant people. The very first Christians were Jewish believers. Jesus was not being racist or arrogant, but instead lovingly straightforward with her. The Son of God possessed the unique ability to be unbending in the truth with people while at the same time sincerely expressing love for the person. What's important is that you be a true worshipper of God, He told her. He then defined further what this kind of worshipper looked like. Should this

person be Jewish? Male? Religious? Educated? Wealthy? Not divorced? No to all these.

Jesus' two stipulations were that whoever worships God simply do so *in spirit and truth.* It makes sense that since He is God, He alone determines the conditions for acceptable worship, right? So let's find out what each of these requirements for worship really means.

The Heart of worship

True worship involves the spirit because it is primarily a spiritual activity. This has to be so because God is a Spirit. He doesn't possess a body. Though the Son took on human flesh and now dwells in a glorified body in Heaven, God in His nature is Spirit. He doesn't have arms or eyes, though Scripture sometimes uses anthropomorphic (human) terms to help us comprehend certain things about Him (like His strength or His knowledge). That's why we have to worship Him in our spirit. Your spirit is the part of you that's you. It's the part of you that can have a relationship with God. To worship in spirit means our worship is primarily inward, not outward. Though there are outward physical expressions of worship, such as the ones we have already seen in previous chapters, worship begins on the inside and is an overflow of the heart. That was one of the biggest problems Jesus had with the Pharisees. Their worship was skin-deep; it was all external. But Jesus wanted His followers to focus on the inside, where the spirit is.

> "Beware of practicing your righteousness before men to be noticed by them; otherwise you have no reward with your Father who is in heaven. And when you pray, you are not to be as the hypocrites; for they love to stand and pray in the synagogues and on the street corners, in order to be seen by men. Truly I say to you, they have their reward in full. But you, when you pray, go into your inner room, and when you have shut your

door, pray to your Father who is in secret, and your Father who sees in secret will repay you." (Matthew 6:1, 5–6)

For the Pharisees, worship was just another show. It was never about touching their spirits or connecting with their hearts—only about appearing religious and spiritual to others. For them, it was a performance. *Not so for you*, Jesus says. So whether you're alone in your inner room or in a crowd of thousands, worship has to be an inward matter of the heart. True worship springs from the innermost part of who you are. It is in your spirit that you feel the deepest desires and emotions (John 11:33; 13:21). You serve God in your spirit (Romans 1:9). You cry out to God with your spirit (Romans 8:15). The Spirit bears witness with your spirit that you are His child (Romans 8:16). You pray in the Spirit (Jude 1:20). And you worship in the Spirit (Romans 12:1–2; Philippians 3:3). God desires for His own children to worship in spirit, and that involves the whole heart—all of you. That was something this woman at the well had certainly never heard before. But there is another requirement God makes concerning our worship.

The integrity of worship

There are at least three areas touched by Jesus' statement of worshipping in truth. The first relates to hypocrisy. You may already be aware that the word *hypocrite* originally referred to Greek actors. They wore these masks when they were playing a role on stage—one was a sad face while the other was a happy face. These drama masks helped them portray their characters. They were pretending, just like actors do today. *Don't wear a mask when you worship*, Jesus is saying. *Don't pretend to worship when your heart isn't in it. Let us see the real you.* In other words, worshipping in truth means you are true to yourself. The Pharisees, however, were spoke one way and lived another. They fulfilled Isaiah's prophecy of those people who honored God with their lips, but their hearts were far away from Him. Jesus said their worship was empty and meaningless to God (Matthew 15:7–9). As leaders, the

Pharisees became the blind leading the blind. They prayed, but didn't really mean what they said. It was just an exercise in religiosity to them. Their worship was all about *them*. It was about appearance. They looked great on the outside but on the inside, Jesus said they stunk (Matthew 23:27). Wonder what Jesus sees on Sunday mornings all across our country as well-dressed churchgoers sing, pray, serve, and give? Wonder how much that spirit of the Pharisees still haunts us? Jesus warned His disciples, "Therefore do not be like them" (Matthew 6:8). And the Pharisees should have known better, considering they were supposed to be experts on the Bible.

"Now, therefore, fear the Lord and serve Him in sincerity and truth; and put away the gods which your fathers served beyond the River and in Egypt, and serve the Lord." (Joshua 14:14)

"Only fear the Lord and serve Him in truth with all your heart; for consider what great things He has done for you." (I Samuel 12:24)

"Since I know, O my God, that Thou triest the heart and delightest in uprightness, I, in the integrity of my heart, have willingly offered all these things; so now with joy I have seen Thy people, who are present here, make their offerings willingly to Thee." (I Chronicles 29:17)

A Prayer of David: "Hear a just cause, O Lord, give heed to my cry; Give ear to my prayer, which is not from deceitful lips." (Psalm 17:1)

"How blessed is the man to whom the Lord does not impute iniquity, And in whose spirit there is no deceit!" (Psalm 32:2)

"Behold, Thou dost desire truth in the innermost being,

And in the hidden part Thou wilt make me know wisdom."
(Psalm 51:6)

God desires a truthful heart from those who worship Him. That's why Jesus exposed this woman's sinful lifestyle. He wanted her to be a true worshipper, but before that could happen, she would first have to be true to herself. She would have to be honest about who she was and about her sinful condition before God. Her problem wasn't that she was a Samaritan or a woman. Her problem was that she was living in sin, and Jesus wanted her to acknowledge that in her heart to God.

But to worship in truth goes beyond being true regarding yourself. It also means to have integrity concerning the truth about Jesus. Later in their conversation, Jesus told this woman He was the Messiah. That was a pretty bold claim considering it made Him out to be equal with God! But this was a truth He asserted on many occasions (John 8:58–59; 10:29–33). So part of worshipping in truth means to worship God through Jesus Christ who is the Truth. Therefore the only true worshippers are those who worship out of a right relationship to Him. The implications of this are obvious, not the least of which is that Christ is the only way to Heaven. As Messiah, He would naturally be the only way to the Father (John 14:6). He was the truth and full of truth (John 1:14). Period. End of discussion. He leaves no room for the worship of Buddha, Confucius, Mohammed, Allah, or any other religion, faith, or belief system. Jesus made it clear that salvation is exclusively through Him alone. Again if that sounds narrow-minded, it's because it is! But truth is a very narrow-minded concept. Twelve inches will always equal one foot no matter what anyone says to the contrary. Sixteen ounces will always be one pound. It is very narrow-minded to assert that two plus two is four instead of five. But that's the nature of absolute truth. It's unbending and forever fixed. Jesus claimed to be *the* truth (John 14:6) and there is just no way to wiggle around that.

But there is a third implication of worshipping in truth. It's that we must also be true to Scripture. Since the written revelation of God (the

Bible) is everything we need for life and godliness (2 Timothy 3:16–17; 2 Peter 1:3), it stands to reason that our worship should conform to the truth of Scripture. That means our worship of God is not based on what we think God is like or what we feel to be true about Him. Our knowledge of God is according to the word of truth. This means our worship ought also to have substance and depth, just like the Bible does. As we talked about earlier regarding the character of God, we should think deep thoughts of God—thoughts worthy of Him. No matter how long you have been a Christian or how much you have studied or think you know about God, there is still an eternity's worth left to discover about our awesome Lord. Remember Paul's words to the Philippians?

> Not that I have already obtained it, or have already become perfect, but I press on in order that I may lay hold of that for which also I was laid hold of by Christ Jesus. Brethren, I do not regard myself as having laid hold of it yet; but one thing I do: forgetting what lies behind and reaching forward to what lies ahead, I press on toward the goal for the prize of the upward call of God in Christ Jesus. (Philippians 3:12–14)

These verses give us a window into Paul's personal walk with Christ. In them, He confessed that he wasn't satisfied with where he was spiritually. There was a healthy discontentment in his life. He knew he hadn't arrived yet. He still had miles to go before he could consider himself as having made it in his journey of spiritual maturity. He hadn't yet achieved the level of Christ-likeness he desired. He wanted more. He wanted depth. Depth of knowledge. Depth of experience. Depth of relationship. But what makes all this so incredible was that at the time he wrote this letter, Paul had known Jesus for over thirty years! Even then, he still wanted to know Him more (Philippians 3:10)! What about you? Do you still desire more? Do you want to know Him in a more intimate way? Still want to go deeper, like you used to? To be honest, from the start of this book, we wanted this book to go a little deeper than most. We didn't want to give you just another devotional, though we love devotionals. Instead, we wanted to challenge you to take your worship to the next level. A deeper one. We don't want to worship God at the infant or adolescent level. We want to praise Him with maturity and depth! Our desire is to worship in truth, friend—with personal integrity, exclusive loyalty to Christ and with faithfulness to the Word of God.

Rare and well-Done worship

Finally, Jesus tells this Samaritan lady something about God she had not known before. He reveals to her the real purpose of His visit to Sychar.

> "But an hour is coming, and now is, when the true worshipers shall worship the Father in spirit and truth; for such people the Father seeks to be His worshipers." (John 4:23)

We've already discussed what it means to worship in spirit and in truth, but two questions still remain: 1) Are these kinds of worshippers common? and 2) Why does God long for these kinds of people? The answer to the first question is that those who worship in spirit and truth are not as common as we might wish. It's pretty common for people to worship mindlessly, without thinking. It's easy to worship because it's that time in the service. We've all done that. It goes without saying that most of us have engaged in outward expressions of worship without ever plugging in our hearts. That's unfortunately normal. But we do this because we all tend to be a little self-centered. We also have a common tendency to worship worship, or find ourselves worshipping merely out of habit or peer pressure. We worship when it's convenient to do so. But when our lives are a mess, we often give up or complain. But that's not being a spirit and truth worshipper is it?

Of course, there are those who paint a bleak and depressing picture of the body of Christ. Everything going on in the Christian community is worldly, they say. It seems these people actually enjoy being negative as they attack their fellow believers. Such persons say true worshippers are more than just rare. *They're nearly extinct!* they claim. But we think that's way too unrealistic and reveals a very low and limited view of God. Though they may not be as common as we would like, they're still there. Do you remember how negative and depressed Elijah became shortly after his great victory at Mount Carmel? After defeating the 450 prophets of Baal, he sat down under a tree and asked God to take his life. Then he went into a cave and continued his personal pity party there, lamenting to God that he alone was left as a true servant of God. *It's just me, God. I am the only true worshipper you have.* But the Lord was quick to inform His pitiful prophet that He had seven thousand in Israel who had not bowed to Baal (1 Kings 19:18). You see, that's how wonderful our God is. He has true worshippers all over your town, state, country and world. There are other worshippers in your school, profession, and community. You're not alone! A God as great as ours will have true worshippers! That's how awesome He is. But while we are confident God has true worshippers all over the world, its sometimes seems like a minor miracle to get a group of them in the same room. That's why we aspire to be uncommon worshippers and to inspire others to be the same. We should all desire God's best for our lives. Sure, no one of us is any different or better than anyone else. We struggle with the same temptations and difficulties. But we do believe God has called imperfect vessels like us to help this generation become a people strong in spirit and truth. But it first has to be true in our own hearts before we can lead anyone else there. Each of us is a work in progress, aren't we? Every one of us is a project God has promised never to abandon (Philippians 1:6). And that's great news.

Okay, so why does God long for these kinds of worshippers? Why does He seek them? What is His motivation? What's the reason behind His quest? We believe God desires spirit and truth worshippers because that's the kind of praise that best glorifies Him. It's like this: When we worship the one true God with real hearts, based on true information about His greatness—*that's* when He is greatly glorified. He loves it when we declare the truth about Him with sincere, whole hearts. It honors Him. It lifts His name up. For example, when a musician is inducted into the Rock and Roll Hall of

Fame (or pick your favorite music hall of fame), it is customary to play his or her greatest hits during the course of the induction ceremony. And why? Because by rehearsing the artist's accomplishments, you can better appreciate who they are and why they deserve the honor and immortality of the Hall of Fame. Now check this out: when you begin listing God's accomplishments—what He did in the Bible, what He has accomplished in history, and what he has done in your life and generation; when you rehearse the things that are truth about Him; when you play His greatest hits in your heart over and over again; a chorus of praise swells around the throne of God. It's almost as if your praise becomes like wind under the angels' wings, prompting them to exalt Him all the more. And doing this with all of your soul, in sincerity of heart, means God is genuinely praised.

And you become a genuine worshipper.

guess who?

So did this Samaritan woman get it? Did she need to sell all she had and go buy a clue, or was her heart open to the things Jesus was saying to her? After Jesus' revelation concerning true worshippers, she told Him she was aware that the Messiah was coming, and that when He did, He would reveal all things to (John 4:25). Now wouldn't you agree that this was a woman in desperate need of some good news? After all, what did she have to look forward to? What was waiting for her at home but another day of despair? Though she had led a sinful lifestyle, there was still a small glimmer of hope in her heart that the Messiah would come and fill in the blanks about God. Little did she know that the great Hope of the world was seated opposite her and was about to rock her world in a matter of seconds. Though His words so far had been surprising, informative, and even convicting, Jesus was ready to give her one more revelation. The sun had now set over the Mediterranean and it had gradually grown dark. However, with each new sentence, Jesus had progressively turned up the light for her, revealing more and more of who He really was. He decided that now was the time for her to hear the whole truth about Him. She already knew He wasn't an ordinary Jewish man. She was also convinced He wasn't your average, run-of-the-mill orthodox Jewish Prophet. He was way too kind for that. Way too genuinely interested. Too caring. Too personal. She may have had suspicions about Him before, but nothing in her mind could have prepared her for what He was about to say:

"Jesus said to her, 'I who speak to you am He.'" (John 4:26)

At these words, no doubt this girl felt an earthquake in her mind, with aftershocks reverberating throughout her heart. Talk about dropping a bombshell! This was the first time in Scripture that Jesus had specifically declared himself to be the Christ. And would you note that this monumental and historic revelation wasn't made to the Pharisees or the religious leaders. It wasn't made at a religious gathering. It wasn't made on the Sabbath, but rather at the end of a long ordinary day's journey. He didn't reveal Himself in Jerusalem, but instead did it in a relatively obscure little town. He made this statement not in the Temple, but at the city watering hole. He shared this truth with a woman, not a man. With a Samaritan, not a Jew. In a conversation, not a sermon. But what He said was even more significant than where, how and to whom He said it. Literally, Jesus declared to her, I am. Because the Samaritans believed the first five books of Moses, she would have likely been familiar with the story in Exodus 3:14 where God reveals Himself to Moses at the burning bush. Asked His name, God simply replied, I am that I am is My Name. Those two English words I am are just one word in the original Hebrew—the word Yahweh. It's the most personal, intimate, true, and revealing name of God. It's the name He calls Himself. Jesus could have told her many things that day, but He chose to let her know He was the great I am.

sail on!

Now, how would you feel if you suddenly discovered the man who had asked to borrow fifty cents at the drink machine turned out to be God

Almighty in human flesh? Would your mouth go bone dry? Possibly feel a chill gallop like a wild stallion up and down your spine? Feel a little weak in the knees? *Drop* to your knees? Maybe feel a little embarrassed because you had been treating Him like an ordinary person? You think you would pass out? Call a friend? Use a lifeline? And what would you have said to Jesus? Well, for this woman, whatever was about to come out of her mouth was put on temporary hold because at that very moment the disciples walked up with dinner. They all had a surprised look on their faces upon discovering Jesus was talking to the woman. But He was the Teacher, the Man in charge, so nobody said anything to Him about it. Meanwhile, the woman took this as her cue to make like a tree and leave. Too many Jewish men approaching. Time to go. So she hurriedly left Jesus, the well, *and* her water pot. No big deal though, because she wouldn't be needing it anymore. From that moment on, she would be making use of an altogether different kind of well and water. She had gone to the well to get some cool water, but in reality, the Well had come to her! And He filled her up so much that she began overflowing with living water. Jesus saw her as a person with great worship potential. She was ripe for a spiritual harvest in her life. The timing was perfect, and so was Jesus' approach. The Lord never did get that drink from her, but she sure got one from Him. Can you see her now? Eyes brimming with tears of joy and excitement, racing back into town in the dark? She immediately ran to tell the men (most likely her former husbands and lovers) about this wonderful Stranger she had met. "Come, see a man who told me all the things that I have done; this is not the Christ, is it?" (John 4:29) More accurately translated, this phrase reads, "Is this not the Christ?" The implication is, it *is* Him! And they listened to her as these men and others began coming out to Him (30). Meanwhile, the disciples were trying to get Jesus to eat something. But He wasn't hungry anymore. "I have food to eat that you do not know about. The disciples therefore were saying to one another, No one brought Him anything to eat, did he? Jesus said to them, My food is to do the will of Him who sent Me, and to accomplish His work." (John 4:32–34)

In other words, Jesus was telling them, *Guys, gather around and listen up.*

There is something more satisfying and fulfilling to Me than a hot meal after a long day's journey. Something even more thirst quenching than a cold cup of this well water. You need to know that My greatest desire is to seek lost people and turn them into true, spiritual worshippers of God. Look around you! There are potential worshippers all over this place! Think of how much glory the Father can receive through these people! That's what motivates Me. That's what occupies my mind. Not food.

It is almost certain this woman became a worshipper of God that day. But not just any ordinary, average, common worshipper. When Jesus dropped anchor that day, her world was injected with a full and healthy dose of heavenly hope. He did way more than just locate her. He dove down to the bottom and met her where she was, right there at the same well she visited every day of her dull existence. He spoke her language, revealing the whole truth to her. But He did something even better than that. He raised her wreckage to the surface. Then, in a way only a real Messiah could do, He completely restored her. He made her ship seaworthy once more. A brand new hull. New railings and decking. A new mast. A re-hoisted sail complete with complimentary wind. Then Jesus charted a whole new course for her. The past was the past. Her boat was re-christened and she discovered for the first time that hope does indeed have a Name. And as a result of becoming a worshipper of Christ, from that city many of the Samaritans believed in Him because of the word of the woman who testified.

That's what happens when the world sees a true worshipper.

Are you one?

CHAPTER 12

Travelin' Music

practicing a lifestyle of worship

Brothers! What we do in life echoes in eternity!
—MAXIMUS DESIMUS MERIDIUS
(RUSSELL CROWE) IN THE GLADIATOR

The trouble with life is that there is no background music.
—FROM AN OLD BUMPER STICKER

We began this book together with the premise that worship is far more than just praise and worship music. We conclude the book by issuing a challenge for you to write your very own soundtrack to life. We want a lifestyle of worship to become your background music, creating some great travelin' music for the long journey ahead. But in order to do this we have to translate the principles of worship we have learned into vernacular living. In other words, we need to put it into common language. We've seen that worship is more than just an act; it's a way of viewing life. It's a perspective about a Person that impacts the present. Through the stories told in Scripture, we've discovered that our worship of God is displayed through daily acts and attitudes. And that attitude is revealed through every word on our tongues and each thought in our heads. So how can we complete our bridge from the theoretical to the practical? What does all this look like in real life? How do we translate our desire to be men and women of worship into our daily experience? We have to be convinced that worship is more than a nice-sounding idea. It's a reality that is proven every day in millions of lives all across the world. Now here's how you can keep that reality fresh in your life.

Never Lose the wow

Our great-grandparents were in awe of the groundbreaking invention of electricity. The mere idea that light could come from a generated source other than the end of a candle or a gas lamp was virtually unthinkable in the nineteenth century. Fortunately for the world, Thomas Alva Edison thought beyond those limits. At the age of twelve, young Thomas worked at the Grand Trunk Railway in Michigan. During that time, he saved the life of a station official's child. As a reward for his act of bravery, Thomas was given the chance to be taught telegraphy. Having attended school for just three months, and because of his innate curiosity, young Edison was eager to learn. Soon he began integrating his knowledge and his creativity into his work, and the repeating telegraph was born. That was all Thomas needed to spur his imagination. Years later, in 1876, after selling telegraphic appliances, he received some forty thousand dollars (which was a lot back then!). He took this money and established a laboratory with it. Three years later, following thousands of experiments, he unveiled his incandescent electric light bulb.

And the whole world was changed.

For your grandparents, the post World War II wow was television. There were no big screen TV's then. No home theater systems. No digital signal. No cable. No pay-per-view. No Cartoon Network! No TV Land and no ESPN. In those days, a television was a big, heavy box with a very, very small screen. And it was in black and white. And the picture was kinda blurry. But hey, when you've been used to staring at a radio dial, seeing a moving image on any size screen was a big deal.

Computers were a definite wow when they first came on the scene. The very first computers were used primarily to solve math problems and were as big as entire classrooms. It was unimaginable back then that virtually every home would one day have a Mac or PC. But with the innovation of the microchip, computer technology mushroomed. Now we have microchips in everything from our coffee pots to PalmPilots, from cell phones to credit cards. What's next? What's down the road for us in this area? The point is that our generation wants and demands more. And we're getting it. This is due largely to the technology and talent available in our country as well as the time in which we live. And because of this, we're not as easily impressed.

So what is the big wow for this generation? Will it come through space travel? Medicine? Digital or computer technology? Maybe a cure for AIDS or cancer? Will it be through education or the economy? Or will it be some other incredible human accomplishment? We strongly believe that for our generation to have any real hope, we have to find our sense of awe and wonder in something even greater than an earth-shattering new invention or technological innovation. We have to find our amazement in something more significant than a gadget man can create. We need something beyond ourselves. Where then is the wow?

It's in God.

If our attention is to be captivated, then it must be by something more meaningful than the final episode of a long-running TV sitcom. We need to see God for Who He is, in all His true splendor and glory. We need to see Him fresh everyday. We can't lose the perspective we gained when we got that first glimpse of His glory. We need what those early believers had. We need the faith of Abraham, who worshipped a God so great He could be trusted with the sacrifice of his only son. We need the courage of Joshua, who defied his own people, choosing instead to believe in God when no one else would. We need the heart of David, who worshipped his God in the midst of great personal pain. We need the conviction of Daniel, who worshipped in spite of ridicule and persecution. We need the determination of Samson, who finished strong despite a history of personal failure. We need the humility of John the Baptist, who continually pointed others to Jesus instead of himself. We need the devotion of Mary, who never grew weary of being at the Master's feet. And we need the boldness of Stephen, who was willing to lay down his life for the cause of Christ. All these had the wow factor in their lives. It was something that kept them from giving up. It was something they never lost. It was something no one could take away from them. They never recovered from their encounters with God. They never got over Him. And if we are to ever convince this generation our God is real, we have to be consumed with that same sense of Wow Worship. We can never look at Him in apathy or indifference. To do this would be to invent a lesser God in our minds. To see Him as he is always produces awe and worship. And this is not something we have to work up on our own. We don't have to worry about maintaining this perspective all by ourselves. All we need to do is simply look intently at Him. Think on Him. Meditate on Him. Every day. Shake your head in amazement as you contemplate the magnitude of Who He is. Never lose the wow.

Remember It's still about Relationship

More than anything God wants a relationship with you. More than obedience. More than doing something for Him. More than serving Him. More than sacrifice. More than music. More than writing a book. It's a relationship, not a performance, remember? And therein lies the ultimate mystery of salvation. Why would God desire a relationship with us? Answer: It pleases Him to do so. Go get lost in that truth and leave your map and compass at home. Talk about a wow moment! He values your love above all else (Matthew 10:37). God knows that if you love Him, you will worship Him. And just how important is it that you have a love relationship with Him? It's more valuable than all the worth of the world put together.

> "For what does it profit a man to gain the whole world, and forfeit his soul?" (Mark 8:36)

And the only way to love Him is through a relationship with Him. As we have said, this goes far beyond mere knowledge about Him. It means we obey the greatest commandment of all:

"Love the Lord your God with all your heart, and with all your soul, and with all your mind." (Matthew 22:37)

But what does this mean? It means to love Him with your heart (or will). To love God is a choice we make, right? When Jesus invited the first disciples to follow Him, it meant they would submit their desires to Him. Of course, any love-based relationship involves choosing. That's because real love is more than a feeling. It's a choice we make to commit ourselves to someone else, ultimately for his or her greatest good instead of ours. When you love someone, you don't have to be told to serve him/her. You don't have to be forced to spend time together. Love automatically does this, doesn't it? It spontaneously seeks to please the one loved. And in this case, love also produces a voluntary obedience to God. Ever notice how couples that are in love rarely forget to call each other or to go out to eat together? On the contrary, they skip class, run up long-distance phone bills, drive for hours, and pay almost any price just to be with the one they love! And that kind of commitment lasts for as long as they're in love. When it comes to a relationship with God, nobody loves us like He does. We discover that we enjoy loving Him. We even find ourselves thirsting to be with Him (Psalm 42:1). That's a small bit of what it means to love God with our heart. But Jesus wants us to love Him with our soul as well.

The soul here refers to our emotions, or our feelings. And how do we love God with our feelings? Two thoughts: First, we all agree that our emotions can be like a roller-coaster at times, up one minute and down the next. As we saw in Chapter Two, our emotions are not quite as stable as they were originally intended to be. So we first demonstrate our love by allowing God to control our unsteady feelings. We submit them to Him, especially because they have a tendency to control us at times. But secondly, we take comfort in knowing that God also truly understands how we feel. Because Jesus experienced virtually every emotion we do, He can identify with us and help us with our emotions. He went through it all (Hebrews 2:17–18; 4:15–16) and understands all our hurts, joys, sorrows, and weaknesses. After all, isn't that what a relationship is all about? That makes it okay for us as Christians to hurt. God gives us permission to feel. You love Him by sharing your every emotion with Him. You love Him by allowing Him to control those emotions. That way, He will prevent your disappointment from becoming bitterness and your distress from turning into full-fledged depression. He is Lord over your emotions. But there is a third way Jesus says we keep our love relationship with God. He also wants us to love Him with our *minds*.

Isn't it great that as a Christian you don't have to disengage your mind in order to worship? In other words, you don't have to check your brains at the door of the church. Christianity is a rational faith, founded and grounded in fact. We don't dismiss our ability to reason, doubt, or question just because we follow Christ. So with that in mind, how can we love God with this part of our person?

First, we should yield our thoughts to Him (2 Corinthians 10:5). The human brain retains untold memories in high-resolution images. Stored as if in a mega-computer, those images are forever logged in our memory banks. So to protect ourselves from damaging data, we should guard our minds, allowing Christ to influence and control what we think. Careful not to be legalistic, we should however be careful what music we listen to, what movies we watch, what magazines and books we read, and what websites we surf on the Net. And it's more than just asking What Would Jesus Do? More specifically, it's what would Jesus have *me* do? Having Jesus on our minds is a matter of obedience. It's a choice that blesses Him and benefits us. But second, we also should use our minds to think often about God. Deep thoughts. High thoughts. Thoughts that challenge our thinking. Consider reading books and listening to messages that cause you to stretch your thinking about God. Your brain is like a muscle, and by using it you make it stronger. Third, we should allow God to renew, cleanse, and purify our minds as we love Him and submit to Him (Romans 12:2). Finally, we should glorify God by using our minds in culture and society for good. There is a good chance God has given you a unique ability to think, reason, imagine, or create. So use your God-given talent in this area to enrich the world around you. In science. In the arts. In business. In technology. In relationships. In theology. In apologetics. Use your mind for Him! Love Him with all your heart (will), your soul (emotions), and your mind (thoughts). It's the greatest and best commandment of all!

know that you're in process

If you'll recall, we discussed in Chapter Two that among the many things Adam and Eve lost in the Garden was their sense of *identity*. Through sin's impact on them, they forgot who they were. But through the Second Adam—Jesus —our identity is restored. And for the rest of our time here on earth we get to live the adventure of becoming who God made us to be. Because of this, we should never forget who we are in Him. Too often we fail to appreciate who we are in Him because we spend too much time looking at other Christians who appear better or more successful than we. You know who we're talking about. Perhaps you've lived in the shadow of their reputation. Maybe you've felt intimidated by their spirituality. You've wondered what they have that you don't have. We're talking about those successful Christians. You know, the ones who seem to be happy all the time. The ones who don't appear to have a care in the world. They don't even look like they struggle with temptation. There are no glaring weaknesses or obvious failures in their lives.

But why do these people seem to appear so successful? Why do they seem to be enjoying so much prosperity, spiritually speaking? We don't intend to play the comparison game, but it just happens sometimes, doesn't it? Fact is, as fallen humans, we often look at the grass on the other side of the fence (where *those* Christians live) and somehow make ourselves believe it's greener. They have more joy. More money. More ministry. More converts. More friends. More influence and more insight. So why is their grass so green? Why do things seem so good over there? Well, it actually may be a bit fresher over there, and it may be growing faster. But it may also be that there is a little more fertilizer hidden in that grass. Beneath the blades, out of sight from the naked eye, may be more compost nourishment than you realize. Don't worry. Every life has its share of trouble. And this is even true of *those people*. Some Christians are just better at covering it up. Or maybe they just aren't as transparent as you are and are uncomfortable about sharing their hurts with others. Besides, God hasn't called us to live our lives on the other side of the fence, has He? He's called us to live it on *our* side. Admittedly, our grass does at times seem to have more cow patties than the other guy's. But every pasture has its share. We have to get our eyes off others and put them back where they belong—on Jesus (Hebrews 12:2).

Truth is, there is enough about our lives to keep us plenty busy. That's because we are all in a process of growth and maturity that is gradual, sometimes grueling and not always picture-perfect. There are bumps in this road of growth. Potholes. Narrow shoulders. At times there are roadblocks of sin. Seasons when we seem to stand still on the road. Times when we become stalled on the side of the highway. Times when we have a flat tire or when smoke comes billowing out from the hood. Times when we are parked and forced to shut off the engine.

But here is where the hope kicks in. God Himself has uttered an unbreakable oath to you. He has sworn to do something for you. He has obligated Himself to complete the work He began in your heart the day you first placed your faith in Him. He has promised to work in you and for you up until that moment when your foot touches Heaven's shore.

> "For I am confident of this very thing, that He who began a good work in you will perfect it until the day of Christ Jesus." (Philippians 1:6)

This process is a lifelong thing. So gear up your mind for the long haul. Prepare for the marathon. Live one day at a time. You are not what you will be. That's okay. Just be thankful you are not what you once were. This commitment from God on your behalf means that whenever you are discouraged because the spiritual traffic has slowed on your road to maturity, you can know that God is still at work even in those times. Remember that though your grip on Him may grow weak, His never does. He is fiercely dedicated to the process. *Your* process. Don't give up. He will never let you go.

Be faithful

Would you like to be successful as a Christian? Dumb question, right? Of course you would. We all do. But exactly what is success in God's eyes? We all have a different way of measuring success, don't we? In business, it's sales. The bottom line on Wall Street is . . . well, the bottom line. It's profit/loss comparisons. In other words, m-o-n-e-y. But money's not the bottom line of success in Christian life. So what is that bottom line for us? How can you have the assurance that your worship is truly pleasing to God? How is that measured? To find the answer, we have to turn to Scripture. Among the many portraits God paints of us in His Word, three stand out. Scripture affirms that as a part of our new identity in Christ, we are now sons (and daughters), servants, and stewards. We are sons because we have been adopted by God and made a part of His family (Ephesians 1; Galatians 3–4). He is now our Abba Father, our Daddy. We are heirs of God and joint heirs with Christ. As adopted children, we have all the rights and privileges of natural born sons. God is no longer our Judge. He is now our Father. But the Bible also affirms we are servants and stewards. And what does God require of us in these roles? How does He spell success? And how does all this relate to worship?

Have you ever watched the epic movie *Ben Hur*? (If not, put this book down right now, go to your local video store and rent it. It's a classic flick you'll enjoy). Though it was made way back in the fifties, its message is relevant to any generation (it's even in color!). Anyway, in one scene of the movie, the hero (played by Charleton Heston) becomes a slave and is placed on a Roman ship. Made to work in the lower galley amid the filth, sweat, and stench of a hundred men, Heston is forced to become an under rower. This was the worst fate for a slave. To be an under rower meant you were chained to the other slaves and existed for one reason in life—to row. Back and forth. Back and forth. Hour after hour. Day after day. It was these slaves' duty to move the multi-ton Roman ships through the water. The captain of the slaves sat in front of them, directing the beat of a drum. And they were required to row to the beat of the drum. Fast or slow, depending on the cadence and speed of the beat. But either way, their lives were reduced to one mindless activity. Talk about monotony! They were the most menial, unenvied, and despised of all the slaves. All these slaves had a common rank —the lowest. They experienced some of the most difficult labor, the cruelest punishment, the least appreciation, and in general, the most hopeless existence among slaves. They rowed in obscurity, hidden in the bottom of the ship. But this word for under rower is the very same Greek word Paul uses to describe us as servants of Christ. This imagery brought to the Corinthian's minds these low-life galley slaves, the ones rowing on the bottom tier of the ship. The life of a servant is not a glory position. There aren't many perks and the job can be very difficult, even demeaning, at times. Life as a servant is not the lifestyle of the rich or famous. You just serve. You serve your church. You serve your family. Your roommate. Your friends. But ultimately, it is Christ whom you serve. Colossians 3:22–24 gives a word of wisdom to slaves. Paul points out that we are to serve:

• sincerely, serving from the heart (verse 22)
• energetically, working hard without laziness (verse 23)
• expectantly, knowing God will reward you (verse 24)
• spiritually, because you are really serving Christ (verse 24)

Paul echoed this exhortation to the Christian slaves who lived in Ephesus (Ephesians 6:5–8). You are a son. But you are also a servant. Not a mistreated slave like those in ancient Rome, but a slave to Christ. And because of this, what you do for Him may not always be seen, acknowledged, or rewarded. Much of your reward may be postponed until Heaven. Are you cool with that?

The other word Paul used in this passage to describe our identity was the word *steward*. The word literally meant "house manager," and referred to a person (often a slave) who would be placed in charge of his master's property—vineyards, fields, finances, food, and general care of the household. He was under his master's authority and yet he himself owned nothing. But just when you thought being a steward wasn't very honorable, God lets you know that He has considered you responsible enough to entrust great responsibility to you. If you're involved in serving in a ministry, then it's an enormous responsibility to help care for others' spiritual well-being. Even more critical than caring for someone's physical health is to care for their souls. If God has entrusted His people to you, then He has allowed you to personally care for the apple of His eye. It is a divine stewardship, so take it seriously if you get to minister to people.

Okay, so I'm a steward. But what does God require of me? What are we supposed to do? And what is success in His eyes?

It might interest you to know that nowhere in Scripture does God ever call His servants to be successful. According to Paul, the responsibility of a servant and a steward was simply to *be faithful* to his Master. Faithfulness. That's it. Simple. Short. Succinct. Try to imagine if this one word appeared on the application for membership in your church.

Name _____

Are you faithful? ____ yes ____ no

For office use only

____ Accepted ____ Rejected

Faithfulness. Nothing more. Nothing less. Nothing else. Just please your

Master through faithfulness. Don't strive to please the other servants, just the Master alone. God does not require cleverness, creativity, popularity, or giftedness. He doesn't require that we have the coolest T-shirts, the smoothest programs, the most envied summer camp, or the newest ideas for Christian activities. God simply says, "Be faithful to Me." All of the above things are negotiable. Faithfulness is not. It's a case of options verses essentials. You can drive a car without the option of a sunroof or an alarm system, but it is required that you have an engine. To have a great paint job on your car but nothing under the hood means you just look good . . . and you go nowhere except in your dreams.

You can be skilled in many areas of life. You can have better than average abilities, incredible administrative skills, and enormous creativity, but if you're not a faithful person, you're not successful in God's eyes. That's because faithfulness is a matter of the heart, not an issue of talent. It's a matter of allegiance and devotion. It's a matter of passion and love for God. That's why Paul saw fit to send Timothy to the Corinthians—because he was faithful (1 Corinthians 4:17). Paul's chosen co-laborers in his ministry to the Colossians were two men—Epaphras and Tychicus—described by Paul as faithful servants of the Lord (Colossians 1:7, 4:7). Stewardship and servanthood are inseparable from faithfulness.

> "And the one who had received the five talents came up and brought five more talents, saying, 'Master, you entrusted five talents to me; see, I have gained five more talents.' His master said to him, 'Well done, good and faithful slave; you were faithful with a few things, I will put you in charge of many things, enter into the joy of your master.'" (Matthew 25:20–21)

Success in Scripture is always linked to faithful obedience. Do you recall what God told Joshua in Joshua 1:7–8?

> Only be strong and very courageous; be careful to do according to all the law which Moses My servant commanded

you; do not turn from it to the right or to the left, so that you may have success wherever you go. This book of the law shall not depart from your mouth, but you shall meditate on it day and night, so that you may be careful to do according to all that is written in it; for then you will make your way prosperous, and **then you will have success**.

Success for him was equated with faithful obedience to God's Word. So what is faithfulness for us in the Christian life? What does it practically look like?

One area where faithfulness is seen is in your friendships. Being faithful to your friends means you view them as a treasure entrusted to you by God. This applies to your buddies or girlfriends, as well as to that person you're in love with. You look at them like you would if you were carrying a priceless cargo of precious jewels on a journey for a king. It means you keep current with their needs and how they are doing spiritually. It means your relationship objectives and goals reflect this concern for them. It means you communicate to them by your words and actions that you have their best interests at heart. It means you give them your best at all times. It means you never settle for mediocrity or just getting by. Instead, you strive to give them God's best for them. This commitment to faithfulness tells them they are important to you. Those first Christians certainly were important to the apostle Paul. Looking at his ministry, ask yourself if you feel the same way about your friends as he did about his. Consider that:

- He was willing to go to hell in their place. (Romans 9:3)
- He passionately prayed for those who were lost. (Romans 10:1)
- He called the Roman believers beloved. (Romans 1:2)
- The carnal Corinthians were still called saints. (I Corinthians 1:2)
- The deceived Galatians were nevertheless his children. (Galatians 4:19)
- The Ephesians were the faithful in Christ to him. (Ephesians 1:1)
- The Philippians were his joy and crown. (Philippians 4:1)

- The Colossians always gave him a reason to give thanks. (Colossians 1:3)
- The Thessalonians were his glory and joy. (I Thessalonians 4:20)
- He even bragged on them to other churches. (2 Thessalonians 1:4)
- Timothy was his beloved son. (2 Timothy 2:2)
- Titus was his true child. (Titus 1:4)
- Philemon was his beloved brother and fellow worker. (Philemon 1)

Is it any wonder there was such an emotional and tearful farewell to Paul by the Ephesian elders? (Acts 20:25–38) Do you get the idea here that people mattered to Paul? That's because people matter to God and Paul's heart was singing harmony with Heaven's throne. Faithfulness to God's people is faithfulness to God. To minister to them is to minister to Jesus (Matthew 25:31–40). Your friends, no matter how few or how many, are people whom God loves, people for whom Christ died, people in whom the Holy Spirit dwells. Isn't it an awe-inspiring truth to think that the Sovereign, self-sufficient God of the universe should elevate puny, sinful, dirt-dwellers like us to such an important and intimate place in His heart! But such we are!

And so part of being faithful to God involves dedicating ourselves to His people. God did not call you to an organization or to a denomination. Those things are all temporary and earthly. God called you to *people*. And it is to those people that we all must be faithful. And it doesn't matter what role He has given you in their life, just as long as you're trustworthy in that role. Faithfully encouraging them, listening to them, leading them, loving them, rescuing them, correcting them, being with them, fighting for them, praying for them, being an example for them, being available to them. We all know there is a special joy that comes from having been faithful to God. Just knowing you gave your all to your friends for Christ's sake. Man, there's nothing like it!

There is just something special about the example of a faithful servant. It's so uplifting to see somebody who lives that kind of lifestyle. There's something about a guy like Cal Ripken Jr., the great legendary third baseman for the Baltimore Orioles. Several years ago, he broke Lou Gherig's long-standing record for consecutive baseball games played. To you non-baseball fans, that's like never missing a day of work for about eighteen years! Cal never missed a game. Not one. Did he play every game perfectly? Nope. Did he make errors and mistakes while in some of those games? Yep. But for nearly two decades, he just got up every morning and reported to work at the ball field. And that's why the crowd at Camden Yards gave Cal Ripken Jr. a nine-minute, uninterrupted, standing ovation the night he broke Gherig's record. He was faithful. And he is a guaranteed future Hall-of-Famer because of it.

One of the reasons you have even heard of MercyMe is because of a special group of people called youth pastors. We know youth pastors from all over the country, and over the years, they have brought us in, fed us, housed us, and given us an opportunity to minister to their kids. Were it not for them, who knows where we would be? Being a youth pastor can be a thankless job. Often it involves low pay, long hours, and very little recognition. One of our youth pastor friends (we'll call him Rick) ministers in a bedroom community of a large metropolitan city. To be honest, Rick is not much to look at. Kinda short and dumpy. He doesn't wear designer clothes. He doesn't own a cell phone or a computer (so how does he minister?). He's not a great communicator. He doesn't drive a cool car and he's not much of a comedian. Worst of all, he can't play guitar or sing (and he's in youth ministry? Get outta here!). There are no big budgets in his church. No real salary perks. No recognition by the other youth pastors in the city. He serves as a literal unknown. You'll never see him addressing a stadium full of students or a conference packed with other ministers. He just wasn't born for that. You see, Rick is an under rower. A servant. A slave for Jesus Christ. But our friend has something that seminary and giftedness could never give him. He has something more admirable than talent, good looks, or a hit record. Rick is simply faithful to God right where he is. And you know what? His students think he hung the moon and stars. He loves those kids and they know it. He is enormously effective and successful in God's eyes because of his simple faithfulness. He has yet to realize he needs all the bells and whistles of ministry. He just doesn't know any better than to daily serve and worship God out of a heart of love.

May his tribe increase.

Rick's faithfulness will take him to places of effectiveness most youth ministers have never even heard of. He'll probably win the Gold Medal for Student Ministry in Heaven one day. Somewhere in eternity, we'll all be following him around with a wheelbarrow, carrying his many crowns.

We live to please God, don't we? We work for His approval. And we long for Him to say, *Well done, thou good and faithful servant, enter into the joy of your Master.* But God's definition of success is faithfulness. Translated to a lifestyle of worship, faithfulness means you don't worry about what other people are doing. You don't bother yourself wondering if you're worshipping long enough. You just worship Him everyday. Just be faithful to do that one thing. If you concentrate on being faithful in your worship, He'll take care of the rest. A life of worship is measured in inches, not miles. It's a daily thing. It's worship in the ordinary moments of life. It's worshipping on those days and during those times when you just don't feel like it. All of our ordinary days are like the base of a great pyramid that points up to God. You will have more regular days than any other kind, so train yourself to focus on Him during those days. Your daily routine will be what most of your life is made of. Occasionally, you will have those exclamation points of the unusual and the spectacular. But the rest of the time, the normal moments will reign. The real key is to see the supernatural in those normal times. Open your eyes. They are there. To redeem an ordinary Monday for eternity. That's worship. Capturing the everyday routine for His glory. That's what it's all about! Keeping our perspective and bowing before Him every day, through all that we do, consciously or subconsciously, it's ultimately all from Him, to Him, and through Him! Having this perspective makes theoretical Christianity practical. It transforms the laboratory into real life. It can even turn ritual into relevancy. And that's what we hope this book has done for you—transformed the way you look at worship. We want you to be aware that every day Someone is waiting for you in the secret place of your

228 • i can only imagine

heart. Waiting to see your face fill with wonder. Waiting to hear you say, "I love you." Waiting to hear you confess how desperate you are for Him, to hear you say how badly you really need him. And He anticipates that day when you will come to the place he has been preparing for you. Then you will praise Him the way you have always wanted to. Unhindered. Uninhibited. Unreserved. Unending.

Unbelievable.

So why would you want to worship God? Simple. Because God is worthy. That's it. He deserves it. All of it. Like a black hole, He is worthy to consume every ounce and molecule of adoration in this universe. But here's another reason. Deep down in the core of your heart there burns a passion to praise God. Down in the part of you that fuels most everything you do is a love for a God who has extended an invisible, inaudible, yet divine calling to you. It's undeniable and irrevocable. It causes you to dream the impossible and endure the unbearable. And the only reason you haven't packed it all in before now, sold the farm, and moved into the suburbs of complacency is because of one thing . . . He is worthy.

Never lose the wow. Remember, it's still about relationship. Know that you're in process, and just be faithful.

Somewhere in side you, your spirit is screaming out loud to the rest of you . . . Worship Him!

Dear friend, listen to that inner compulsion. Heed that inward prompting. Pay close attention to what your heart—your true self—is telling you. Are you listening? Can you hear it? It's a melody. A song. Your song. Your personal composition of worship. It is unlike any other and resonates not from the speakers in your car, but rather from the stereo of your soul. It's your own background music to life. Your worship soundtrack. Your own travellin' music. Your anthem of praise. Go ahead. Turn the music back up again. Look down the road. Throw back your head and sing.

And enjoy the ride!

Jeff Kinley is President of Main Thing Ministries, a non-profit organization whose mission is to communicate the relevancy of Christianity to this generation. When he isn't writing, Jeff is traveling and speaking across America at camps, retreats, and rallies. He is a graduate of the University of Arkansas (BA) and Dallas Theological Seminary (ThM). Jeff and his wife Beverly live in Little Rock, Arkansas with their three sons.

Jeff is the author of ten books:
Through The Eyes Of A Champion
No Turning Back
Never The Same
Done Deal
Do You Know This Man?
Take Me To The Cross
Embracing The World As Jesus Did
Handling Opposition As Jesus Did
Connecting In Prayer As Jesus Did
Trusting God As Jesus Taught

notes

1. 1 Thessalonians 4:16
2. Psalm 147:7
3. Psalm 150:3–5; Psalm 147:7; Psalm 149:3
4. Psalm 147:1
5. Deuteronomy 4:7; Psalm 139:7–12; Acts 17:27
6. While Christ bore the punishment for our sins on the cross, we still have earthly consequences for our actions.
7. Hebrews 12:5–11
8. Ecclesiastes 2:25; John 10:10
9. Jeremiah 29:11; Romans 12:2
10. James 4:3; 1 John 5:14–15
11. John 1:18; 17:3
12. John 1:14; 1 Peter 5:7
13. Genesis 1:26–27
14. Genesis 1:26–2:25
15. Genesis 2:18
16. Genesis 2:23
17. Genesis 2:24–25
18. Genesis 2:15, 19–20
19. Genesis 3:1
20. Genesis 3:2–5
21. Hebrews 11:25
22. Genesis 3:7
23. Genesis 3:8
24. Ephesians 2:1
25. Romans 3:10; Acts 17:26–27
26. Genesis 3:8–11
27. Isaiah 40:8
28. 2 Samuel 6:16

29. 2 Samuel 6:21–23

30. Matthew 9:9

31. Luke 5:28

32. Matthew 9:10

33. Matthew 11:9

34. 1 Kings 7:9

35. Matthew 8:10; 15:28

36. Mark 7:24–29

37. Matthew 6:1–2

check it out! get involved! make a difference!

Habitat for Humanity
Build a home for a low-income family.
www.habitat.org

Compassion International
Help make a difference in the life of a child.
www.compassion.org

Drop the Debt
Learn how to help rid Africa of poverty and disease.
www.j2000usa.org

check out these other groovy products from extreme for jesus

wait for me
Rebecca St. James
$13.99
0-7852-7127-9

30 Days with Jesus
Audio Adrenaline
$7.99
0-7180-0165-6

genuine
Stacie Orrico
$13.99
0-8499-9545-0

unfinished work
Kevin Max
$16.99
0-7852-6630-5